In Honor Of

Ed Krauel
on his

100th Birthday

Monroe County Library System
Monroe, Michigan

LEGACY, VISION, AND IMPACT

W e all need compelling reasons to invest our time and money in a book or in an organization. The author of *Four Percent*, Michael S. Malone, presents the amazing legacy of over 100 years of Eagle Scouts by bringing individual Eagle Scouts to life on every page. From the early days of Scouting when the design of the Eagle badge had to be created quickly after the first Eagle Scout rank was earned, to the impact that the Knights of Dunamis organization had on generations of Eagle Scouts, to the vision being carried forward by the National Eagle Scout Association (NESA) are all interwoven on the pages of this book.

The vision of NESA goes well beyond the role of steward of all things Eagle Scout. We are focused on supporting Boy Scout councils, where the important work of helping Scouting units be successful and to grow takes place. To accomplish this objective we have created new and exciting adventures for Eagle Scouts—Argonauts traveling the planet with Dr. Bob Ballard the discoverer of the *Titanic* or astronomers attending the creation of the largest telescope mirrors ever created by human kind. Eagle Scout adventurers of all persuasions are finding opportunities to be exceptional in the legacy of great Eagle Scout explorers of previous generations like Neil Armstrong, the first man to walk on the moon, and Dr. Paul A. Siple, who as a young Eagle Scout of 21, explored Antarctica with Admiral Richard E. Byrd in 1928. He went on to invent the term "wind chill factor" after a life-long career of exploring places where no humans had gone before.

NESA is very proud of its accomplishments through its forty plus years of existence, but especially over the past few years. It's reached a much higher level of service and benefit to its constituency, the highest achievers of the BSA program, Eagle Scouts.

Some examples of recently successful projects include the first nationwide search ever done of where Eagle Scouts currently are. Conducted in 2008 and again in 2010, well over half of the over 2 million Eagle Scouts since the first one in 1912 have been located and are being welcomed back.

And college scholarships: NESA awards over 200 college scholarships annually valued at nearly $600,000—an increase of almost 300% in six years. The largest of these scholarships is the NESA STEM Scholarship, a $50,000 scholarship awarded annually to an Eagle Scout who plans to study and have a career in a STEM subject in science, technology, engineering or math.

A requirement for earning the Eagle Scout rank is to plan and give leadership to a project benefitting the community. NESA has established the *Glenn A. and Melinda W. Adams National Eagle Scout Service Project of the Year Award* to recognize the most outstanding Eagle Scout projects at the council, regional, and national levels. The national-level winner is considered to be the best Eagle Scout project in the USA out of over 50,000 of them annually.

Nearly everyone believes that being an Eagle Scout means something and that it makes a big difference in a person's life. But has it ever been studied by academics? In the results from the 2010 Baylor University study, *Eagle Scouts: Merit Beyond the Badge,* conducted by the university's Program for Pro-Social Behavior, the researchers found statistically significant differences between Eagle Scouts and men that never were in Scouting. In summary, Eagle Scouts:

- Establish greater lifelong connections to family, friends, and neighbors
- Exhibit a higher sense of responsibility to give back through volunteering and donating
- Gain a greater connection and concern for their community
- Exercise more self-discipline to plan ahead and set and achieve goals
- Hold higher self-expectations
- Demonstrate greater appreciation and concern for the environment
- Display increased respect for religion and religious diversity
- Enjoy an increased variety of hobbies and interests
- Develop greater commitment to lifelong learning

Now we know for sure.

Yours in Scouting,

Glenn Adams
NESA President

Dustin Farris
NESA Director

FOUR
PERCENT

THE EXTRAORDINARY STORY OF EXCEPTIONAL AMERICAN YOUTH

MICHAEL S. MALONE

WIND RUSH
PUBLISHERS

Dallas, Texas

Published by WindRush Publishers, Dallas, Texas.
WindRush Publishers and colophon are trademarks of
WindRush Ventures, LLC.

Second Edition 2015

10 9 8 7 6 5 4 3 2

WindRush Publishers
PO Box 670324
Dallas, Texas 75367
www.WindRushPub.com

Book design and layout by Charito Jones, Dallas, Texas
Creative Direction by John K. Shipes, www.ShipesShooter.com
Cover image copyright John K. Shipes 2015
Production assistance by David C. Scott

Eagle medal, Eagle neckerchief, and BSA uniform tunic courtesy of Robert Reitz, Museum
Director of the Harbin Scout Museum at Camp Wisdom, Circle Ten Council, Dallas, Texas.

www.4percentbook.com

ISBN-13: 978-09859097-5-8

**Scan for more
resources.**

To those who wear the Eagle medal—
and to all who helped them earn it.

FOUR
PERCENT

THE EXTRAORDINARY STORY OF EXCEPTIONAL AMERICAN YOUTH

ACKNOWLEDGMENTS

B eing an Eagle, and having now mentored nearly fifty Scouts on their Trail to Eagle, I can say with certainty that no boy ever gets to Eagle easily. Most Scouts, of course, don't make it at all —and of those who do, some stall at the lower ranks, others in merit badges, and nearly all with the service project. And even if you do get through the long, arduous process quickly and earn your Eagle young (as I did), you still will find yourself learning about what it means to be an Eagle for many years to come.

And along the way, both before and after you earn your Eagle, there will be scores, even hundreds, of people who will help you along the way—some for hours and some for decades, and you will never be able to thank them all for what they did for you. But, thanks to this book, I'm at least getting this chance to try.

It always begins with your parents. My father had a terrible, Depression era childhood. Boy (and Sea) Scouting gave him just about the only structure in his life. He was also one of those '30s Scouts who never got his Eagle because of the Bird Study merit badge. When I joined Scouting in 1965, he rejoined as well, becoming Assistant Scoutmaster and mentor the troop's future Eagles—exactly the leadership path that I have followed. Meanwhile, my mother sewed my patches and washed my filthy clothes after my camping trips—often getting poison oak in the process.

Scouting is also about your fellow Scouts. You learn something important from each of them; from the boy who stays in the troop for a few weeks; to the ones you know the rest of your life. My fellow Troop 480 Eagles, as you might expect, have all gone on to successful careers and impressive lives— and they stand in perpetual reminder to me of what it means to be an Eagle.

Then there are the Scoutmasters. I had four as a Boy Scout—Mr. Thompson, Mr. Habermeyer, Mr. Rinfret, and Mr. Henderson. Each showed me what it means to be a man, to be a leader, and to be a teacher. Each took on the enormous responsibility and time commitment of being a Scoutmaster—and though each approached it differently, each did the role great honor.

The second phase of being an Eagle begins when you leave Boy Scouting and continues until you die. I now am well along that path. And over the years I have met thousands of my fellow Eagles, usually serendipitously—and they too have all taught me about what it means to be an Eagle. The fact that these lessons almost have been universally positive is yet more evidence that America's Eagles are an extraordinary group and a national treasure. And it was that realization that both impelled me to write this book and to pull no punches on the story. I believe Eagle Scouting can withstand any level of scrutiny.

Finally, more than a decade ago, and like many middle-aged Eagles, I returned to Scouting when my oldest son turned 11. He earned his Eagle—and far more impressively than I did—and now is being followed along that path by his younger brother, 16-years-old as I write this, who is about to embark on his own Eagle service project. My wife has been involved with their Scouting careers from their very first troop meeting—these days she sits on the Eagle Board of Review, an experience that, she says, gives her hope for the future.

We joined Troop 466 in Sunnyvale, California because of a remarkable figure, Norm Ehmann, who had served as the troop's Scoutmaster for more than 30 years (I had even earned a merit badge from him as a teenager). Ehmann called our troop "the Eagle Makers," and 200 Eagles later we continue to live up to that name. And along the way, I have been honored to serve a number of terrific Scoutmasters: John Rugo, Chris Early, and Dave Holt. Seeing them close-up I am only more in awe of what it takes to be a Scoutmaster. They are remarkable men, indeed.

As Assistant Scoutmaster in charge of the troop's older Scouts, I've had the honor of mentoring almost 50 new Eagles. Each one is different, and each is a kind of miracle. And each also is a chance—one largely lost on your younger, dazed self—to experience with a clear eye what it is like to take the Trail to Eagle. What I've learned, all of the myths aside, is that this generation of Eagles may be the most impressive of all. I am honored, and more than a little intimidated to serve them. And I have been inspired by their parents to try to be a better parent myself.

There were a number of individuals who helped with the production of this book, most notably David C. Scott, a fellow Eagle. Given all of the vicissitudes of the last two years within Scouting and without, he has shown tremendous courage in taking on the project. I also would like to thank BSA counsel Richard Mathews for convincing me of the need to publish this book. Rich Goldman, Silicon Valley, Eagle Scout and fellow Scout parent, did superhuman work to connect me with Dr. Neil Armstrong to assure the accuracy of his biography. And Jason Stein, Ron Schoenmehl, and Jake Carlson of the Santa Clara County Council (on whose board I serve), John Richers of the Fresno Council, and Matt Myers of the National Office, remind me every day of the great calling of being a professional Scouter.

Finally, to all of America's Eagle Scouts, past and present, I hope that this book captures at least a part of the story of Eagle Scouting's first century —and does so in a way that honors your medal. I'm humbled to be counted among your ranks.

Michael S. Malone
ASM, Troop 466
Sunnyvale, California

The title of *Four Percent* was chosen for this book as it is the historical average of a century of Eagle Scouts to total Boy Scout membership. The raw statistics were given to the publisher by the National Office of the Boy Scouts of America and interpolated.

The key column on that document was "cumulative individual members." That amounted to about 54 million Boy Scout youth that were eligible to attain the rank at the time of the request and nearly 2 million Eagle Scouts had done so. This resulted in an average of 3.62 percent—hence, *Four Percent*.

CONTENTS

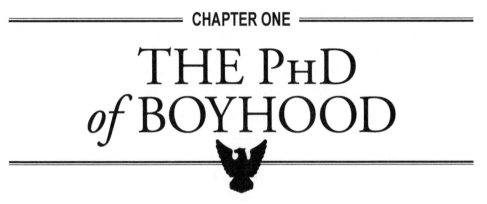

CHAPTER ONE

THE PhD
of BOYHOOD

*It is a ceremony that takes place
more than 50,000 times each year.*

S OME OF THEM ARE AS SIMPLE AS A MEDAL pinned on the pocket
of a young man's uniform, followed by a firm handshake; others
are as elaborate as a stage show and feature VIP guests. But most
are comparatively intimate: a few dozen people including close and
distant relations, a grandparent or two, schoolmates, a group of other Boy
Scouts in uniform, often a religious leader or favorite teacher and, despite
the stereotype of the awkward Scout, usually a girlfriend sitting with the
recipient's family. In the past, the ceremony typically took place at a school
or public building but, thanks to the cultural debates of the last half-century,
it now almost always takes place at a church, temple or mosque.

But for all of the variations in style, the substance of the Eagle Scout
Court of Honor is almost always the same. There is an opening invocation, a
welcome, a flag ceremony, and the recitation of the core texts of Scouting—
the Scout Oath and Law—often with some form of candle lighting ceremony.
The Eagle usually stands at center stage, joined by his parents, flanked by an

"Eagle Court" of other, older Eagles—often quite elderly—who announce the date and location of their own Courts of Honor.

At some point, many of these ceremonies step away from the formalities. The lights dim, and a movie or slide show runs that presents the Scout's "Trail to Eagle," beginning with baby photos but mostly focusing on the boy's Scouting career. Given that the honoree is usually 16- or 17-years-old, and may have joined Scouting as a seven-year-old Tiger Cub, that trail is pretty long for such a short life. Indeed, there may not be much of the young man's life that he can remember when he *wasn't* a Scout.

The images are usually pretty standard and predictable: baby pictures to elicit *oohs* from the audience, first day of school, family vacations, a class pageant, perhaps a first communion or bar mitzvah, and then a run of Scouting photos. If the honoree was a Cub Scout, there are the inevitable Pinewood Derby and Webelos bridging ceremony (the transition to Boy Scouts) images.

The 11-year-old Tenderfoot Scout who appears in the next few images—frightened, excited, and overwhelmed by the new world in which he finds himself—seems impossibly small in light of the full-grown young man who now sits confidently in the front row.

The next few images are of the Scout's career: troop campouts, district-wide camporees, 50-mile hikes, summer camp, and perhaps even a jamboree. Through it all, the Scout continues to grow—not only physically, but through taking on ever-greater responsibilities—and, as he advances through the ranks and earns more than a score of merit badges, one of them perhaps giving him the first glimpse of an adult career, his competence increases as well.

But the veteran viewer knows to look for something else. It is the moment when the Scout—whether he is 15 or just short of his 18th birthday—makes the decision to pursue his Eagle community service project; not just to formulate the idea of the project—but to *accept* it as his own. At that moment, he takes full responsibility for the biggest project of his young life; and, in relation to his skills, perhaps in his whole life. He will have to learn time management to organize the project; create a list of materials, and either purchase them or solicit businesses for donations; manage a small army of fellow Scouts, classmates, and friends; deal with adults in positions of power; and most of all, complete the project on time to the satisfaction of the nonprofit organization that is its recipient.

In doing so, the prospective Eagle will be making his own contribution to the largest youth service program in American history. In the last 50 years since the service project has taken its place as the signature requirement of the Eagle rank, it is estimated that these projects have contributed as much as 100 *million* hours of targeted service, changing the face of America in the process.[1]

Challenging as the project will be—and *all* Eagle projects are challenging, whether they involve painting benches at a local school or devoting thousands of hours to an international initiative that wins the Adams Award for best Eagle project of the year—the single most difficult moment comes with the acceptance of that responsibility. There is no going back and with that understanding comes the beginning of maturity.

That decisive moment never is captured on film but its consequences are there to see for anyone who knows to look. The goofy teenager of a few images before metamorphoses into the serious young adult leading his team through the project. You don't so much earn the Eagle rank as you *become* an Eagle—a fact only the Eagles in the audience and the Scout's parents, fully appreciate. And in becoming an Eagle, you are changed forever.

When the lights go back up, and the Scout takes the stage, it is this transformed young man who accepts the Eagle medal from his mother and the patch from his father. Because many Scouts take right up until the last moment to earn their Eagle before the official cutoff of their 18th birthday, and thus, their Court of Honor is held after they "age out," sometimes just days before they leave for college—the odds are about even that the honoree never will actually wear his Eagle patch.

But he will wear his Eagle medal again; perhaps soon, as a member of a fellow Scout's Eagle Court just a few weeks hence or 40 years distant at his own son's Eagle ceremony. As he has been reminded throughout the ceremony—and will continue to be reminded in the years ahead—"once an Eagle, always an Eagle." You were a Boy Scout, but you are, and will always be, an Eagle Scout. It is a message that will continue to resonate in the decades ahead, long after the new Eagle's memories of details about his Scouting career, even of this ceremony, begin to fade. And its impact starts now, as the new Eagle steps up to the podium to thank all the people who helped him reach this moment. The young man who now speaks with such assurance and command is the transformed boy of those last few images on the Trail to Eagle. For good reason, the Eagle award has been called the "PhD of Boyhood"; and this is a graduation ceremony in which recipient— with a hard-earned new perspective on life and achievement—gives his own final address.

Then, after *Taps* or some other official adjournment of the Court of Honor, it is time for cake and punch, handshakes, and a visit to the table that holds the congratulatory letters from national figures and the display of all the honoree's other awards. Soon, the younger Scouts will fold the flags and chairs, and the ladies will pack up and hand out the remaining food. And the honoree, as he prepares to leave with his family and friends, will put the patch in his pocket and the medal in its box. He already has begun to experience what it is like to be an Eagle Scout. He will spend the rest of his life learning the rest.

ANTECEDENTS

Founded in 1910, the Boy Scouts of America (BSA) is the largest, and most enduring, training and development organization for young men in the United States.

Created during the Progressive Era, it was born largely out of the perception that, with the end of the frontier and the rise of industrial cities, something profound in the American character was being lost, especially among youth. The Scouting movement itself was founded in the United Kingdom in January 1908 by a retired Lt. General, Robert Baden-Powell, who feared the same forces at work on British life.

Casting about for an operating philosophy for his nascent movement,

Baden-Powell settled on a hybrid between his own experiences working with young messengers during the Siege of Mafeking in the Second Anglo-Boer War, and the work being done in the United States—the Woodcraft Indians—by naturalist and author Ernest Thompson Seton.

Thus, even though Scouting began as a British institution, its philosophical roots were equally American. And that may be the reason, when Scouting was brought to the States in 1909 by Chicago publisher and promoter William Dickson Boyce after his fateful (and perhaps apocryphal) encounter with the helpful "unknown Scout" in the London fog—the BSA's founding myth—it met with an immediate and strong response from American boys. Indeed, numerous independent Scouting organizations had spontaneously sprung up throughout the country creating something of an identity crisis for the U.S. movement in its first decade until the BSA emerged as the dominant organization.

Ernest Thompson Seton (left), Robert Baden-Powell (center), and Dan Beard (right) atop BSA headquarters in New York City on September 23, 1910.

Two additional factors were crucial to the triumph of the BSA. The first was the incorporation of a second, older, domestic boys' outdoor group—the Sons of Daniel Boone—created by Daniel Carter Beard, who would go on to become the most famous of all Scout leaders. Beard brought a patriotic (jingoistic, some complained) attitude to Scouting that not only nicely balanced Seton's pacifism but also distinguished BSA from the international Scouting movement as a uniquely American institution.

The second factor was the appointment, in early 1911, of Washington, DC, attorney James E. West as the first chief Scout executive. West, a comparatively bloodless bureaucrat, brilliantly navigated between these various passionate and self-promoting advocates, all while placing the BSA on a stable financial footing, backed by both the nation's leading industrialists and the United States Congress. The Boy Scouts of America was on its way.

In the century since the organization's founding, more than 115 million American boys (and girls as well, beginning in 1969 with the Exploring— now Venturing and Learning for Life programs) have passed through Scouting. There are 2.6 million Scouts today, with another 1 million adults in 125,000 packs, troops, and crews.[2]

The impact of these tens of millions of Scouts over the last century on American life and culture is all but immeasurable. Scouts served on the home front in both World Wars, selling millions of dollars in war bonds and assisting in war rationing programs. Scouts also have devoted millions of hours to the preservation of the nation's

Young YMCA lawyer James E. West in 1909 prior to becoming BSA's chief Scout executive.

national parks, to collecting food for the indigent, and assisting in disaster relief. Former Scouts can be found in the top leadership positions in American industry, government, academics, the military, and nonprofit institutions.

So deep and profound has been the impact of Scouting on American life in the twentieth, and now in the twenty-first, century that it is hard to imagine the United States without Boy Scouts. The image of the Boy Scout— especially as rendered by a half-century of Norman Rockwell paintings—has become as much an American icon as Uncle Sam. And, like most icons, it also has been a ripe target for cartoonists, satirists, and social activists. The earnest young man in puttees and campaign hat (or later, the baggy uniform and baseball cap) quickly became a symbol not only of resourcefulness and integrity, but also of wide-eyed innocence and tiresome earnestness. The noble Scout heroically saving a life through skill and resourcefulness has long lived alongside the wide-eyed and ardent Scout dragging an unwilling old lady across the street as his daily "good deed." And thus, even before it was a half-century old, to be a "real Boy Scout" had entered the language as both a compliment and a pejorative.

ALWAYS AN EAGLE

But there is one part of Scouting that always has stood apart from the rest, largely immune from the various cultural winds that have swept back and forth across the rest of the organization—Eagle Scouts.

If, in everyday parlance, "Boy Scout" is, for good or bad, a description, then "Eagle Scout" is almost always an explanation. "Well, he's an Eagle Scout" has become shorthand for an entire body of skills that has enabled a man, young or old, to accomplish something—build a fire, lash down a roof load, splint a broken arm, organize and lead a group—that surprises his peers.

Even in the tumultuous years of social upheaval in the late 1960s when every American institution, not least the Boy Scouts, was under assault, Eagle Scouts were somehow were immune. Scouts, with their gaudy patriotism and uniforms, might have been decried as a paramilitary organization—but Eagles, after all, were college professors and forest rangers, scientists, and social workers.

They also were seen (ironically, because of their roots in Scouting) as the nation's premiere environmentalists. When the hippies went back to the land at the end of the decade, many, as with generations of reconstructed naturalists before them, depended on people who knew how to build and cook on fires, lash together wooden structures, and provide first aid for injuries. Eagle Scouts, some with ponytails and tie-dyed shirts led the way— and it was with good reason that the *Whole Earth Catalog* listed the *Boy Scout Handbook* as its outdoor guide.

Forty years later, at the height of the national debate over the refusal of Scouting to accept homosexuals in adult leadership roles, when municipalities were throwing Scout troops out of public facilities those same Scouts had built decades before, Americans momentarily paused to honor the passing of the nation's only Eagle-president, Gerald R. Ford. Not only did the encomiums from both sides of the political divide mention Ford's Eagle Scout award, but they also noted its central role in his life and the creation of his character. And when the Ford family asked 200 young Eagles in the region to serve as the honor guard to the former president's casket, not only did no one object, but it also was praised as being perfectly appropriate.

Every Eagle Scout during the course of his life experiences this exceptionalism. Colleges and universities, to one degree or another, are known to give the Eagle applicant the advantage over an equal contender—largely (and probably accurately) based upon the perception that, with the service project, the Eagle already has shown the discipline to successfully manage a complex project and see it through. Join the military as an enlisted man, and the Eagle award rank usually confers an instant advancement and a leadership position.

College Eagles quickly discover, once the word gets out, that they are expected to take over every time a barbecue or bonfire needs to be built, whenever anyone in the dorm is injured or when a team needs to be formed and led.

Adult Eagles come to appreciate the full implications of the phrase "always an Eagle." It is the only childhood award that appears on your resume—and likely will be included in your obituary. You become accustomed to the flicker of respect in the eyes of others when they learn you are an Eagle—suggesting as it does unseen skills and strength of character; and the quick affirmation from others you heretofore never suspected of being in the brotherhood.

It also means a lifetime of assumed responsibility and the perpetual risk of failure and humiliation. When the luggage needs to be lashed to the car roof, the wood chopped, the accident victim's bleeding stopped or when the group is lost in the woods, everyone looks to the Eagle Scout to fix the problem, tend the wound or save them. Any failure is not just your own, but of Eagle Scouting itself. They don't mention this at your Eagle Scout Court of Honor.

Not surprisingly, given what it once took to earn the award, most Eagles step up to this added responsibility. Eagles are disproportionately represented in the high-responsibility professions of modern American life, including the military, universities, politics, and senior management at Fortune 500 companies, law, and medicine. A midshipman or cadet at one of the service academies or a White House Fellow candidate will find him or herself surrounded by Eagles.

Hollywood, while it may not employ many Eagles, hasn't hesitated over the last century to use the Eagle rank as quick shorthand to confer added ability or integrity to its characters. It's not surprising, then, that Steven Spielberg put the badge of the penultimate Scouting rank (Life) on the most iconic modern cinematic hero, Indiana Jones, in *The Last Crusade*, implicitly suggesting that the adult Indy is an Eagle—just like Spielberg himself.

Real heroes, especially when their achievements are a matter of daring, often turn out to be Eagles as well. No one was surprised to learn that Neil Armstrong was an Eagle Scout, along with least a dozen other astronauts. Nor were they surprised to learn that aerial adventurer Steve Fossett considered earning his Eagle equal to all his round-the-world balloon and small plane records or that six of the nation's Medal of Honor recipients were Eagles.

By the same token, Eagles, young and old, also are disproportionately represented in the relief efforts of every major U.S. disaster. If they aren't leading the Scout troops that are providing assistance, then they are leading the nonprofit organizations that are managing the relief, are officers in the National Guard or Army units providing help and order on the scene, are covering the event for the national media or advising the president of the United States as he flies over the destruction.

It can truly be said that in good times and bad, more than any other discernible category of citizens, Eagle Scouts lead America. And, consciously or not, their fellow citizens recognize that fact and honor it.

PATTERN IN THE FABRIC

To merely list the extraordinary achievements of a century of Eagle Scouts is to at least partially confuse cause and effect. It only proves the obvious fact that young people of achievement gravitate toward the opportunity for achievement.

What hasn't yet been explained is why this particular award has come to assume a place so honored in American life that it alone, of all childhood achievements, follows its recipients throughout their lives; why it remains important as a résumé highlight decades after the honoree has aged out of the program; why newspapers still devote precious editorial space to coverage of Eagle service projects and Courts of Honor; and why at a man's funeral, three score or more years after he earned the award, his eulogy likely will include the fact that he was an Eagle Scout.

SUPREMACY

The Eagle Scout award is, of course, the highest rank in Boy Scouting. Everything beyond (bronze, gold, and silver palms for earning additional groups of merit badges; the Distinguished Eagle Scout Award for life achievements as an adult Eagle) is merely gilding on the award itself. But Scouting has other supreme awards: the Silver Award in Venturing, the Quartermaster Award in Sea Scouts, the Hornaday Medal for Conservation, the Honor Medal for saving a life but none have caught the public's imagination in the same way. The Gold Award in Girl Scouting is at least the equivalent of the Eagle (and some say it is even harder to earn) but few outside of the Girl Scouts of America (GSUSA) ever have heard of it. The Little League, American Youth Soccer Organization (AYSO), and other youth sports organizations have their MVPs and All-Stars, but those honors are all but forgotten by the time the next season begins.

Only the Eagle stands apart. Young Scouts are reminded constantly of the sheer rarity of its achievement. They are told that in the history of Scouting, only 4 percent of all Scouts ever have earned their Eagle. And though that ratio today may be two or three times that historic average, it remains reserved for only a tiny fraction of the millions of boys who join Scouting. And for that little 11-year-old, looking ahead at the prospect of seven ranks, 21 merit badges, and hundreds of requirements, that Trail to Eagle can look very, very long. Six or seven years later, as that same boy stands on stage, having completed that climb, the notion of having reached a pinnacle of childhood is no longer an alien concept.

VENERABILITY

Not only is the Eagle medal the most famous award in American childhood, but it is also the oldest. As has often been noted, childhood as we know it was a Victorian invention, the product of reduced infant mortality, greater leisure time, and the need to spend more years educating young people and preparing them for the complexities of an industrial world.

But the increasingly attenuated childhoods that resulted provoked their own backlash toward a greater structure and a more empirical approach to self-improvement, skill development, and good citizenship in children's upbringing. The first such institution dedicated to keeping the young from going astray was the Young Men's Christian Association (YMCA), brought to the United States in 1851. Its primary focus was on saving young men's souls.

The turn of the 20th century saw numerous movements arise through the industrialized world, all designed to avert the perceived impending catastrophe from a generation of "soft" young people (a widespread belief that disappeared overnight in August 1914 as World War I began) as well as to apply to youth the same empirical "scientific" principles then in vogue everywhere from factories (Taylorism) to Sociology (Social Darwinism) to population management (eugenics). Fredrick Jackson Turner's famous 1893 paper "The Significance of the Frontier in American History" on the closing of the American frontier had stunned intellectuals, politicians, and industrialists. America, they realized, was changing rapidly and the new century would be very different from the last. Were America's young people, the leaders of this new century, prepared for this emerging new world? Were their characters strong enough? Did they have the requisite skills to make it America's century?

The answer, many concluded, was that America's youth needed a new kind of training; that had one foot in the traditional values that had built the country—skill in the outdoors, resourcefulness, leadership, and independence—and the other in the new world of the industrial nation-state—patriotism, organizational management, skill with technology, and community service. Just how all of these components were to be mixed and matched was the subject of considerable dispute.

Scouting, as much through the clash of competing visions as conscious design, stumbled on the right mix for the American zeitgeist of the early years of the twentieth century, and it became as synonymous to that era as President Theodore Roosevelt. The result was explosive growth—there already were 182,303 Boy Scouts by 1915 and that number climbed to 541,000 by 1925.[3]

Theodore Roosevelt hosts Boy Scout Troop 1 of
Long Island at his Sagamore Hill estate in 1915.

With the support of the nation's leaders, Scouting also became quickly embedded into the fabric of American life. It was Scouting that was enlisted to help with the war effort on the home front. Congress formally chartered the BSA in 1916, giving it special rights and privileges unavailable to other youth organizations for many years (such as the right to retire flags and to serve as the honor guard at inaugurations, national funerals, party conventions, and so on). And, during the depths of the Great Depression, Franklin Roosevelt—who had been a major supporter of Scouting since 1915 when he was a young assistant secretary of the navy—turned to Scouting as a way to bolster the spirit of American youth, ultimately playing a key role in the creation and production of the first BSA national jamboree in 1937.

As the "best" of Scouting, Eagle Scouts were at the heart of all these events. Indeed, in one of the most noted events of that first jamboree, FDR awarded

President Franklin D. Roosevelt examines the Eagle medal of Troop 7's Frank St. John of Poughkeepsie, New York, during the BSA's 1st National Jamboree parade on July 7, 1937.

the Eagle medal to one Scout and then invited a dozen other Eagles to join him at the major league baseball All-Star game at nearby Griffith Stadium.

Scouting earned its chapter in the American national identity and Eagle Scouting embedded itself into that chapter as the exemplar of the movement—the apparent hero of the narrative.

By comparison, most of the other youth movements in the United States got their start two generations later, powered by the demographic engine of the baby boom. As large as many of them became, they were in a sense too late for history. Even Girl Scouts, almost as old Boy Scouting, didn't settle on its Gold Award until 1980—meaning its story, however memorable, has comparatively just begun.

PROMOTION

It would be wrong to credit the success of Eagle Scouting to successful public relations and advertising over the course of the decades by the Boy Scouts of America, but it also would be a mistake to assume that it had no part.

Scouting always has tried to push its Eagles front and center. And, of course, why not? Every institution wants to put its most successful members on display—not just to honor them and to use them in recruiting new members—but also just to keep them from leaving to pursue other achievements.

That's why, since the mid-1920s, Scouting always has had a separate organization for Eagles: first the Knights of Dunamis and then the National Eagle Scout Association. It also is why almost every major Scouting event, especially national jamborees, has separate events for Eagles. One reason Eagle Courts of Honor stories are so popular in community newspapers is precisely because local troops, districts, and councils promote those stories. And, on the big-ticket events—such as presenting the *Annual Report* on Scouting to the president of the United States—it almost is always an Eagle Scout being tapped for the job.

It is amazing, given the enormous amount of attention Eagle Scouting receives, just how *little* the BSA spends promoting it. For example, Scouting almost never contacts the media about an individual Eagle project—rather, that is usually done ad hoc by the Scout's family, a troop leader or often by the recipient institution. News coverage of Eagles helping in disaster areas (or of adult Eagles earning high honors) typically are just sidebars to a larger story. It can be said that beyond some pro forma press releases from Scouting headquarters, almost all of the attention given to the nation's Eagle Scouts is organic and grassroots in origin. Eagle Scouting is its own promotion.

In fact, so effective is this marketing that it regularly spills over its own boundaries. For example, Wikipedia has compiled a list of famous individuals who are assumed to be Eagle Scouts but who are not: Henry Fonda (Scout and Scoutmaster), Walter Cronkite, Bill Gates (Life Scout), Jimmy Stewart (2nd Class Scout), Hank Aaron, and Harrison Ford (Life Scout). Some of the confusion comes from these individuals having earned other Scouting honors (such as the Silver Buffalo) or from doing Scouting advertisements—but most of all it is because they are such quintessentially American characters that it is assumed if they are in any way connected with Scouting then they must be Eagles.

The BSA's Annual Report to the Nation *delegation salutes President Harry S. Truman in the Oval Office in February 1951.*

Meanwhile, in the fictional world, as in the real one, while Boy Scouts have made thousands of appearances in books, television shows, and movies over the last century, the Eagle usually is reserved for the smartest, most accomplished or noblest characters—not just Indiana Jones, but everyone from the Professor on *Gilligan's Island* to Will Smith's character in *Men in Black* to *Snoopy* ("Beagle Scout").

ACHIEVEMENT

In the end, what truly keeps Eagle Scouting in an honored, almost-impregnable position in American culture are the achievements of the Eagles themselves. If the Eagle rank was only the highest achievement in Boy Scouting, its reputation still would be strong but far more circumscribed—and it would wax and wane with Scouting's own reputation.

But as we've already shown, it is all but immune to such cycles. No, there is something larger at work.

Eagles always have made news, but most of that news was made by adult Eagles for whom this childhood achievement was just the first step to eventual fame. But beginning in the 1960s, with the ascendance of the service project over the simple accumulation of merit badges as the key requirement of the Eagle rank, the actual achievement of the Eagle rank not only came to be seen as a peerless achievement of childhood but also as a major news event in its own right.

From that moment on, while there was (and always would be) the story of the new Nobel Prize winner who also was an Eagle Scout, that comparatively rare story now was joined by a steady drumbeat of new stories of teenagers accomplishing amazing, even landmark, things in every corner of the country.

In the last half-century, those stories only have increased in number and quality as something of an arms race emerging among the most ambitious young Eagle candidates—and Scouting itself has begun to recognize the best of those projects with awards and scholarships. It now is easy to imagine a Scout earning national attention at age 17 for his Eagle project, local coverage six months later for his Eagle award; then 30 years later entering the public again with a major career achievement (an Oscar, a Nobel Prize, election to national office, ascending to the CEO job at a major corporation or becoming the President of a university)—and then, after another decade, being recognized as the newest recipient of the Distinguished Eagle Scout Award.

That's a lot of attention both for the Eagle and for Eagle Scouting. And it guarantees that the Eagle medal and the men who wear it will be a part of the nation's story for many years to come.

BADGE OF HONOR

There is no small irony to the fact that the Eagle Scout award, which began with a different name and was less a considered strategy than an institution's stopgap response to overachieving young members, has proven to be the most respected and best-known award for American youth. What began as a badge of honor for a small coterie of dedicated teenagers has become not only the most enduring award for youth in American life but also the most consistently rewarding award in their own lives. And perhaps most amazing of all, what at first was considered just the next step in the accumulation of skill badges have over the course of a century, generated the greatest outpouring of youthful community service in history.

In the pages that follow, we will look at the story of the Eagle Scout award. We will be on hand for its awkward beginnings in the general confusion of Scouting's early years. Then we will look at how it assumed the role as the "Ambassador of Scouting" during the Roaring Twenties and its shift to becoming a beacon of hope for America's youth during the Great Depression.

After the Eagle goes to war for the second time, we will look at the 1950s and early 1960s and the golden age of American Scouting, and then at the chaos of the late 1960s and Scouting's greatest crisis—and the near-fatal mistake of trying to make the Eagle award "relevant." We'll then look at the slow renaissance of Scouting and the Eagle. And we'll end with the centennial—first of American Boy Scouting and then of the Eagle award—and at the growing professionalization of the Eagle rank and its service project as the value of the award becomes universally known.

Finally, we'll close with a look at Eagle Scouting as it enters its second century and what roles it is likely to play in both Scouting and American life in the decades to come.

Along the way, we will meet some of the most remarkable Americans of the last 100 years and hear the stories of achievements that are touching, heroic, and in some cases almost superhuman. For some of these individuals, these successes represent the most important accomplishments of their lives; for others, it is the first glimpse of future fame.

The Eagle is ambitious, yet humbling; the height of achievement, yet devoid of competition; the ultimate challenge of childhood, yet accomplishable by any boy with the courage to pursue it, no matter what their physical or intellectual gifts. It is straightforward and plain in its requirements but complex and subtle in their execution.

The Eagle Scout award has taken its place at the heart of American life not only because it reflects what is best about the United States but also because it captures some of the quixotic, even contradictory, nature of that life.

To understand how that came to be, we need to start at the beginning: with the very first Eagle Scout.

CHAPTER TWO

PATHFINDER

In April 1912, Arthur Rose Eldred of Troop 1 of Rockville Center,
Oceanside, Long Island, completed his 21st merit badge
and threw the Boy Scouts of America into a panic.

S couting in the United States was, at this point, just two years
old—and still more of a spontaneous movement revolving around
a couple of best-selling books rather than a formal and cohesive
organization.

In fact, the BSA was only one of a number of Scouting entities in the
United States competing for new members and the blessing of Englishman Robert Baden-Powell and British Scouting. Besides the Boy Scouts
of America, there also were the more militaristic American Boy Scouts
(the largest competitor to the BSA), the Rhode Island Boy Scouts and Sea
Scouts, the (Mormon) MIA Scouts, the Boy Scouts of the United States,
and the National Highway Patrol Association Scouts—not to mention the
Woodcraft Indians and the Sons of Daniel Boone that Ernest Thompson
Seton and Dan Beard, respectively, continued to operate in case the BSA
failed or didn't award them proper credit.

How the BSA emerged from this chaos as the sole winner is a long and convoluted story. Ultimately, it was the result of backing by the large and established YMCA, recruitment of the biggest figures in the field (not just Seton and Beard, but Baden-Powell himself), absorbing failing competitors, and the superior diplomatic and financial skills of first Chief Scout Executive James E. West.

The initial shakeout in U.S. Scouting would continue until 1918. And so, in early 1912, as Arthur Eldred completed his final merit badge, it was no sure thing that the BSA would emerge victorious—or even survive.

In fact, Arthur himself almost didn't join the Boy Scouts of America. A tall, quiet boy with a thick shock of black hair, Eldred had been born in Brooklyn, NY in 1895. After his father's death, the family moved to Oceanside. Arthur was raised by his mother and a brother, Hubert, who was a dozen years older.

In 1910, Hubert, the unsung hero of the story, joined thousands of other young Americans caught up in this new Scouting fad. An American Boy Scout (ABS) troop had been formed in Rockville Center—and Hubert resolved to join the ABS and bring along his baby brother—no doubt to give 15-year-old Arthur some structure and a greater male presence in his life.

New members of the American Boy Scouts drill with dummy muskets and a bugler in 1910.

But Hubert Eldred was a bit put off by all of the drilling, marching, and other martial activities that characterized the local ABS troop, so he decided to start a troop of his own and set off for ABS headquarters in New York City to obtain a charter. Then while he was in Manhattan, Hubert decided to stop by the YMCA building and visit the offices of the Boy Scouts of America. In the end, he found the BSA's ideals a better fit to his own and filed for a charter as BSA Troop 1 on Long Island for which he would be the first Scoutmaster.

The story of Long Island Troop 1 captures something of the improvised, low-budget nature of Scouting itself in those early years. For example, the handful of boys who comprised the troop met in the loft of the Eldred barn—suggesting neither a lot of money nor adult supervision. It also became known quickly as one of the few troops in the country in which every Scout owned a uniform. One story tells of a Scout in Troop 1 named Melvin Daly (we will meet him again) who came to a meeting in a snowstorm wearing shoes with just scraps of soles having apparently spent his shoe money on his first Scout uniform.

To the children of today who can pass through an entire K–12 education without ever once having walked to school, this image of young Scouts tramping through snow to meet unsupervised in a barn, raising money for their own uniforms, and being led on camping trips by a post-adolescent may seem like life on another planet. But it was precisely this spirit of independence, self-sufficiency, and naturalism that Seton, Beard, and Baden-Powell espoused, and that struck such a powerful chord in young men of the era. Many of them were, after all, the sons and grandsons of Civil War veterans, pioneers, immigrants, cowboys, and Indian fighters—and the chance to experience that disappearing world must have exerted a powerful pull.

And no Scout in the troop thrived more in this world than Arthur Eldred. He had, after all, joined at 15, likely making him the senior Scout in the troop. And that fact, perhaps combined with an adult perspective that sometimes emerges at that age, made Arthur a classic young man in a hurry.

RANK AND FILE

In 1911–12, advancement in Scouting was just about as undefined as everything else in the movement. The first Boy Scout *Official Handbook*, written in 1910 by Seton, was essentially a reworking of Baden-Powell's seminal 1908 British *Scouting for Boys*—which Seton (rightly) believed had borrowed extensively from Seton's own 1906 *Birch-Bark Roll of the Woodcraft Indians*. This first *Official Handbook* (of which nearly 29,000 copies were printed) was rushed out to give the Boy Scouts of America a clear and distinct identity.[1]

Not surprisingly, the result was a hodgepodge. Given Seton's reputation as a famous naturalist and writer, the manual worked best in establishing the philosophical foundation of American Scouting in the outdoors, woodcraft, Indian lore, camping, and natural science. It offered a vision of wildlife conservancy that wouldn't be seen in Scout handbooks (or American life) for another half-century. And it also was one of the best books of games for boys ever written.

Ernest Thompson Seton combined the contents of Robert Baden-Powell's Scouting for Boys *(left) with his own* Birch Bark Roll of the Woodcraft Indians *(center) to produce the BSA's first* Official Handbook *(right) in July 1910.*

But when it came to structuring, organization, and advancement, Seton's notoriously unsystematic mind failed him. Ranks, such as they were, were divided into Red, White, and Blue classes, with honors and "high honors" levels. Many of these requirements were relatively straightforward—ride a horse, be trained in archery or study geology—but others can only be described as romantic nonsense; notably, the high honor requirement to hunt a gorilla, grizzly bear or elephant. As you might imagine, the first year of the BSA didn't see a lot of advancement.

The next year, the BSA tried again—with much greater success. The Boy Scouts of America's *Handbook for Boys*, which would go through 37 printings and more than 3 million copies by mid-1927, was one of the most popular American children's books of all time. As a measure of Scouting's growing influence, the *Handbook* soon sported a cover, by leading illustrator J.C. Leyendecker that originally had appeared on the cover of *Saturday Evening Post* (creating a precedent that ultimately would lead to Norman Rockwell). Reinforcing his position as chief Scout executive, James E. West even sent out, with much fanfare, 4,500 reader's copies of the first printing to educators and civic leaders around the nation to solicit their suggestions—knowing full well that it already was too late to incorporate those suggestions into that edition.

Though no better organized than Seton's *Official Handbook* edition (and often more retrograde in its attitudes), the new Handbook was infinitely more structured in its message. For the first time, Scouting had its Oath, its multipart Law, and just as important, precise requirements for the Tenderfoot, Second Class, and First Class ranks—requirements that, in some form, largely survive today. And as soon as the book fell into the hands of enthusiastic young Scouts like Arthur Eldred, they set about tearing through those requirements as quickly as school and chores permitted.

The BSA's first Eagle Scout, Arthur Rose Eldred, as announced in The Brooklyn Eagle *newspaper in 1912.*

Eldred may not have been the first Scout to earn his First Class badge, which he reached in March 1911, but he must have been very close. Indeed, since the *Handbook* wasn't even officially published until August of that year, Arthur must have learned about the requirements early, perhaps through a newspaper (*Boys' Life* magazine wouldn't begin publishing for another year) or Hubert's contacts at BSA headquarters.

But now, having reached the official pinnacle of Scouting, young Arthur Eldred found himself entering into an unknown country. After First Class, where did a 16-year-old Boy Scout go next?

The answer was merit badges—awards for the mastery of a particular Scouting skill for basic apprenticeship in a potential adult career. They were the crucial step in turning Scouting from being just an exciting adventure for 11-year-olds to being a life-enhancing experience for 17-year-olds. Baden-Powell had invented merit badges (known as proficiency badges) and they had been a part of the British Scouting movement from the beginning. With its founding, the Boy Scouts of America had imported the idea and had initially announced just 14 badges—none of which had yet been manufactured or awarded. With the new *Handbook*, the BSA announced a total of 57 merit badges and this time actually began to make them.

BADGES OF MERIT

Then as now, the BSA's merit badges were an eclectic and intriguing bunch. Some of those original badges, in fact, still exist today—and even (in the case of architecture, art, athletics, bugling, chemistry, electricity, first aid, lifesaving, music, painting, public health, and scholarship) still look the same after a century. Other than a few badges that grew anachronistic in the modern world and were retired (e.g., taxidermy, stalking, not least because the meaning of the term changed, masonry, interpreting, pathfinding, blacksmithing, and bee farming) most still survive in some form under the same or slightly different name.

It is a measure of the thought that the BSA put into its merit badge program that there was only one real clunker—and only then because it was just too difficult. That was the Inventing merit badge, which required a Scout to not only invent a new device or mechanism but also to obtain a U.S. patent for it. Needless to say, not many Scouts ever attempted this badge during its four-year existence and it is something of a miracle that nine Scouts managed to earn it.

But if the BSA's merit badge program was a model of thoughtful planning, the new ranks these badges created were anything but. In the original *Handbook*, as is true today, the accumulation of earned merit badges created three special honors. But whereas those three ranks—Star, Life, and Eagle—today have very specific and distinct requirements, in 1912, they were little more than counters, a kind of super-merit badge designating a milestone in the total number of badges the Scout had earned. First Class, as the name suggested, was still considered the pinnacle rank of Scouting.

The original order of these "Merit Scout" honors was Life, Star, and Eagle, and they required 5, 10, and 21 merit badges respectively (Star and Life were reversed in the 1920s when it was determined that the five points of the Star insignia fit neatly with the five merit badge requirement). The Life insignia, shaped like a heart, was chosen because the first cluster of required merit badges dealt with health and fitness (first aid, lifesaving, public health, personal health, and athletics). The Star rank had its own set of required merit badges and likely was designed to be like Polaris, the North Star, to guide the Scout to the zenith rank of Scouting: the Eagle.

This explanation sounds much more straightforward and logical than it really was. For one thing, because the merit badges for the first two ranks were so tightly specified and mutually exclusive, it was possible to earn either without earning the other. By the same token, it also was possible to work directly toward Eagle without earning the other two ranks in between.

And, in fact, that's what Arthur Eldred did: he went straight for Eagle—and soon discovered that the Boy Scouts of America wasn't ready for him.

JUGGERNAUT

It's not as if Scouting didn't see Arthur coming. At the BSA's first great rally held at the 71st Regiment Armory in New York City in February 1911,

Second Class Scout Arthur Eldred and Troop 1 wowed the crowd (and their fellow Scouts) by lashing together a 20-foot sapling tower, then climbing it, and putting on a semaphore demonstration. So impressed were the other troops at the event that the Scouts of Troop 1 spent the next few months following up on invitations to teach their skills to other troops around the region.

A month later, Arthur completed First Class, studied the requirements of those first 14 merit badges, and was on his way. By August, with the publication of the *Handbook*, Arthur's universe of merit badge opportunities nearly quadrupled. Now nothing would stop him because merit badge sashes were a sartorial innovation still more than a decade in the future and because the BSA assumed that most Scouts never would earn more than a couple of merit badges. Eldred and his handful of peers in the vanguard of Scouting were required to sew their badges (embroidered circles on a square of khaki cloth) on the right forearm of their uniform. And by the end of 1911, Arthur's right sleeve was growing thick with them.

Baden-Powell was scheduled to review American Scouting with a visit in late January 1912. Wanting to put on the best face to the founder of worldwide Scouting—the BSA still was, after all, competing against a half-dozen other pretenders for official International Scouting designation—Chief Scout Executive West and his staff remembered the troop with the full set of uniforms, the precise marching drills, and the impressive signaling tower. The invitation went out to Long Island Troop 1 to join a second local troop to serve as the honor guard for Baden-Powell's arrival by ship.

It is telling about the precarious nature of most Scouting units of that era that Scoutmaster Hubert Eldred wrote back to West to politely decline the invitation because his troop could not afford to pay the train fare for the 21-mile trip to Manhattan. West quickly wrote back to say that the BSA would pick up the tab.

And so, on January 31, 1912, as Baden-Powell stepped down the gangplank of the *SS Arcadian* to begin his multiple city tour, he was met by a contingent of 40 Scouts forming two ranks on each side of his path. Baden-Powell would tell Hubert that "his finest memory of his entire trip around the world was sailing up beautiful New York Harbor and seeing the long line of straight-backed, uniformed Boy Scouts with the American flag on the right hand side of the line and the British Cross of St. Andrew on the left with the Boy Scout flag in the center."[2]

As he passed through the ranks, the retired Lt. General, whose career had been built on being a quick judge of character, found his attention drawn to one particular Scout. This boy, older than the rest, stood a head taller than the others. His right arm bore an astonishing number of merit badges and he wore a shiny First Class pin on his tunic. To the surprise of everyone, including the VIPs waiting at the end of the gangplank, Baden-Powell reached out and gave Arthur Eldred the left-handed Scout handshake and quickly began peppering him with questions. Eldred tried to answer the best he could but the unexpected attention of the great man, along with his fear that he was screwing everything up in the eyes of the event organizers waiting at the end of the ranks, combined to make him both red faced and increasingly inarticulate. Finally, to his immense relief, Baden-Powell moved on. And rather than annoyed, it is easy to assume that West and the rest of the BSA leadership positively were thrilled that the founder had paused to meet and approve the flower of American Scouting.

After all this, the BSA surely must have seen Arthur Eldred heading its way, at the front of a cohort of Scouts all of whom had made the Eagle rank their ultimate target. And yet, Scouting still seemed oblivious.

THE SELECT FEW

Legendary business efficiency consultant Joseph M. Juran first proposed the "Pareto principle" (named after an Italian economist) popularly known as the 80–20 Rule. As most people know, and many have seen in practice in their daily life, this rule suggests that the minority accomplishes the majority of the work in most human organizations. That's the standard definition but it also comes in many variations. Twenty percent of the members of a group represent 80 percent of the creativity, revenues, net worth, productivity, wealth, and achievement.

Scouting is not immune to this rule: a quick inspection shows that only about 20 percent of all Scouts stay in the organization and earn ranks beyond First Class. By the same token, 80 percent of all merit badges seem to be earned by about 20 percent of those who pursue them. Meanwhile, nearly all leadership positions in a troop are held by about one-fifth of the boys.

Looking at the early years of Scouting, it seems pretty obvious that by the time Baden-Powell walked down that gangplank, this 20 percent cohort of achievers already had emerged in the BSA.

But it doesn't end there. As anyone who ever has been a part of a major social movement or hugely popular technology start-up company knows, this emergent 20 percent begins to undergo its own 80–20. This "Pareto of Paretos"—an elite 4 percent—represents the superstars of any organization. They aren't just overachievers; they break through any boundary set for them, rewrite what it means to be successful in the organization, and very often establish legends and precedents that can last for generations. It is not a coincidence that the ratio of Eagles to total Boy Scouts has hovered around this same 4 percent over the last century.[3]

The uniform sleeve bearing the merit badges earned by the BSA's first Eagle Scout Arthur Eldred in 1912. Photo courtesy of NESA.

In retrospect, we can see in 1911 that the first 20 percent of successful Scouts emerged. But we also can recognize that in 1912, especially after the widespread availability of the *Handbook*, this super-elite was making its first appearance. The Boy Scouts of America, in creating the Merit Scout honors, thought it had dealt shrewdly with the challenge of overachieving Scouts for years to come. Within months, it already had fallen behind.

Arthur Eldred took Scouting to a whole new level in 1912. By April, eschewing both Life and Star (in fact, of the first nine Eagle Scouts, eight— including Arthur—did not earn either Life or Star Scout ranks as they were not required to do so before October 1914). Eldred had earned the 21 merit badges he needed for his Eagle rank. Arrayed in a three-by-seven grid on his sleeve, they began with Personal Health—then Plumbing, Gardening, Cooking, Painting, Swimming, Civics (symbolized by a fasces that soon would be abandoned), Lifesaving, Public Health, Cycling, Pathfinding, Interpreting (French), Electricity, Dairying, First Aid to Animals, Chemistry, Business, Handicraft, Firemanship, Horsemanship, and culminating with Poultry Farming. Six of Arthur's badges were from the original 14—suggesting that he, in a superhuman achievement, had earned the remaining 15 badges in less than six months.

But that doesn't capture the full magnitude of Arthur Eldred's achievement. In 1911 and early 1912, he was to Boy Scout merit badges what Babe Ruth was to home runs a dozen years hence. When he reached that 21st merit badge, a grand total of just 141 merit badges had been awarded to 50 Scouts in the *entire* BSA. Not only did Arthur Eldred at that moment own 15 percent of all of the awarded merit badges in Scouting, but he likely had more merit badges than all of the Scouts in entire Scout districts, councils, and perhaps even some regions. No Scout ever again would—or could—enjoy that kind of dominance.[4]

Arthur compiled affidavits from local city leaders confirming that he had been tested successfully for all of his merit badges and then sent the whole package off to BSA headquarters in New York City.

And there it sat for weeks, creating no little consternation. No one knew quite what to do about Arthur Eldred. Like many institutions, the BSA had, as a kind of theoretical exercise/membership motivator/publicity vehicle, established what it figured was an impossibly high achievement and assumed it wouldn't have to sweat the details for many years if ever. Instead, it posed a challenge to every boy in Scouting—a challenge that now had been met in just seven months.

VALIDATION

What now? Was it enough that Arthur Eldred could prove that he had earned the requisite merit badges and had passed muster with some local committee? Or was some of national certification required—and if so, of what would it consist? Certainly by this point, James E. West and the rest of BSA leadership had come to the realization that there were other near-Eagles queuing up out there across America, and that how they handled Arthur Eldred would set an important precedent for the approval of other new Eagles for years to come.

In the end, the BSA decided on a "board of review"—the name would stick forever—during which young Eldred would be invited down to Manhattan and tested on his Scouting knowledge by learned adults in each field.

The exact date of this board of review was not recorded, but it was likely sometime in early summer 1912. We also don't know whether the board met as a single gathering or was a series of individual interviews—that is, whether it more resembled a star chamber or a gauntlet. But one thing is certain: out of the more than 2 million Eagle Courts of Honor that have taken place, this not only was the first but also easily the most intimidating.

Facing 17-year-old Arthur Eldred were the founding fathers of Scouting: Chief Scout Ernest Thompson Seton, National Scout Commissioner Daniel Carter Beard, Chief Scout Executive James E. West, and Wilbert E. Longfellow, who had drafted the swimming and lifesaving sections in the Scouting *Handbook*. Seton and Beard were living legends and considered the leading experts in their fields. Worse, while Beard, West, and Seton held each other in enormous respect, they also mostly despised one another because of their gigantic egos as well as their nearly antithetical views about the philosophy of Scouting.

Seton, with his floppy hat, walrus moustache, and poor hygiene, was not just a brilliant storyteller (he was in many ways the precursor of Jack London) but also one of those Edwardian man-children who served as a philosophical bridge between the Romantics and the Hippies. His Scouting was a kind of pre-lapsarian mash-up of personal freedom, adventure in the woods, Native

American ceremonies, rites of manhood, and pacifist libertarianism. Beard's Scouting, by comparison, focused on woodcraft and other outdoor skills, and was highly patriotic. Beard himself was crisp and neat, even when dressed in white-fringed buckskins.

Tellingly, Seton had wanted to name the highest rank in Scouting the Silver Wolf, likely after his famous story about capturing Lobo the Wolf, the "King of the Currumpaw Valley" in New Mexico in the 1890s. It was not a title destined to sit well with Scoutmaster/Ranchers in rural America, who dealt daily with wolf predations. Beard lobbied for and won the American eagle for the award.

For West, meanwhile, the Boy Scouts of America was a nonprofit institution that had enjoyed considerable initial success but soon would fail unless it rationalized its operations, developed new sources of sponsorship from the wealthy and the powerful, continued its recruiting and marketing efforts, and beat the various contending Scouting-like organizations to official Congressional or White House certification. Even if it was about kids, West believed, it was time for Scouting as an institution to grow up. He had little time for the antics and self-aggrandizement of either of the other two men, and within three years, he had driven Chief Scout Seton out of the BSA and co-opted "Uncle Dan" Beard to serve for the next 40 years as the new unofficial Chief Scout.

Exactly how Arthur Eldred managed to navigate through the shoals of these competing interests may have been the biggest miracle of his miraculous year. The fact that each of these powerful men was looking for answers that often were the opposite of the one sought by the others—and each man presumably held a veto vote—it would seem to make it impossible for Arthur to survive the process. And yet he did.

We only can speculate as to why. It may be because all four members of the board realized that the BSA could use an Eagle Scout for organizational promotion. And in front of them sat not only a sterling example of American boyhood but also someone who already had been singled out by the worldwide founder of Scouting himself just a few months prior.

Nonetheless, an exhausted Arthur Eldred went home to Long Island to await the board's decision.

Ultimately, Arthur Eldred earned his Eagle. He deserved it. And the feuding founding fathers of Scouting put aside their differences to give it to him.

HERO

You might think this would be enough of an accomplishment for one summer for this young man. But, incredibly, he only had begun. While he waited for news, Arthur Eldred went on a camping trip with his troop to Orange Lake, New York. At some point during the day, Melvin Daly, the Scout who'd walked through the snow to the meeting, decided to wade in the lake. But he went out too far, slipped off an underwater ledge, and being a non-swimmer, sank beneath the surface.

Arthur, realizing that Daly was drowning, dove into the lake, swam to the bottom, found the boy, and pulled him to the surface. He quickly was joined by another Scout, Merritt Cutler, who grabbed Daly to help pull him to shore. Unfortunately, at this point, Daly revived and panicked. He wrapped Cutler in a death grip and the two boys went under water.

Arthur again dove in. He managed to pull the two boys apart and then, using his lifesaving skills, dragged Daly to shore. He then swam back out and helped in the now-struggling Cutler. This feat of heroism had numerous witnesses, and thanks to their reports, Arthur Eldred was awarded one of Scouting's first Honor Medals, reportedly by Chief Scout Seton himself.

On August 21, 1912, a letter from Chief Scout Executive West formally informed Arthur Eldred, now five days past his 17th birthday that he had been awarded the first Eagle Scout rank of the Boy Scouts of America. It was a historic letter—diminished somewhat by the fact that, after he had congratulated Arthur, West apologized that, well, his Eagle medal wasn't quite ready. It seemed that the dies for the top scroll and the Eagle dangle hadn't yet been fabricated.

Had it been known, this bit of news would have stunned thousands of Boy Scouts across America. They assumed the Eagle medal was real. After all, they'd seen a drawing of it in the *Handbook*—a rectangular ribbon of solid-colored satin, suspended from an unmarked metal bar, culminating at the bottom with a metal Eagle (presumably gold) in flight from right to left.

Arthur Eldred's Eagle Scout medal from September 1912. Photo courtesy of NESA.

No doubt that was what Arthur Eldred was expecting too. But that image never had been more than a preliminary artist's rendition. So Eldred undoubtedly was surprised, when the package finally arrived on Labor Day 1912, to find a very different Eagle medal inside. This one, possibly manufactured by the T.H. Foley Company, had a silver scroll at the top, bearing the Scout motto "Be Prepared," with a wire square knot (representing the Scout slogan "Do a Good Deed [later: Turn] Daily") dangling beneath— just like the bottom of the Scout insignia. Meanwhile, the satin ribbon suspended from the scroll was much more triangular and red, white, and blue. Finally, at bottom, hanging from three interlinked rings (the largest one inside the ribbon) was a very different—and as many noted, scrawny— Eagle: rampant, wings outstretched, and apparently gripping a narrow segment of perch or a bundle of arrow shafts. Across the Eagle's narrow chest, in raised relief, were the letters "B S A."

Eldred was the first recipient to see the true Eagle medal. The design has changed slightly over the years—the square knot took different lengths, the BSA lettering disappeared in the mid-1950s and reappeared in 1969, and the Eagle itself mercifully grew more robust. But after more than a century it remains so similar to Eldred's medal that only a collector can quickly tell the difference. And, in fact, that comparison can be made easily: Arthur Eldred's Eagle medal still survives and is scrutinized by young Scouts each day in its display at the National Scouting Museum in Irving, Texas. Its satin ribbon has been reduced partially to threads and the Eagle itself has lost much of its silver plating to reveal the bronze beneath the surface. But it is unmistakable as to what it is: both the prototype and the first awarded copy of the Eagle medal.

That September a proud, but obviously embarrassed, Arthur Eldred stood for a photographer (probably brother Hubert) in his full Boy Scout uniform— trousers and puttees, campaign hat tucked under his arm, and high-collared long tunic-jacket—with the 21 merit badges on the sleeve and his new Eagle Scout and Honor medals prominently displayed on his chest pocket. He posed for two photos (apparently in the yard in front of the screened porch of his house): one facing forward, with his arms crossed and a confident look on his face; the other holding his hat and looking away with the beginning of a smile—as if he's about to answer a question from a curious onlooker.

*Eagle Scout
Arthur Rose Eldred
around 1913.*

And that was it. The only public notice of Arthur's achievement was his inclusion in a merit badge honor roll in the August 1912 issue of the new *Boys' Life* magazine and an article in several local newspapers including the *Kingston* (NY) *Daily Freeman* that described him as a "sturdy, well-built, keen-eyed little fellow" who was the first of 2 million Boy Scouts to earn the award.

And then Arthur Eldred disappeared from Scouting history.

AFTERMATH

He didn't disappear from the world, of course. But, like all Scouts, when he moved on in life he packed away his medal and other Scouting mementos. Troop 1 soon disappeared—Scout troops in those days were often little more than a fraternity of schoolmates—and Hubert Eldred moved away from Rockville Centre.

Meanwhile, with a world war on the horizon, both Scouting and Scouts had much bigger concerns than preserving history.

Arthur Eldred attended Cornell University, ran on the cross-country team, and was president of the university's Agricultural Association. Graduating in 1916, he served in World War I as a Navy machinist on a submarine chaser based out of Corfu, Greece, patrolling the Strait of Otranto. He served honorably and saw combat on several occasions. During the 1918 Spanish flu epidemic, Eldred became sick while still on Corfu and was hospitalized. So horrific were the conditions at the hospital that a semi-delirious Eldred had to crawl to a stream for water at one point—permanently scarring his hip in the process. Eventually, he was shipped home, a process that, after more than two months, had only gotten Arthur as far as Gibraltar. There, he was given a choice of continuing the six-month long route home or taking his discharge on the spot and making his way back.

LEFT: Arthur Eldred (center) watches his son Willard (right) receive the Eagle Scout medal. RIGHT: Tennessee Abbott (right, great grandson of Arthur Eldred) holds his celebratory Eagle Scout cake with fellow Eagle recipient Sam Crane.

The intrepid Eagle chose the latter. He officially was separated from the Navy in March 1919. Luckily, soon after that, he met a group of U.S. Army soldiers who took a liking to him, put him in one of their uniforms, and sneaked him on as a stowaway on their troop ship. Eldred played soldier by day and slept each night in a lifeboat on the voyage home to the United States.

Life back stateside proved much less exciting for Arthur and he seemed to welcome the peace and quiet. He went to work for a dairy and by 1921 had worked his way up to become Agricultural Agent for New Jersey's Atlantic County. He served in that role for seven years, during which time he was credited with creating the Atlantic City Municipal Farmer's Market.

In 1928, Eldred joined the Reading Railroad as a specialist in promoting the railroad transportation of produce. In time, he was named manager of the Motor Carrier Committee of the Eastern Railroad Association. It was a position he would hold the rest of his life. In later years, Eldred also served on the Camden County Council and the local school board.

Through the years, Arthur Eldred never forgot Scouting, nor ever left it. As early as the 1920s, he served as a board of review examiner—no doubt for Eagle candidates who imagined that their experience was the toughest ever. Later, Eldred served as committee chairman for his son Willard's Troop 77 in Clemeton, New Jersey. A

Theodore Gaty Jr.—the BSA's 38ᵗʰ Eagle Scout as announced in the August 1913 issue of Boys' Life *magazine.*

photograph from 1944 shows Arthur, in a suit with thinning hair, looking on as an Eagle medal is pinned on Willard's uniform. Sons in three generations of Eldreds now have earned their Eagles.

About this time, Eldred did something else that would prove crucial to Scouting's understanding of itself: he compiled his documents, including his brother's record of Baden-Powell's visit, his Honor Medal citation, James E. West's letter informing Arthur that he'd become an Eagle and perhaps most important, a carbon copy of an account of his Scouting experiences that he'd written in 1940 and sent to his old high school principal.

Perhaps he'd had a premonition.

On January 4, 1951, Arthur Eldred, the first Eagle Scout, died of colon cancer. He was 55 years old. He had lived long enough to see nearly one-half million Eagle Scouts follow the path he'd cut but not long enough to participate in his own rediscovery.

By the 1960s, as the first generation of Scouts began to fade away and a vast new generation of Scouts appeared on the scene, the Boy Scouts of America finally began to look back on its history and its story. And it found Arthur Rose Eldred. Books about Scouting, many of them featuring brief mentions of Eldred and his achievement, were being published.

Unfortunately, and with the inexplicable confusion that always seemed to characterize Scouting's relationship with its first Eagle, the photo that accompanied these stories was of the wrong boy. That photo was of Theodore Gaty Jr., the 38th Eagle, whose good looks and square jaw were right out of a Leyendecker illustration. The puzzle only was solved in 2005 when Gary Twite, a commissioner in BSA's Chief Seattle Council purchased a pair of antique photographs—the two described earlier—and realized they had a much closer resemblance to the 1944 Eldred than the official photo. The truth was confirmed by Willard Eldred, now himself a senior citizen.

But if Gaty looked the part of the first Eagle, Arthur Eldred lived it. In his three short years in Boy Scouts, Eldred had transformed the Boy Scouts of America. He had set a shining example to Scouting's founder, earning the great man's approval, and thus helped establish the primacy of the BSA over its rivals. He had saved the life of another Scout. He had permanently restructured Scouting's own operating philosophy to make the merit badge ranks the true second phase of the Scouting experience. And, by dint of his hard work and ambition, he even had forced Boy Scouts to make the Eagle

Scout rank both real and the new pinnacle of Scouting. Most of all, quiet, serious Arthur Eldred had set a high standard for what a Boy Scout—an *Eagle* Scout—could be. He had honored the BSA in a way no other Scout ever has.

Like most Eagles, Arthur Eldred never became a famous man, but in his quiet way, he was a great man and a great Eagle Scout. He was a pillar in his community, a man who committed himself to serving others throughout his life, and a person who left the world a better place than he found it. Baden-Powell had been right that day on the ship dock: Arthur Eldred would do just fine as the first Eagle Scout.

CHAPTER THREE

SIR KNIGHT

Raymond O. Hanson was a haunted man.

I t was 1925, and the Boy Scouts of America had experienced profound changes in its first 15 years. For one thing, in the years since Arthur Eldred had earned his Eagle, the BSA had seen tremendous growth— its 62,000 members had exploded to 760,000, a twelvefold increase. The number of Eagle Scouts had seen a similar leap—Scouting now had produced a total of 10,746 Eagle Scouts, with many of them still active as Scoutmasters and Assistant Scoutmasters.[1]

The last figure was the one that had come to obsess Scout Executive Hanson for the San Francisco Council. What he, like many other professional Scouters around the country, saw was young men rising through the ranks of Scouting and at last achieving not just the Eagle rank but the level of leadership and skill competence that came with being an Eagle and then leaving Scouting.

Many of these Eagles simply left because they turned 18 and left—and, if Scouting was lucky, they might return a quarter-century later with a 12-year-old son. But others, perhaps even more, Eagles quit Scouting well before their 18th birthday simply because Scouting no longer appealed to them. They had earned all the merit badges that interested them, held all the leadership positions in the troop, and been to the same summer camp too many times. But most of all, they had found Scouting—enthralling when they were 12— now simply too *juvenile* in light of their growing adult interests.

And so they quit. So much talent and experience lost—a reality made even *more* painful by the recognition that even with its remarkable growth, Scouting could have grown even more had it been able to recruit more leaders. So why, Hanson asked himself, was Scouting consciously jettisoning the best of its newly trained young leaders simply because of an arbitrary retirement date? Why did Scouting devote so much time and energy bringing boys to a peak of competence and confidence and then abandon them? Why couldn't this soon-to-be lost intellectual capital be retained and put to good use now—instead of waiting until, say, 1950?

Hanson asked himself, why had Scouting, which had proven itself so brilliant in creating a program that captured the imaginations of the nation's 12- to 15-year-old boys, not done the same for its 16- to 18-year-olds? Why did Eagle Scouts, the crowning achievement of the movement, young men who should have been savoring what they had accomplished, instead grow bored and walk away?

For Ray Hanson, each departing Eagle Scout in his council was like a body blow—an unrestorable waste of potential and a small betrayal to the Eagle himself. And sitting in his office in San Francisco, he would look down Market Street, past the Ferry Building and across the continent, and wonder why BSA national headquarters wasn't seeing the same thing.[2]

RESISTANCE

What Scouters on both coasts—and everywhere in-between—understood was that the Boy Scouts of America wasn't the same organization in 1925 as it had been in 1913. And it wasn't just the growth of the membership rolls, or the final rationalization of ranks and requirements, or the geographic expansion of troops, or even the ongoing experimentation with a new "Cub" program for younger boys.

No, Scouting had changed because the world had changed. The movement had been born in the Progressive Era, that tenuous marriage between scientific empiricism and romantic environmentalism, buoyed by the belief that the world had entered into a more enlightened age of continuous progress. Boy Scouting had been devised in part in the belief that even boyhood was a problem that could be solved.

But that confidence had died in the flooded trenches of Passchendaele on the Western Front and in the Hall of Mirrors with the signing of the Treaty of Versailles. What was left now was either disillusionment (as exemplified by the Lost Generation wandering about Europe) or a new, less-idealistic pragmatism.

By its very nature, Scouting was destined to choose the latter. The days of ad hoc groups meeting in barns and playing Indians or Frontiersman were gone. Scouting was now a giant organization, as big as any domestic corporation, and one of the largest institutions in American life. Thanks to the efforts

Chief Scout Executive James E. West sends off Eagle Scout Raymond Wood of Columbia, South Carolina, to the Holy Land as BSA's International Golden Rule Ambassador in July 1924.

of James E. West, whose 30 years as chief Scout executive would provide the stability and continuity the organization needed, Scouting had been organized, systematized, and recognized.

The requirements for each of the ranks now had been set and made universal across the program. The number of merit badges had increased continuously in both number (by 1930 there would be 92) and scope (new badges included Zoology, Weather, Salesmanship, and Railroading).[3] And the "patrol method" from which Baden-Powell first had built Scouting now had evolved into a sophisticated and multi-tiered management structure for troops that included patrol leaders, senior patrol leaders, instructors, and even librarians and chaplains. The adult volunteer/professional apparatus of districts and councils, Scoutmasters, committees, and commissioners now was largely complete as well.

Purists, not least Ernest Thompson Seton, complained that Scouting had lost something important—the innocence and freedom of childhood that had characterized the movement at its conception—in its transformation to respectability. But West's answer was a simple one: under his leadership Scouting had both survived and thrived and soon would soon be delivering its experience to 1 million American boys. None of that would have been possible with the 1910 version of Scouting. Scouting's extraordinary success was the prima facie counterargument to any of its critics.

But, West also could point out, much of Seton's original vision of Scouting had, in fact remained. It had merely been packaged into, or channeled through, the more formal organization. Thus, Seton's vision of younger Scouts was emerging as Cub Scouting, his worship of Native American culture had been the foundation of Scouting's camping fraternity—the Order of the Arrow (created in 1915)—and when it came to his belief that boys should spend time in the outdoors, how could he argue with hundreds of thousands of American boys now out camping and learning woodcraft skills at least one weekend per month?

Scouting may have lost some of its innocence (though not in the public's imagination) but it also had gained something far more important than good bookkeeping: a new purpose.

The transformative event had been the World War I. Here again, the conflicting visions of the BSA founders had unwittingly forced the best possible compromise. It was a middle ground between Seton's pacifism and Beard's jingoism—a position that could best be described as staunchly patriotic *non-militarism*.

What this meant in practice was that the BSA was deeply committed to the war effort as a U.S. organization and went to enormous lengths to instill the values of duty and love of country into its young members. It also was dedicated to teaching its young charges the kind of skills—bravery, resourcefulness, first aid, camping and hiking, and survival—that would make them *become* superior soldiers. But Scouting itself refused to take the next step to the teaching of American boys to *be* good soldiers. Scouts wore uniforms but they weren't military uniforms. They marched, but never with weapons. They played war-like games but never held war games.

This was, at least initially, a difficult position to maintain. As the fighting intensified in Europe, and as older brothers—and eventually older Scouts themselves—began to volunteer or be drafted, considerable pressure from the highest levels was placed on the BSA to become a kind of Junior ROTC and assume some of the duties of military basic training.

Scouting resisted—and that, other than the actual founding of Scouting in America—may have been the single most important decision the BSA ever made.

By not following the path that led to being merely an extension of the armed forces, BSA made itself much less vulnerable to the cultural swings between pro-military and anti-military eras that characterized American life during the rest of the 20th century. Radicals of different decades still accused BSA of being a paramilitary organization—an argument that would have had a lot more teeth had the BSA chosen the other path—but those claims found little support.

By taking the position it did, the BSA never faced the danger of being hijacked by political interests pursuing a sinister objective. There were no *Hitler-Jugend* or Soviet Young Pioneers in the future of American Scouting—in the end those who tried, like the German-American Bund with its *Jugendshaft*, obviously were transgressive imitations.

BSA's choice to resist was so important because it also forever changed the *orientation* of Scouting. Until the outbreak of the World War I, Scouting had remained a comparatively introverted organization, focused mainly on camping, woodcraft, and advancement. What encounters these early Scouts had with their communities mostly was restricted to those daily "good turns"—hence the eternal association of Boy Scouts, especially younger ones, with walking little old ladies across the street—and merit badge instruction.

SAVE A SOLDIER

And so it might have remained had war not erupted. Now the Boy Scouts of America faced an existential challenge: how could it, as a patriotic organization, help the nation in its war efforts while remaining true to its non-militaristic charter?

One last time, the parent Scouting organization in England provided a model solution. From the beginning, Baden-Powell's program had been accused of being too militaristic. He was, in fact, still on active duty in 1907. Ultimately, several competing organizations formed in reaction to this perception—the Order of World Scouts, which still exists today in 14 countries, and the British Boy Scouts (BBS), which at one point represented one-third of Scouts in the UK. There were even British Peace Scouts. The success and growing internationalism of these organizations—indeed, the BBS appears to have only failed because of financial mismanagement—had forced Baden-Powell to move Scouting away from a strong military connection, a stance he was in no position to abandon in 1914. Instead, he directed Scouting to immerse itself in service on the home front.

Baden-Powell's definition of home "service" was a pretty fluid one—perhaps not surprising given either his background or the fact that Britain was under direct attack. British Scouts not only joined agricultural work and other activities, but also served as military messengers and coastal guards. One Scout, 15-year-old George Taylor, was killed during the siege of Scarborough—and was buried with full military honors at a service filled with his fellow Scouts. Taylor was the only active Scout known to have been killed during the war.

As for Baden-Powell himself, he placed himself before the War Office in search of a command. But Lord Kitchener refused to give him one, saying he "could lay his hand on several competent divisional generals but could find no one who could carry on the invaluable work of the Boy Scouts."[4] Whether or not that was the real reason, it was a wonderful publicity message, and it underscored the importance of British Scouting to the war effort. During the war, it was regularly rumored that Baden-Powell was engaged in espionage activities—an activity never proven, but also shrewdly never denied by intelligence officers.

A young Boy Scout assists two aging Civil War veterans at the Gettysburg Reunion in Pennsylvania on July 1, 1913.

Three years later the Boy Scouts of America, facing the same challenge, chose the same solution—and with a vengeance. Scouting already had begun to find its public footing with Scouts (many of them Eagles), who had served on the honor guard and support staffs at the Star-Spangled Banner Centennial ceremonies in 1914 and at various 60th anniversary reunions of Civil War Veterans beginning in 1913. It also had found considerable success with its National Good Turn, begun in 1912 with a "Sane and Safe Fourth of July" initiative.

On June 15, 1916, the BSA finally reached its goal of a congressional charter. From now on, it would be the sole Scouting organization of the United States. Henceforth, it would be an official American institution. Now, with America entering the war—and with their big brothers, including former Scouts and Eagles like Arthur Eldred, heading off to France—Scouts were anxious to do their part. The BSA, filled with its own patriotism and recognizing a unique opportunity, quickly created programs to help the boys do so.

Begun in 1917, first was the Veteran Scout program 1917 to help retiring Scouts, wherever they were, maintain contact with Scouting. Then, when the United States declared war at last, Scouting was ready with a "Help Win the War" campaign. This campaign, which was built on the BSA's ready-made motto—"Be Prepared", incorporated a wide range of programs designed to

Boy Scouts collect their harvest of corn at a World War I Boy Scout Farm in 1918.

empower even the youngest Scouts to be part of the war effort. For example, the "Every Scout to Feed a Soldier" initiative instructed Scouts to plant their own victory ("war") gardens—a total of 12,000 were created. In another program destined to become a trivia question, Scouts collected 100 railroad cars' worth of nut hulls and peach pits to be used to make charcoal filters for gas masks. They also identified and charted the location of 21 million board feet of black walnut trees for use in gunstocks and airplane propellers and

Boy Scouts pose with a 1917 War Bond campaign poster.

distributed 30 million pieces of government literature to the citizenry.[5]

These achievements were impressive enough and did much to capture the public imagination but they paled in comparison to the showpiece initiative for Scouting during those years—war bonds.

It began with the huge government-sponsored "Wake Up, America!" rally held in New York City on April 17, 1917. Ostensibly held to commemorate the 1775 Battle of Lexington, the rally was in fact a military recruiting event. In an enthralling photograph from that day published in the *National Geographic* (and used nine decades later by the U.S. Post Office to promote a stamp series about the decade) scores of Scouts in full uniform and carrying tall staffs bearing American flags can be seen running down Fifth Avenue as if leading the charge of the 60,000 parade participants into battle.

War bonds—officially "Liberty" Bonds—were an array of government script ranging in valuation from $50 or more for the official money-like bonds, down to just 25¢ for War Savings Stamps. Strictly speaking, these bonds were IOUs covering the principle and interest for the loan made to the government by citizens with their purchase.

Flag waving Boy Scouts race down Fifth Avenue in New York City for the "Wake Up, America!" rally on April 17, 1917.

War bonds quickly became synonymous with "doing something for our boys 'over there,'" and Liberty Bond rallies often drew thousands—especially when the entertainment featured the likes of Charlie Chaplin, Mary Pickford, or the Ziegfield girls. Boy Scouts across America were enlisted into the program as foot soldiers for the bond drives: handing out promotional flyers, going door to door to either sell bonds or seek out rally attendees, serving as ushers, and perhaps most of all, acting as the very embodiment of "what we're fighting for."

This last was most brilliantly visualized in one of the most celebrated (and collected) posters of the era (called "Weapons for Liberty"). It was created by J.C. Leyendecker for the third Liberty Bond drive in 1918, and as was often the case, began its life as a March 1918 *Saturday Evening Post* cover. It is still a knockout: Lady Liberty atop her plinth has come to life and is now draped in an American flag and carrying a golden shield bearing the Great Seal of the United States (that looks like a giant military officer's dress uniform button). Girded for war, Liberty gazes out into the distance, apparently at an emerging threat and, without looking, is reaching down for her giant broadsword. That sword has been etched with the words "Be Prepared", and it

Scouting's early moves toward racial inclusionary policies are evident during the 1917 War Bond campaign.

is being lifted to Liberty by a kneeling young Boy Scout wearing a campaign hat, neckerchief, and khaki shorts. On the plinth has been carved: "Weapons for Liberty".

As a piece of propaganda, the poster for the third Liberty Bond drive is a masterpiece. As a bit of over-the-top patriotic theater in poster form (perhaps driven by Leyendecker's self-consciousness about his German birth), it is one of the best ever done by an American illustrator. It is so influential in the Scouting story because of a critical aesthetic decision made by the artist.

Leyendecker was and is justly famous for his images of impossibly handsome men (he did invent the iconic Arrow Collar Man, after all). But with the Scout set beneath the battle-tested, androgynous Lady Liberty, Leyendecker makes a very different choice: he portrays a real boy: skinny, a bit gawky, and a bit overwhelmed by the situation in which he finds himself. To understand why this is important, you need only imagine the Scout replaced by a classic Leyendecker square-jawed young man out of an Interwoven Sock or Pierce-Arrow ad: what would be gained in artistic coherence would be more than lost by distancing the viewer. The genius of Leyendecker in putting the real-life boy in the poster is that, for adults, it placed Boy Scouts at the heart of American life during wartime; and for boys, it enabled them to see *themselves* in the poster.[6]

J.C. Leyendeker's famous Third Liberty Loan campaign poster features a kneeling Boy Scout handing the sword of preparedness to a battle-ready Lady Liberty.

A third impact of this famous poster wouldn't be seen for almost two more decades—in Leyendecker's most faithful follower, Norman Rockwell, who already was painting covers for *Boys' Life*. Rockwell, who one day would be a pallbearer at his mentor's funeral, learned much from this poster—not least that no matter how mythical the subject, the Boy Scout in the image had to look like the kid next door.

In the first Liberty Bond drive held in April 1917, the Boy Scouts under the slogan "Every Scout to Save a Soldier" (the Girl Scouts ran an identical campaign) stunned everyone by raising $23 *million*. They topped that in October, in the second campaign, by raising $102 million.[7] By now, Scouting was becoming as synonymous with Liberty Bonds as Douglas Fairbanks and Al Jolson—not a bad place to be in 1917—and the best was yet to come.

For the third campaign, to be held in April 1918, Scouting went all out. Secretary of the Treasury William Gibbs McAdoo made a special appeal to James E. West that Boy Scouting shift from the high-profile/high-ticket fundraisers and focus instead on a house-to-house appeal. President Woodrow Wilson himself asked that Scouting be the "gleaners and reapers" of the Liberty Bond drive, focusing on private citizens and small organizations that the national campaign might not reach—and then to sell the lower-cost instruments like the War Savings Stamps.

The third campaign kicked off with a major rally for Scouts at Liberty Loan Park in New York at Madison Avenue and Thirty-Eighth Street. Afterward, Scouts, armed with their new Government Printing Office pamphlets instructing them on successful salesmanship using the points of the Scout Law and under the banner of the Leyendecker poster, fanned out across America to do their patriotic duty.

What happened next cemented Scouting forever into American life. A few weeks later, when the numbers were tabulated, it was found that the Boy Scouts of America had sold a seemingly superhuman $205 million *more* bonds—nearly all in the smallest denominations available.[8] By war's end, over the course of five Liberty Bond drives, America's Boy Scouts sold 2,328,308 bond subscriptions for a total of $354,859,262. They also sold more than 2 million War Savings Stamps worth $43,043,698.[9]

In just 20 months, the BSA had mobilized its 400,000 members, re-oriented its energies towards the community and supporting the war effort and, in the process, had raised almost $400 million—more than $6.2 *billion* in 2015 dollars—toward that effort.[10] The organization then made a quick turn and provided nationwide first-aid service during the 1918 Spanish influenza epidemic.[11]

Together, this was the largest youth service initiative in American history to date. It is little wonder, as the decade ended, that the Boy Scouts were almost heroes as celebrated as the nation's returning doughboys.

PROTAGONIST

Where were Eagles during this great transformation in Boy Scouting? As always, they were in front, leading. But, at this point in the Scouting story, only other Scouts and their leaders noticed.

After just a decade, Boy Scouting was one of the most celebrated new cultural institutions in the land; and the boys who wore its uniform were instantly recognizable almost anywhere. This new celebrity was driven home in 1923 when, joined by Jackie Coogan, the most famous child star

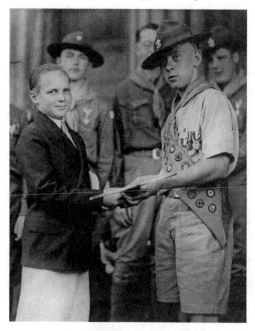

of the age, Scouting took part in the national Milk Campaign that made the humble carton of milk a standard feature of school cafeterias for generations to come.

But beyond that, to the general public the Scouts themselves were essentially indistinguishable. They were young and a little older, short and tall, and they all wore khaki uniforms, neckerchiefs, campaign hats, and a variety of patches and pins of obscure meaning.

It would be several decades more before the badges and ranks of Scouting—especially Eagle—would be distinguishable to most Americans. And that process would begin in the 1920s in the world of entertainment and the media.

An Eagle Scout hands young Hollywood actor Jackie Coogan the keys to the city of Detroit in the 1920s.

Scouts emerged from the war years as both amusing and heroic figures—amusing because they were so young and ardent, heroic because of their extraordinary service to the country—and the stories created about Scouting for a hungry audience in the 1920s reflected that schizoid perception.

Beginning with silent films, first in the UK (*Scouts to the Rescue*, 1908) and then in the United States (*Universal Boy Joins the Boy Scouts*, 1914), Scouting was basically a new leitmotif on which to play out traditional adventure stories. Early fiction on Scouting was much the same, notably the Boy Scout series of books begun by author Herbert Carter in 1913 (e.g., *The Boy Scouts through the Big Timber, The Boy Scouts in the Maine Woods, The Boy Scouts'*

First Camp Fire). In these productions, the Scouts are young and competent but usually played to comic effect. This narrative thread has continued right up to the present, constantly adding new layers—postmodernism, cynicism, social conflict, optimism, technology—to essentially the same tale of do-good Scouts made to look foolish out of a combination of too much sincerity and naivety, but ultimately succeeding through their unique skills and determination.

The "good deed daily" Scout stereotype found in the earliest movies, books, and cartoons about Scouting, survives to this day—often slightly disguised to circumvent Scouting's copyright demands—in everything from TV episodes of *The Simpsons* and *South Park*, to comic strips featuring "Calvin and Hobbes" and the "The Berenstain Bears" series of children's books.

This is the Boy Scout patrol reviewed by President Woodrow Wilson in the film The Making of a Scout.

A more nuanced version of this Scout can also be found in productions such as the classic film *Mr. Smith Goes to Washington*, and even in the guise of a drag queen in the musical *Rent*.

But there is a second, more complicated narrative thread about Scouting that began to emerge during the World War I, exploded in the 1920s, and has made subtle and often unexpected appearances ever since. In these books, movies, and television shows, the Scout is older, more accomplished and almost never a fool—on the contrary, he is often the hero and protagonist of the story. And though it is rarely said—at least not until the last 30 years when the title finally distinguished itself in the public mind—the Scouts are most certainly Eagles. And when their title is stated—as with the Will

Smith character in *Men in Black*, or Captain Jonathon Archer in *Star Trek: Enterprise*, or even the Professor on *Gilligan's Island*—"Eagle Scout" is almost always code for clever, brave, and resourceful. This fictional Eagle first appears in a spate of very popular books published through the 1920s with titles like *Boy Scouts on Motorcycles*, *Boy Scouts in the Northwest Fighting Forest Fires*, and *Boy Scouts of the Air on Lost Island*—potboilers all. Additionally, they appear in classic ripping yarns where older Scouts behave like proto-action figures (soon-to-be-invented Eagle Scout Indiana Jones comes as no surprise to anyone who has read these books) taking on adult responsibilities, acting bravely, and using their unique Scouting skills to best their evil opponents.

These stories introduced an older, more responsible, and more adventurous image of Scouting not just to the American public but also to Scouts themselves. And they wanted to be those heroic characters. The 1920s saw the birth of the first glimmerings of Scouting's future high adventure program, as these same older Scouts began testing themselves with 50-mile hikes, wilderness survival camps, and other feats.

One positive result of the influenza epidemic for Scouting had been that the BSA had taken a hard look at its emerging collection of summer camps (military camps had been the breeding ground of the epidemic), concluded that too many were unacceptable, and established a set of standards for these sites—which in turn laid the groundwork for a growing number of special outdoor programs (climbing, rappelling, and so on) at these camps. Needless to say, Eagles soon found their place serving on camp staffs and running these programs.

Other older Scouts migrated to specialty versions of Scouting, notably the Sea Scouts, where they could be with their chronological peers and take part in activities that were riskier, more demanding, and more rugged than most of what traditional Boy Scouting could offer. Besides the Sea Scouts, a number of other specialty Scouting programs emerged over the next 20 years. In a brochure for "Senior Scouts" published by the BSA in 1938, Chief Scout Executive West noted "the surprising fact" that more than 200,000 registered Scouts were more than 15 years old:

> *There never has been any upper age limit to Scouting. Hundreds of thousands of young men have carried on as Junior Assistant Scoutmaster or Assistant*

Scoutmasters, upon reaching the age of sixteen or eighteen respectively and then have become Scoutmasters. Many others have preserved their membership with their Troop even while away at college as associate Scouts.

During the years, Sea Scouting as a program for older Scouts, has steadily grown in its appeal until today there are 29,500 young men and leaders registered in this branch of the Movement. The experiences gained in our contact with these young men has been invaluable.

In recent years there have been experiments with Rovering (British Venturing program) throughout the country. On the college campus, the Alpha Phi Omega, an honorary society for Scouts who are in institutions of higher learning, has come into being. In addition, certain Local Council organizations for older Scouts have come into existence. In the far West, much success was attained in the experiment with an Explorer Program for older Scouts.[12]

The passive language ("have come into being") betrays an organization faced with a fundamental paradox—one that still bedevils Scouting. As its name suggests, Boy Scouting is about *boys*, these days between the ages of 11 and 14—that is, roughly between fifth and eighth grades, or in Scouting terms, the final "Webelos" year of Cub Scouting and, in Boy Scouting, the achievement of First Class and the leadership position of Patrol Leader. Everything before is basically an after-school program for children; everything after is an adventure/senior management/career training program for young adults.

This isn't to say that the activities on either ends of this spectrum are superfluous to Scouting. On the contrary, the Pinewood Derby for Cub Scouts is as iconic to American life as anything in Scouting. And much of the glory of Boy Scouting lies in its high adventure camps (such as Philmont) and, as we shall see, in its Eagle service projects. But the mass of Scouting will always lie within those four years, with its focus on the patrol, the troop, weekend campouts, and outdoor skills. *That* never can be compromised.

And there is the problem. The better Scouting does its job, the more Scouts who will want to stick with the program after they turn 14, when troop meetings and fourth time around at some of the same campsites is no longer enough. Demography plays a part as well: one reason Scouting (and the rest of America) found itself in a crisis in the late 1960s was because the mass of baby boomers had rolled through and were now in their late teens.

Not wanting to lose this vast source of intellectual capital today, and adult leadership tomorrow, institutions inevitably responded by creating specialty programs for its veteran members that walked a fine line between allowing them a certain amount of independence while still keeping them tightly bound to the organization.

And that is exactly what Scouting did, with those various Senior Scout programs—some of which, such as Sea Scouting and Exploring still survive today.

But these separate programs inevitably brought with them a whole new set of problems. For one thing, they drew away talent and resources from the main organization—a major problem for Scouting in the 1920s when it was short on leaders, and in the 1930s when it was short on money. Another problem was that, if successful, these operations tended to exacerbate the very problem they were created to solve: that is, if all of the older Scouts ran off to join Rovering or Sea Scouts, who would be left to lead the troops?

Finally, there was the problem of expectations: young men joined senior Scout organizations to live out the dreams of adventure they read about and watched in movies—could Scouting provide that? Did it want to? At the same time, almost by definition, these senior Scouts were the members most committed to advancement—did Scouting want to allow them to continue their march through the ranks even if, strictly speaking, they weren't involved in Boy Scouts anymore? Or did each of these groups need its own advancement program?

Scouting's answer to the first—high adventure—proved to be brilliant. The Senior Scout organizations came and went according to the interests of that age cohort and were free to develop their programs in any way, as long they didn't violate Scouting rules. As for the second, advancement, Scouting mostly failed. Each program did develop its own ranks and supreme award, many of them more difficult than Scouting's own, but the Sea Scouting Quartermaster Award, and the Exploring/Venturing Silver Medal (to name the most popular) never achieved anything like the public acclaim afforded to the Eagle medal—a fact that no doubt led the majority of Scouts to stick with their Boy Scout troops, even as they became increasingly irrelevant to their teenaged lives.

It is hard not to conclude that this was exactly the way the Boy Scouts of America wanted it. It understood the desire of these older boys to continue their Scouting experience (or join and catch up on what they missed) and was happy to allow these institutional "safety valves" to pop up on the fringes of the program. But each year, a half-million excited new 12-year-olds were showing up at troop meetings around the country—and the BSA's first duty was to engage those boys, give them an experience they'd remember the rest of their lives, and help them reach the summit of basic Scouting—the First Class rank.

But there was one other group of older Scouts who shared the same desire to stay engaged with Scouting, combined with a desire to create their own special program that was so central to Scouting that the BSA could neither ignore nor marginalize it: Eagle Scouts. By 1921, Scouting already was producing 1,000 Eagles per year. As the finest flowering of the Scouting philosophy and the *ne plus ultra* of the movement, Eagle Scouts were too important for Scouting to lose—and yet, by the mid-1920s, several thousand were leaving every year.

The BSA had rested its hopes on the belief that, being among the most committed of Scouts, Eagles would want to stay associated with the program straight through into adulthood—hence West's almost wistful comment about older Scouts becoming Junior Assistant Scoutmasters, Assistant Scoutmasters, and then Scoutmasters in the years to come. Certainly that would prove true for many Eagle Scouts—but often after an interregnum of decades. The flaw in Scouting's logic—once again it had been surprised by its Eagles—was that it had failed to understand that overachievers rarely stick around to admire their handiwork; instead, they race off for the next mountain to climb.

Still, if Scout headquarters did not yet understand the problem, a continent away there was one Scouting professional who did: a born entrepreneur who would have felt right at home in the world of high- tech start-up companies that would define his community a half-century hence. And he would build the most mythic (literally and figuratively) among the most influential, and the least celebrated, organization in Scouting history.

A RETINUE OF KNIGHTS

Raymond O. Hanson was the right man for the challenge. A slight man with horn-rimmed glasses who most resembled a college professor, Hanson was in fact—in the great Northern California tradition—one of the great mavericks of American Boy Scouting. And as he pondered the conundrum of the Lost Eagles, it slowly dawned on him that the solution might not be to reform Scouting but to lead a friendly revolt against it.

In early 1925, the BSA not only was experiencing spectacular growth but was also looking forward to even more as a baby boomlet created by the war was about to enter its teenage years. This expansion in both membership and units combined with the chronic shortage of leaders was putting considerable stress on the organization—and the last thing it had time to worry about was either the retention of older Scouts or the care and cultivation of Eagles. Meanwhile, most of the Senior Scouting programs described in the 1938 brochure were either just being born or as yet unimagined.

As Hanson studied the situation, he realized that the wealth and youthful excitement of the Roaring Twenties was sparking the creation of a number of new organizations for young people, and many—his attention was drawn particularly to the phenomenally successful Masonic youth society DeMolay, founded in 1919—seemed to be doing a much better job of attracting and keeping older teens than Scouting.

Investigating these competing organizations, Hanson discovered several common themes: exclusivity, a commitment to service, "adult" activities such as dress balls and dinners, rituals and ranks of distinction, membership that continued to age 21 and beyond, and a small amount of mystery.

On April 19, 1925, Hanson invited 10 local Eagle Scouts (**Jack McDonald, Lou Mulloy, Clement Schnabel, Scott McDonald, Raymond Moyle, Ralph Gilley, Stewart Ebner, Prescott Blatterman Jr., Joseph Roger**, and **Ted Blockley**) to his Market Street office and presented his thoughts to them.

He was shrewd enough to leave just enough of its elucidation to the boys to give them ownership of the idea, while still keeping the plan within the boundaries of his own thinking, notably in terms of an overarching mystical theme. With Indians, pioneers, explorers, pilots, and sailors already taken, Hanson took a cue from DeMolay and chose knighthood—an inspired choice given the implicit chivalry of the Eagle Scout image.

This wasn't the first such meeting Hanson had attempted. Nine years later, the organization's newsletter would recall "several other meetings previous to this one were held at which ways and means were discussed to bring about a permanent organization. Several attempts failed. Something was lacking..."[13]

Reading between the lines, it seems pretty obvious that rather than tripping over the idea for this new organization through trial and error, Hanson was in fact slowly moving the boys toward a consensus. and on that Sunday night (the day is important to show that, from the beginning, this was a nonofficial group) he got it.

The program was to be called the Knights of Dunamis—the final term derived from the Greek word for "power" or "spirit."

The Knights of Dunamis, Hanson suggested and the boys agreed, would follow the theme of the Knights of the Round Table with swords, capes, and even on occasion, helmets. New members were to be called Squires, and established members were designated Knights (and addressed as "Sir Knight") or Knight Commanders (chapter presidents), and there would be a series of requirements, initiations, and award ceremonies for each position. Eventually the Knights of Dunamis (KD) would create its own ultimate rank, Knight-Eagle, which would unofficially become the highest honor for a boy in Scouting.

It was also agreed by the little group that:

1. The Knights of Dunamis would be an honor society dedicated exclusively to service to both Scouting and the community.

2. Membership only would be open to Eagle Scouts.

These two little spur-of-the-moment decisions would prove to be momentous in the story of the Boy Scouts of America. The first would turn Scouting, for

The patch version of the logo and symbols of the Knights of Dunamis.

the first time, permanently away from its hermetic world of camping and woodcraft and dedicate it to full-time public service, a move that eventually would lead to the Eagle service project and a permanent transformation of the face of America. The second would, also for the first time, make Eagle Scouting a distinct entity, part of Scouting yet apart from it, and a lifelong brotherhood. "Once an Eagle, always an Eagle" began that day in Raymond Hanson's office.

Having completed their vote, the 10 Eagles then were presented by Hanson with a preliminary program for new member initiation and other rituals, as well as for new ranks and their requirements. Scribed in the KD newsletter in 1934, "The plans were enthusiastically received and it was voted to organize a chapter immediately and to adopt a Constitution and by-laws."[14] The 10 Eagles then selected the officers for Chapter Number 1 of the Knights of Dunamis and named Hanson Patron General in perpetuity. After this, Hanson led the newly elected Commander Jack McDonald into another room and read him the ritual and administered the oath of office. He followed that with similar ceremonies for each of the Chapter's new officers. The secret side of KD, a source of consternation in years to come, had begun.

The ten new Sir Knights ended the meeting by performing the newly written closing ceremonies for the first time and then made their way home in the darkness. The Knights of Dunamis had been founded formally.

In the months ahead, the details of the society's rituals and regalia were elaborated. It was classic secret society mumbo jumbo; here's a scene from an induction ceremony that sounds to modern ears like something out of Dungeons & Dragons:

Senior Councilor: Has he satisfied you that he is qualified to do this?

Third Guard: He has proven himself worthy of our confidence.

Senior Councilor: Very well. We will escort him further—(to Candidate) but I warn you, my friend, that you have not yet reached the goal of your ambition, and that beyond this door, Seven Knights who are seated at the Round Table will demand further proof that you are a true Eagle Scout and that you are continuing to practice daily the Scout Oath and Law.

The Senior Councilor knocks five times and the same is answered in like fashion by the First Sir Knight of the Castle, after which the door is opened with sound effects.[15]

One of the founding Sir Knights, Clem Schnabel, designed the emblem of the Order: an Eagle, taken from the BSA medal, clenching a broadsword ("the sword of Galahad") in its talons, atop a triangular shield bearing "KD" in blue letters. According to the Order's history, the Eagle symbolized service, the sword symbolized leadership gained in that service, and the three sides of the triangular shield stood for the three parts of the Scout Oath.

This emblem, as a lapel pin, jacket patch, neckerchief and slide, and even on the end of a blue-and-white uniform pocket "dangle" (similar to that presented by the Order of the Arrow) would come to distinguish the Knights of Dunamis from the rest of Scouting and extend the image of the Eagle further in public life. Eighty years later, they also would become among the most prized and valuable Scouting collectibles.

(The Knights of Dunamis wasn't the only Eagle organization to emerge during this period—only the most successful. A number of adult Eagle groups popped up in the mid-West to offer their help to local councils. Across the Bay from the KD in Oakland, the "Ohitekah Tribe" had a brief existence. And most interestingly, the Diocesan Troop, created by the Roman Catholic Archdiocese of Chicago, was created to serve as honor guards at priest ordinations and to provide future candidates for the priesthood.)[16]

That October 27th, chosen because it was the birthday of early Scout supporter Theodore Roosevelt, the KD held its first public installation. It took place at the Golden Gate Commandery (Knights Templar Hall) in San Francisco and featured public speeches, a music concert, and a new Eagle Scout Court of Honor—very different from traditional Scouting events and a first glimpse of the new organization's new trajectory. So too were the semiannual past-commander's banquets, first held in January 1926, and the annual semiformal balls, both dress-up affairs in which a Scout uniform was a rare sight.

By December 1929, when the Bay Area chapters met to create a Grand (Headquarters) Chapter, the Knights of Dunamis had 13 chapters, including Chapter 3 in Atlantic City, New Jersey. By 1933, the KD had 27 chapters across the United States, mostly within major cities, 750 members and 130 adult associates, and a new slogan: "Power and Service."[17]

By "power," KD was playing off the meaning of the "Dunamis," but the underlying message was clear: the Eagles who now comprised the Knighthood were the zenith, the princes, of Scouting—and as such, they wielded considerable power inside Scouting as leaders and role models and outside Scouting as its shining emissaries.

As for "service," this was an evolving notion for the Knights. During its first decade, this meant service to Scouting. The Order regularly published for its members long lists of ways in which they could help Scouting, from hosting Courts of Honor to serving as merit badge counselors, and from working as summer camp staff to even serving as temporary Scoutmasters for orphaned troops. Said a 1936 flyer:

> No one can deny the lack of adult leadership at the present time. This is due not so much to [a] lack of volunteers but rather to their lack of experience … The Knights of Dunamis can aid Scouting in great measure by serving as leaders, instructors, and examiners in Troops where the Scoutmaster is handicapped by his own inexperience, and by a lack of efficient junior leaders.[18]

This contribution by the Knights of Dunamis to Scouting in the BSA's difficult middle years during the Depression and the war has gone largely unrecognized. But that certainly wasn't the case at the time with its recipients. In the late 1930s, when Hanson decided to audit the impact of the KD and requested comments from executives of councils where the Knights had a chapter, he was inundated with letters lauding the KD for its contribution. Sir Knights filled the staffs of summer camps, merit badge midways, Scout circuses (a popular advancement gathering of the era), and camp-o-rees. They also served as Assistant Scoutmasters to new troops and staged nearly all of the Eagle Courts of Honor.

QUEST

The Knights of Dunamis now seemed perfectly positioned to move ahead of the other pretenders and claimed ownership of the now-empty 18- to 21-year-old wing of Boy Scouting. Raymond Hanson could look on with satisfaction that his little brainstorm had grown in just a dozen years into the most visible, and in many ways the most influential and new movement in Scouting. The organization was still Western-heavy, but new chapters that were popping up in Washington, DC; Boston; and Kansas City were beginning to change that as well.

The future of the Knights of Dunamis looked very bright indeed.

What Hanson didn't realize was, almost from day one, he had made a strategic blunder that would one day prove fatal to the KD. In fact, in many ways he already was at the climax of the KD story because he was about to crash into two roadblocks unique to his Eagles, which no one had foreseen.

Hanson's strategic mistake dated all of the way back to that first meeting in his office. He had imagined an independent organization, part of the BSA but still detached from it in terms of ranks, rituals, and membership requirements. In this way, Hanson believed, the Knights of Dunamis could be a tremendous asset to Scouting, bringing its unequaled intellectual capital to bear wherever the BSA's operations were weak.

And, as the letters to Hanson showed, the KD was just that. However, James E. West and the staff at BSA's National Headquarters in New York City saw a lot more. Beyond the standard East Coast skepticism that anything new and of value could come from the West Coast, the BSA also saw other problems: an exclusive club inside an organization that stressed its lack of exclusivity; a group that often behaved as adults with dates, dances, cars, and parties when Scouting was designed to be a final respite from the complexities of adulthood; a new locus of power—a praetorian guard with unmatched credentials—that eventually could challenge Scouting's leadership; and perhaps most important of all, an organization of the elite of Scouting that was so appealing that it was actually drawing young leadership talent away from troops.

Secret societies for good (Elks, Shriners, Rotary, and Lions) and evil (the KKK, European fascists) were all the rage in the 1920s and 1930s, but Scouting, probably rightly, feared them. And if the Knights of Dunamis obviously was benign, there was no guarantee it would stay so, or that this valuable asset wouldn't one day prove a parasite on the organization.

Had he been as calculating as he was clever, Ray Hanson would have traveled to New York at the very beginning of the KD, built support, and lobbied to have the Knights fully recognized as part of Scouting. Instead, by the time he requested that certification, it already was too late. To read the minutes of the annual KD conferences of the 1930s shows, in the midst of all of the good news, a persistent effort by the Knights toward recognition by the BSA turning into a forlorn hope. It's not that the KD didn't try: Chief Scout Executive West was invited and attended the KD national convention one year in San Francisco. Other senior Scout executives were invited to join the KD national council. And even the Chief Scout of the World, Lord Baden-Powell was invited and accepted an honorary membership, while stopping in San Francisco in 1935 on his last world tour.

The aging founder responded to the honor with a message that was, in part, a warning:

> I have been watching with interest the growth of the Knights of Dunamis among Eagle Scouts, and am especially gratified to see its members have realized the truism that it is one thing to be in a state of mind for doing things but that it is quite another to do them.
>
> The Knights of Dunamis have a hunch that it is a good thing to render service, in some form to Scoutcraft ... This is of great potential value to the Scout movement; it not only prevents the Knights of Dunamis from becoming a class of superior beings distinct from their younger brothers, but also it is a big help to our organization as a whole in keeping the older boys still under the influence of Scouting.[19]

In other words, *Don't get above yourselves*. Dedicate yourselves to Scouting and Scouting will find a place for you.

But that place was still up in the air. For all of KD's efforts, the BSA continued to keep the Order at arm's length—even as it began to embrace other peripheral organizations. In 1938, in what was perceived as a breakthrough,

Boy Scouts finally recognized the Knights of Dunamis but nothing more. The KD was now officially a member of the Boy Scout family—but with limited support and almost no recognition.

Still, it was assumed that full recognition was just a matter of time. In fact, it would be more than 30 years before Scouting fully embraced the Knights of Dunamis—and that was only as a prelude to killing it. If Hanson had pressed for full recognition early, the history of the Knights of Dunamis might have been very different. As it was, the organization ended the 1930s watching helplessly as it was eclipsed by Exploring—open to all older Scouts, even accepting new Scouts—as the BSA's new favorite organization.[20]

It didn't help that its own success was making it increasingly difficult for the Order even to fulfill Baden-Powell's admonition and stick to service in Scouting. Thanks to the KD, the general public was beginning to discover this singular breed of super-Scout. And even as the Order's members were busy with their service commitments to Scouting, individual chapters increasingly found themselves asked (often by local Scout councils) to serve as honor guards at parades, speeches, conventions, and conferences. KD members themselves also increasingly treated the Knighthood as an extension not just of Scouting, but also of their high school service clubs— and began volunteering at hospitals, soup kitchens, and during disasters. In time, the KD armband would become as well known as the neckerchief or pocket dangle.

These community service activities provided immediate and immeasurable goodwill for the Boy Scouts of America. In the long term, they did even more: they set the stage for the Eagle Scout service project. Indeed, with the perspective of 75 years, it can be said that the modern Eagle Scout award most resembles in its requirements and difficulty, the Sir Knight title (requiring as it did both the traditional Eagle plus extensive service). And if there is a historic precedent for the Adams Award for best Eagle service projects in the nation, it is probably the Knight Eagle award.

But in the short term, these activities drew the KD away from its Scouting activities—making it less vital by the year to the BSA, and opening the door even further to the Order of the Arrow; Exploring; and other more ecumenical, Scoutcraft-oriented groups.

Still, the Knights of Dunamis, given its rapid growth—it peaked at 110 chapters—and immense contribution to Scouting, might still have eventually forced itself on Scouting by its sheer size and importance. However, that is when the two roadblocks appeared that couldn't have been bigger obstacles. The first was the Great Depression. Even at its zenith, the KD found itself begging its chapters to pay their dues—not a major problem for the Chapter 1 kids going to Berkeley or Stanford, but a real burden on other chapters from Northern California and elsewhere. Making the situation worse was the unexpected reality that while parents might scrape together enough money for their 12-year-old's Scout uniform; their 20-year-old Eagle son was on his own. And, because the BSA didn't even allow the Knights to run a capital campaign until 1939, the KD was almost always nearly broke and unable to finance a national recruitment campaign.

In the end, even the Great Depression didn't prove to be the biggest threat to the survival of the Knights of Dunamis. Rather, it was World War II. The KD hit a challenge that traditional Scouting had never faced: its members were all of military age. And, being Eagles—indeed, beyond Eagles: Knight Eagles had to earn 36 merit badges, restore a Scout troop, and perform prodigies of leadership and service—they were the perfect candidates for military officer training.

By mid-1942, the ranks of the Order had been decimated by the draft and enlistment. The KD had performed one last great service to the country. In the hours after Pearl Harbor, members of the Honolulu chapter of the KD rushed to the scene of the attack and volunteered their help. It was a fitting end to the first era of the Knights of Dunamis.

COMING HOME

When the KD was reborn after World War II, it was a radically different organization. Not only had the first generation of Knights disappeared with the war, but so had the founder himself. Ray Hanson retired from Scouting for health reasons in 1942. He died two years later, at age 54.

Almost nothing survived of the old order, but its symbols and rituals and the latter were increasingly honored in the breach. Arthurian sagas and secret societies no longer had as much attraction in the Atomic Age.

The newly emerging chapters—and those that survived, including KD Chapter 1—increasingly dispensed with the robes and the rococo titles. The ceremonial sword now was rarely hauled out, and only for investitures and Eagle Courts of Honor. The new Knights of Dunamis now looked less like DeMolay and more like a college service fraternity.

That was no coincidence: if the KD was never lucky with Scouting, it certainly was blessed with leaders. Hanson's eventual replacement, who would serve the Order for the rest of its history was Dr. Lester R. Steig, a San Francisco school administrator who, tellingly, had been a major figure in the story of Alpha Phi Omega, the national college service fraternity based on Scouting's principles and officially recognized by the BSA in 1931.

Steig would go on to become one of the most honored figures in Scouting history—serving as national president of Alpha Phi Omega and earning its National Distinguished Service Key. In Scouting, he would become not only the national president of the Knights of Dunamis, but also earn Scouting's two highest awards for adults: the Silver Buffalo and the Distinguished Eagle Scout Award.

KD II, as it might be called, was almost exclusively a service organization, now dedicated as much to being the face of local Scouting to the community as to Scouting itself, where the task had now largely been assumed by the others. And though it never grew again to more than a few thousand members, its impact was far out of proportion to its size. In the Golden Age of Boy Scouting, the Knights of Dunamis was the BSA's most famous (if uncredited) public face.

For example, a typical year for the reborn Knights of Dunamis Chapter 33 in San Jose, California, in the early 1970s included serving as master of ceremonies for more than 30 Eagle Courts of Honor; honor guard duties at Christmas, Veterans Day, and Cinco de Mayo parades; flag honor guard at several county supervisor meetings, State of the City, and other events; holding a Christmas party for children at a local hospital; packing emergency supplies; and cooking and manning a wedding reception for a local Scout executive (the fees donated to charity).

Once again, in such a list, one can see the template for the Eagle service projects to come.

But, for all of its achievements—and its tenacious endurance—the Order was still viewed with suspicion by a BSA that still believed the KD to be too independent, too exclusive, and too much of an attraction drawing Eagles away from troops. In other words, the Knights were trapped: whether succeeding or failing, the BSA deemed them a failure and withheld its support.

Well, not always. In 1956, the BSA National Executive Board at last— after 30 years—gave its blessing to the KD. Two years later, shifting its support to the new national rollout of Exploring, it rescinded that certification. And the dreams of two generations of Sir Knights were dashed again.

It is a measure of both the organizational strength and the internal morale of the Knights of Dunamis that, despite this devastating turn, it not only endured, but also continued to grow in both size and influence. Boy Scouting may not have believed in the KD but Eagle Scouts still believed in the Knights of Dunamis.

Remarkably enough, thanks to an interesting confluence of events, the KD was given one last chance at legitimacy. Les Steig was a mild-mannered, courtly man, but he had a will of iron, and he surrounded himself with a young national chapter leadership filled with future college presidents and corporate executives. Steig began by completely restructuring the KD, stripping out the last remnants of the 1920s secret society and making it into an association. Then, in the late 1960s this leadership group, leveraging Steig's reputation at BSA National Headquarters, made one last attempt at acceptance. Amazingly, they got a welcome reception.

The explanation was pure serendipity. In 1967, Alden G. Barber was appointed the fifth chief Scout executive. He is remembered today for having led Scouting not only at its peak in membership, but also through one of the most culturally challenging periods in its history. That Barber was a maverick and risk taker was not surprising given that he had learned adult Scouting from a similar character: Ray Hanson. Alden G. Barber had been, in fact, a

KD chapter commander in Chico, California, in the mid-1930s, and in time, national commander of the Knights of Dunamis.

Barber was not only the ultimate advertisement for the value of the Order, but he also understood it better than anyone. And now, at last, he gave the Knights of Dunamis its break. Suddenly, Scouting was talking about the KD, its surviving chapters were given national support, and there was even a page in the Scout Uniform catalog dedicated KD gear. In November 1967, the BSA Executive Board passed a resolution stating, "the Boy Scouts of America recognize the Knights of Dunamis and cooperate with them in achieving their objectives." The KD had waited 52 years for those 18 words.

To the surviving Knights—and especially chapter alumni—this sudden realization of a half-century-old dream was staggering. Perhaps now the Knights of Dunamis would take its rightful place in the Scouting family. Chief Scout Executive Barber even came and spoke at the Order's 1968 convention—another first.

THE LAST BATTLE

But it was too late. By now, the KD had shrunk to just 44 chapters (many of them inactive) in 22 states. Meanwhile, Scouting itself was beset with its own problems: a toxic combination of trying to be too relevant and urban, combined with changing rank requirements, and the departure of the baby boomers from teenagehood, had devastated Scouting's membership rolls. It had little time or patience to wait for the KD to come around. In giving its support to the Order at last, it was also giving it one last chance.

And so, in 1971, even as the KD was holding meetings and conferences to come up with a strategy to regain its storied past, the BSA already was working on its own study about what to do with its Eagle Scouts. Leading the charge were two members of the BSA National Council, Donald H. Flanders, and J. Kimball Whitney. The concept they developed, the National Eagle Scout Association, would abandon almost all that had made the Knights such a singular program—guaranteeing it would never again steal away young Eagles from their troops—in exchange for full BSA support and (because all Eagles of any age were welcomed) a massive increase in membership.

The bomb was dropped on the KD at its conference in Asilomar, California, in 1973. Steig, accepting the inevitable, agreed to join the NESA transition team and use his influence to convince the Knights to accept the change. Flanders would later say of Steig, "He was a big help to me in trying to fold the Knights of Dunamis into NESA." NESA's new *Eagletter* would go so far as to say, "Les Steig, probably more than any other single individual, provided the impetus for the birth of the National Eagle Scout Association."[21]

Though he would live until 1995, dying at the age of 91, there is no record of Dr. Steig's opinion of that appraisal. He had saved the Order at the cost of its identity. Brokenhearted Knights joined the staff of the two national jamborees in 1973 and put on happy faces as they announced to giant crowds of Eagles the creation of the new NESA. Most wore their KD neckerchiefs and armbands as they did so. In a glimpse of the future, the gathering at the Pennsylvania Jamboree was the largest assemblage of Eagle Scouts in BSA history.

A few KD chapters, notably the one in Long Beach, held out for a few more years. But by the late 1970s, the Knights of Dunamis was gone. Even the board members who joined NESA had moved on.

Today, except among collectors who prize the rare surviving items from the organization and among a few gray-haired men who still pointedly wear fraying dangles on their uniform shirts or KD pins on their suit jacket lapels, the Knights of Dunamis is long forgotten.

A KNIGHT'S FAREWELL

Nine decades after Raymond O. Hanson called that meeting in his San Francisco office; there is one surviving memorial to his creation. It stands 80 miles north of that office in the "Knights of Dunamis Grove" at the San Francisco Council's Camp Royaneh.[22]

Hanson built Camp Royaneh during his tenure as council executive, and each summer from the mid-1920s to the late 1950s, the members of KD Chapter 1 would travel up to the camp and hold a big Saturday night ceremony in front of the other campers. In that ceremony, as many as 50

Eagles would march singing down the hill from their encampment in the grove with their banners and white neckerchiefs, with the robed chapter commander in the lead, and sit at special tables in the mess hall with their Chief Knight Ray Hanson. Later that evening, the KD would put on a campfire program for the younger Scouts, often featuring chapter alumni who had gone on to careers in the arts. The Grove was dedicated in 1942, two years before Hanson's death.[23] Many years later, a black marble headstone was placed there. It still stands and reads:

In Memory of
RAYMOND O. HANSON
1890-1944
FOUNDER
KNIGHTS OF DUNAMIS
Eagle Scout Service Society

Above those words is carved the last surviving public image of the Knights of Dunamis logo.

Raymond Hanson didn't invent the Eagle rank. But more than anyone, he invented modern Eagle Scouting. And, even though, his name and the Order he created may be now long forgotten, his legacy is stronger than ever.

CHAPTER FOUR

FIRE AND ICE

On August 13, 1928, the New York Times,
the nation's most influential newspaper, carried the headline
"Scouts in Race for Honor of Joining Byrd's Expedition."

S couting's most famous adventure had begun. The story picked up by numerous other newspapers electrified Boy Scouts across the country. Soon, thousands of applications flooded the New York offices of Commander Richard E. Byrd. And what had begun as something of a publicity stunt quickly became a national obsession.[1]

It was the era of polar exploration and Byrd was one of the most celebrated of its adventurer-explorers. He had come a bit late to the game. As early as 1908 American Frederick Cook claimed to be the first to reach the North Pole but his claim generally was disputed, and today the credit usually is given to the team led by American Robert Peary and that included Matthew Henson and four Inuit men. They reached the North Pole on April 6, 1909.

The South Pole, by comparison, first was reached by Norwegian Roald Amundsen on December 14, 1911, just 34 days before the doomed second expedition of the Englishman, Robert Falcon Scott.

Each of these heroic—and harrowing—journeys made the history books and fired the world's imagination. All of these men were prodigies of human endurance. In terms of impact on mankind's future, Byrd's expeditions to the South Pole that began 15 years later were far more influential.

Seen from today's perspective, Byrd's polar assaults seem auguries of the future, in which cutting-edge technology and careful project management (at the time credited to "Byrd's Luck") enabled the Commander and his crew not only to embark on high-profile expeditions, but also to conduct scientific research along the way and return alive. From the elaborate staging to the regular radio communications, to the triumphant returns, the Byrd expeditions seem like primitive rehearsals for the Apollo missions.

In the first of these adventures, on May 9, 1926, Byrd and his co-pilot Floyd Bennett flew a Fokker Tri-motor over the North Pole—just three days before Amundsen and his American sponsor Lincoln Ellsworth did the same thing in the airship *Norge*. For this feat, Byrd and Bennett were awarded the Congressional Medal of Honor,[2] a rare feat in peacetime.

It is a measure of the inherent danger in this kind of adventuring that a year later co-pilot Bennett, in a practice run with Byrd and a third pilot in their pursuit of the Orteig Prize for flying across the Atlantic (won by Lindbergh a few weeks later), was seriously injured in a crash. The resulting injury would lead to pneumonia that would kill Bennett a year later during an equally daring flight to northern Canada to save the downed crew of the airship *Bremen*. Byrd was heartbroken by the loss. His co- pilot on Bennett's final flight, Bernt Balchen, would became the chief pilot of Byrd's aerial assault on the South Pole—and the plane they would fly would be named the *Floyd Bennett*.

Most of these details are long forgotten in twenty-first century memories; but they were in the forefront of every boy's dreams in the mid-1920s (as late as the early 1930s, Amelia Earhart would hire Balchen to fly her Lockheed Vega—using his fame to distract the world from her own secret planning for an Atlantic crossing). Once Byrd had conquered the North Pole, it seemed inevitable he would take on Antarctica and the South Pole. But when, in announcing the adventure, he added that he would be taking an American boy—a Boy Scout—the result was a frenzy.

From among the thousands of applications, the Boy Scouts of America winnowed out all Scouts who had not met the basic requirements for the honor. The applicant had to be between 17- and 20-years-old; he had to have been a member in good standing for two years in the BSA; and he had to have earned either the First Class or Able Sea Scout rank. The applicant also was required to have completed a 500- to 1,000-word essay stating his reasons for wanting to be part of the exhibition and his explanation as to why he was uniquely suited for the honor.

To these requirements, the BSA added that preference would be given to Scouts with merit badges whose skills would directly support the expedition, including astronomy, carpentry, hiking, photography, signaling, surveying, and taxidermy. Boating and winter camping experience also were expected.

The six Eagle Scout finalists for the 1928 Antarctic trip inspect Admiral Byrd's flagship, The City of New York.

Given all of these stipulations, the local councils were able to narrow the applicant pool down quickly to just 88 boys. Then, in turn, the national office—making heavy use of the applicants' essays—cut the list to just six boys representing the absolute best of Scouting—**Donald H. Cooper**, **Sumner D. Davis**, **Jack Hirschmann**, **Paul Siple**, **Alden Snell**, and **Clark Spurlock**.[3] All the finalists were Eagle Scouts *and* all were veteran winter campers and had earned at least 31 merit badges. One had earned the Honor Medal for saving a life, another had summited Mount Rainier, and a third had paddled a canoe 180 miles. They also came from hometowns as different as Birmingham, Alabama, and Tacoma, Washington. Arguably, there were no better candidates for this expedition under the age of 21 in the United States.

In August 1928, the six were invited to New York City for the final stage of the competition. There, they spent ten miserable days undergoing a battery of tests in complex skills, the Army IQ test, physical examinations, and personal interviews. Then, with the media in tow (one reporter, Russell Owen of the *New York Times* even would join the expedition to cover the story), the candidates were rushed around the city for a week to be part of various media events—including a trip to Byrd's flagship, *The City of New York*, to meet its captain.

The culminating event was a luncheon hosted by Commander Byrd himself. Like any great leader, Byrd had an ulterior motive for the gathering: it enabled him to watch the six candidates alone and together, and in interaction with perceived subordinates, peers, and superiors. During the course of the luncheon, Byrd made a point to go up to each boy, introduce himself, shake the boy's hand, and look him in the eye. Just from that brief moment, Byrd largely made his choice. It was finalized when he compared his judgment with that of a quick poll taken of the finalists—asking which two other finalists each would pick to go with them on the expedition—and found that the results were unanimous. Every Scout had named one boy as his first choice: Paul Siple.

Byrd had his Eagle.

SCOUTING'S BEAU IDEAL

If Paul Siple hadn't existed, Scouting would have invented him—and, in a way, it already had. The 19-year-old whose image appeared under the headline, "Erie Scout with Byrd" on the front of the *Erie Dispatch-Herald* could have stepped out of one of those potboiler Scouting novels of the era as the resourceful and fearless hero. And he would prove to be more than that.

Born in Montpelier, Ohio, in 1908, Paul's family moved to Erie, Pennsylvania, when he was nine. Three years later, in 1920, he joined Boy Scout Troop 24. With impressive speed—no doubt in part because he was skillful at the one merit badge subject that ruined the dreams of three generations of early Scouts: Bird Study—Siple earned his Eagle medal when he was just 15.

LEFT: Eagle Scout Paul A. Siple in 1928. RIGHT: Siple salutes Byrd in a promotional image taken before the Antarctic Expedition.

As if his Eagle was merely a prelude rather than a culmination, Siple then turned around and joined the Sea Scouts, becoming an Able Sea Scout. Because Sea Scouting allowed him to advance as a Scout, Siple continued to earn merit badges, until by his 18th birthday, he had earned 59 merit badges—nearly all that were available, making him one of the highest-achieving Scouts in the country. (Since Scouting had no upper age limit then, Siple would go on to earn a total of 61 merit badges.)

In June 1926, Paul Siple graduated from Erie's Central High School and went to work as an assistant draftsman at the Pennsylvania State Highway Department. That job helped him pay for tuition at Allegany College in nearby Meadville, where he enrolled that fall.

And there Paul Siple might have remained, ultimately becoming a laboratory scientist at some local company, had that article not appeared in the *Times*. As with many young men his age, Commander Byrd had been a hero of Siple's. He had followed the great man's exploits through his high school years and had dreamed of being along with him on a polar expedition. And now, the opportunity was there before him.

There was every reason for Siple *not* to apply. He was, strictly speaking, out of Scouting now, in college and with a job. But he also knew, as did his family and the people who supported him in this quest, that he was not an ordinary Scout. The early Eagle and the three score merit badges proved that—as did Paul's skills in cold weather camping, taxidermy, and sailing. Looking at the requirements for the honor, Siple figured he had as good a chance as any Scout in the country.

But there was more than that, and this was the distinction that made Byrd take notice at that luncheon: Paul Siple was huge. Six feet tall and 180 pounds in an era when the average adult man was six inches shorter and 20 pounds lighter, photos show him as a Boy Scout sitting on a bench towering over the Scouts around him. He also had the overdrawn features of a hero: a large and long face with hawk-like features, a wide mouth with almost comically large teeth, and huge hands that suggested immense reservoirs of hidden strength. If you were to imagine an Eagle Scout joining a company of tough veterans on a polar exploration mission, he probably would look a lot like Paul Siple.

What the photographs don't capture is what Byrd saw in Siple's eyes. Where many of the other candidates were visibly nervous meeting their hero for the first time, Siple, no doubt at least as frightened, swallowed his fear and stepped forward, looked the legend in the eye, and firmly shook the Commander's hand. At that moment, Byrd knew that Paul Siple was a hero, awaiting his call. And Siple would show his bravery and cool judgment under the most stressful conditions imaginable in the months—and decades—to come. After a few brief days in Erie, where friends, neighbors, and civic leaders feted their now-famous native son, Paul Siple headed back to New York City. On August 25, the first of Byrd's four-ship flotilla, the wooden square-rigged *City of New York*, carrying 200 tons of cargo (everything from thumbtacks to airplanes) as well human passengers—scientists, engineers, expedition veterans, and one Boy Scout—weighed anchor and started down the Hudson River.

Hundreds of people lined the dock waving farewell, including two of the major underwriters of the $500,000 expedition ($6.8 million in 2015 dollars), John D. Rockefeller, and Edsel Ford; representatives of the other sponsors, including Maxwell House coffee and Beechnut chewing gum; Paul Siple's parents and older sister, and, much noted by the media and on-lookers, a contingent of Scouts from Troop 24, Erie, Pennsylvania.

For the next two years—he would return in June 1930 to a very different America—Paul Siple would not only participate in, but also would play a major role in one of the epic adventures of the 20th century. He would be tested every step of the way and on more than one occasion would use his Scouting skills to save his own or another person's life. And the callow youth would return as a veteran explorer and researcher, ready to embark on a career that would make him the most famous of all polar scientists.

ON DECK

With his legendary organizational skills, Commander Byrd had planned for each of his four ships to arrive in New Zealand at the same time. That meant a staggered start, with the old *City of New York* given a head start, followed six weeks later by the steel-hulled *Eleanor Bolling* (named after Byrd's mother) carrying 300 tons of supplies, sailing out of Norfolk, Virginia. Following it, but catching up quickly, would be two smaller whaling boats filled with men and dogs, steaming out of Southern California.

Over the two months of the cruise, Paul Siple endured the usual indignities of a long voyage in an old boat—seasickness, tight quarters, a bunk too small for his huge frame, cabin bullies, vermin, hazing, and practical jokes. He also was initially assigned duty as a messmate in the ship's galley, which meant long days in a cabin without a porthole, breathing greasy smoke and sundry smells, and peeling thousands of potatoes. But he was tough and single-minded, and he learned to endure the misery.

Then, in a bit of good luck, a stowaway was discovered on board. By tradition, the stowaway had to earn his stay on the ship until he could be dropped off at the nearest port—in this case, Panama. When he was made a messmate, Siple was promoted to the duty of port watch. He had at last made it to the open air—though in a job that provided little sleep.

It only got more challenging from there. Just a few weeks into the voyage, the old hull sprung a leak that flooded the engine room. The salt water damaged the boiler, fouling much of the stored fresh water. Siple and others fought to plug the leak and then spent days pumping out the water and working, via added shifts, to repair the engine. Meanwhile, the remaining water was reserved for drinking, so the crew soon grew filthy, wearing salt-encrusted clothes. It was not a promising beginning.

Then Byrd's Luck returned; although, it didn't begin very well. A fire broke out in the radio battery storage room that threatened to engulf the entire wooden ship in an inferno. The crew worked for hours putting out the fire and then collapsed in exhaustion. It was a windless night with a glassy sea, and with no one noticing, a current took the ship nearly 80 miles off course. They awoke to a strangely calm sky and then learned on the radio that a savage hurricane had passed just behind them, hitting Puerto Rico and Florida with tornados in its trail. Had the *City of New York* not drifted off course, it would have been trapped—and likely destroyed—by the storm.

After a stop in the Panama Canal, where Siple was met and escorted about by the local International Scouting Commissioner—and where he learned to put limes and lemons in the ship's drinking water to improve its antibacterial acidity and to fight scurvy (a useful bit of knowledge for the years ahead)—the crew sailed on into the Pacific.

After the tumult of the Atlantic and Caribbean, the immense Pacific was a relatively easy passage. On crossing the equator, Siple tried to escape the Davy Jones ceremony by hiding in a ventilator pipe, but he was caught and with the others, sentenced to have his head shaved and to be thrown into a tank of water. When he wasn't on shift, Siple used his time wisely. The expedition had brought with it a library of 3,000 books, including encyclopedias and technical manuals. And during the long, equatorial passage, Siple studied the books to learn more about astronomy, navigation, bird study, and zoology.

He also had come to appreciate more than ever the value of his Scouting skills, especially knots, rope splicing, and compass work—knowledge that many of the younger expedition members didn't have. Siple later would write that these skills proved to be the difference between being "a humble servant and being recognized as a leader."[4]

The *Eleanor Bolling* caught the slow-moving *City of New York* in Tahiti, and the two ships sailed on into rough weather toward New Zealand.

At one point in this passage, Paul Siple nearly was killed. Caught in high seas in the "Roaring Forties"—strong westerly winds in the Southern Hemisphere—he rushed to answer an "all hands on deck" call. However, the moment he climbed up from the gangway, he was hit in the head by an unstowed wooden crate sliding across the deck. He revived just in time for a huge wave to crash over him, which sent him sliding along the deck towards the scuppers. Still dazed, he managed at the last second to grab the rail before being washed overboard.

He still was clinging to the rail when he heard the chief officer shouting, "Make the upper topsail fast"! Without thinking, Siple made his way to the shrouds and started to climb. At the top of the mast, more than 100 feet above the rolling deck, he joined other crewmen in tying down the flapping sail.

Just as they did, the great ship, hit by a giant wave, heeled over so far that the mainsail, far below Siple, dipped into the ocean—threatening to snap the mast with the men on it. Everyone on deck stared in horror. Then, just as suddenly, the ship righted itself, and the mast rose to vertical again. An exhausted and thankful Paul Siple made his way back down the shrouds and, as he later wrote, was never so happy to be standing on a solid, if pitching, deck.

In late November 1928, the *City of New York* was the last of the flotilla to arrive in New Zealand. On the first day of December, the repaired and restocked ships set sail for Antarctica. On Christmas Day, they reached the great Ross Ice Shelf. They had arrived—now the real adventure would begin.

COURAGE ON ICE

The expedition eventually dropped anchor at the Bay of Whales. Byrd judged this the best place from which to take off on his polar flight. And, not far from Amundsen's old camp, he set the crew to building what would become famous as "Little America".

The location, like everywhere else in Antarctica, was far from safe and secure. Soon after arriving, Siple—who had just been named assistant to the scientific staff—joined Commander Byrd and several others in a lifeboat investigating black specks in the water just beyond the edge of the ice shelf. As they were searching, a lookout atop the edge of the ice began shouting, "Killer whales!"

The men started paddling back to the ice wall—slowly, so as not to arouse the attention of the pod of three orcas. But the orcas saw the lifeboat and began to swim toward it. The men quickly changed direction and headed for the shore. Ominously, the orcas turned and followed.

Now it was a race. As Siple and two other men rowed frantically, Byrd drew his pistol and prepared to fight.

The boat reached the shore first—and the men scrambled out onto the low ice. Siple was last out, and as he dove onto the ice, the lead orca lunged, just missing him with its huge teeth. Falling backward from the attack, Siple nearly lost his balance on the ice and slid back into the water. The other men, sprawled on the ice beyond, looked back just in time to see the orca disappear back into the depths.

The ice too was an ever-present threat. The two big ships had anchored up against a low section of the ice shelf and had begun unloading the next morning, stacking the items from the hold atop the ice "dock". Then, in the middle of this rushed work, the ice shelf suddenly began to crack under the weight and calve off a section of ice-bearing much of the supplies. Within seconds, the entire expedition was at risk.

The men on shore raced to the edge of the shelf and then scrambled down toward the water, the most intrepid jumping onto the nearest large piece of ice and then leaping from floe to floe toward the cargo. They managed to get there in time and haul the goods back aboard the ships.

After that near-disaster, Byrd decided that the low shelf was just too fragile to handle the stress of serving as a dock—and ordered the ships moved to a new location against the full-height ice wall. Unloading there would be a lot more difficult—indeed, at their new anchorage, the top of the ice shelf towered high over the decks of the two ships, which were lashed side-by-side against the ice. This was deemed to be safer, but, in fact, the expedition had merely replaced one threat with another.

Realization of this fact took only another 36 hours. As the men busily unloaded from the ships' decks to the ice above, there was a tremendous groan and a rumbling in the ice wall that knocked the men above off their feet. Below, the men of the *Eleanor Bolling* looked up helplessly to see a giant sliver of ice break loose and come hurtling down to crash on their ship's deck. The concussion and the sheer weight of the ice rocked the ship so far that only the lines to the *City of New York* kept the ship from capsizing.

But no one felt the crash more than the two men standing on the section of ice when it broke loose. One of them, seaman Benny Roth was literally catapulted over the *Eleanor Bolling*—a distance of well over 100 feet— and into the freezing water. Miraculously, Roth surfaced still alive but not knowing how to swim, could only cling desperately to a small ice floe that kept slipping out of his grip. Commander Byrd and several other crewmen heroically leaped into the frigid water to save Roth but they quickly had to retreat before they too drowned.

The second man, meteorologist Henry Harrison, who had been standing just inland from Roth, felt the ice disappear beneath his feet and suddenly found himself sliding down a sheer ice face to the water. With amazing presence in such a shocking situation, Harrison, as he slid spotted the *Eleanor Bolling's* anchor chain (it had been attached to the top of the ice shelf) beneath him. He managed to grab it as he passed and clung for dear life—only to have the chain pull taut as the shipped rolled and drifted out, leaving Harrison dangling 50 feet in the air above the icy water.

As Byrd and the men on the ships scrambled to help Roth, whose location was lost in the sun's glare off the water, Paul Siple and the expedition's physician Dr. Francis Coman ran to save Harrison. In the single most important application in his life of his Scouting skills, Siple, grabbed a length of rope and tied a loop in it using that bane of Second Class Scouts everywhere, the bowline. Shouting for Harrison to slip the loop under his arms—the meteorologist, hanging with frozen hands from the chain, was getting the benefit of the many pull-up competitions during the voyage—Siple flung the rope.

Harrison somehow managed to catch the rope and loop it under his arms. Next came the dangerous part. Unsticking his bleeding hands, Harrison let go, swinging down and slamming into the face of the ice wall. Siple and Coman then pulled with all of their might, dragging Harrison up the jagged wall face and up onto the top.

Within minutes, Roth too was located and dragged from the water by men in the *City of New York*'s lifeboat. Both rescues had taken less than 20 minutes. Harrison and Roth were in bad shape—the former with much of the skin ripped from his hands, the latter with severe frostbite—but they had survived and soon would be back at work.

As for Paul Siple, the Eagle Scout had used his skills to save a man's life and once again had proven his value to the expedition.

COLD COMFORT

Having (barely) survived the disembarkation, the expedition now set about constructing its home for the next year.

The original plan for Little America had been comparatively elaborate (certainly by Antarctic standards) with a half-dozen separate buildings that included sleeping quarters, mess hall, library, scientific areas, and a gym. Half of those buildings, all of the food, and most of the supplies had arrived with the expedition; and now, unloaded on the ice, it all had to be transported the eight miles to the Little America site. Byrd divided the team into three groups: one to manage and unpack the supplies, a second to transport the items inland via dog teams, and a third to do the on-site construction at Little America. When one of the sled drivers was hurt, Paul Siple was assigned his sled. It was yet one more promotion for the young man, but a mixed one, as he found himself with a team of dogs—troublesome huskies and mongrels that no one else wanted.

However, Siple always had been a natural with dogs, in part because of his almost superhuman patience, and he quickly formed his motley pack into an enthusiastic team. Sometimes too enthusiastic: on one occasion, caught in a whiteout in which earth and sky, and near and far, were all but indistinguishable, Paul turned his team the wrong way and headed down a slope toward the ice shelf cliff. The dogs, refusing to stop, only ran faster toward oblivion. It took the quick-witted intervention of Dr. Coman—who used his own sled team to cut off the runaway group, and then dove out and grabbed Siple's gang line to the dogs—to avert disaster.

No doubt in part because of his increasing importance to the expedition, when the time came for Byrd to select the 42 men to winter over at Little America, Siple was among those chosen. And, because he had made himself so popular with the crew with his cheerfulness, competence, and bravery, there was little grumbling about the "kid" getting special treatment by those who had to leave. Indeed, as at the New York luncheon, there seems to have been a general consensus that Siple had earned the right to stay.

With the weather starting to turn, Byrd ordered the *Eleanor Bolling* to be manned quickly—there wasn't even time to get the last three buildings out of its hold—and made ready for a quick dash to New Zealand. The hope was that if it could get away fast enough it might be able to return with supplies in time before the sea ice locked up.

But it wasn't to be. As the men who remained at Little America learned—listening to the radio signals picked up by the three tall masts they had just installed—the *Eleanor Bolling* endured a hair-raising voyage of storms and high seas and barely limped intact into Wellington Harbour. Meanwhile, at the Bay of Whales, the sea quickly froze with thick ice. The *Eleanor Bolling* had gotten out just in time. It would not be able to return now until spring. The immediate impact of this change of plans was that the original six structures of Little America now had been reduced to three. That meant a long winter of crowded quarters (exacerbated by the fact that the reindeer-skin clothes shed and quickly covered everything in fine hairs), greater human friction, and reduced shelter from the elements. It also created a pressing need to get the last remaining supply items inland from the ice shelf, especially as the items already had disappeared beneath the increasingly deep snow.

And so, as soon as there was a break in the weather—that is, when the howling wind had reduced to less than 60 miles per hour—three teams of dogs, sleds, and drivers raced for the coast. The three drivers of one team, Paul Siple and his two new friends, Quin Blackburn and surveyor Mike Thorne, agreed to stay within visual contact for safety.

But within minutes, the snow flurries grew so blinding that the three lost sight of each other. A few minutes more and they were lost in a whiteout. Siple was on the brink of turning back when he spotted one of the markers—an orange flag atop a long bamboo pole—he had emplaced days before to mark the route. He pressed on, knowing he was just a few hundred yards from the supply cache.

When the three sled teams reached the cache, they found the members of the two teams that had preceded them huddled together against the storm. Siple, Blackburn, and Thorne did the same. Linking arms and hunching down against the wind, they searched about until they found the buried 50-pound barrels of fuel. Though the blizzard was worsening by the minute, the three young men didn't stop until they had loaded the barrels on their sleds.

Now they had to get back, and the trail was beginning to disappear under the piling snowdrifts. Once again shouting to each other to stay together, the three sleds took off, Thorne in the lead, Blackburn in the middle, and Siple taking up the rear. But this time, the wind was quartering into their faces and whatever cohesion they had disappeared within seconds.

Now alone, Paul Siple did his best to navigate by the orange markers, driving from one to the next, 100 yards away, by trying to keep the team moving in a straight line. Within minutes, his eyes nearly were frozen shut from squinting—so he closed his eyes and tried to navigate with his feet by feeling for the most compressed snow of the path.

But it was a doomed strategy. Soon, Siple found himself nearly blind in a perfect whiteout, his visibility down to a few inches, lost in loose snow with no idea how to get back to the trail. There was no other sled, no orange marker—no feature of any kind—in sight. It was more than 40 degrees below zero but Paul Siple began to sweat with fear. In Antarctica, this was how men died.

He remembered his Scouting training: when lost, the first step was to stop, stay calm, and evaluate your situation. Holding back his rising panic, Siple did just that. What vital bit of information was he missing?

Then it hit him. His dogs, given the chance, always would turn downwind to keep from having to drive into the teeth of the storm. And they had begun to do just that. So, fighting his impulse to bend away, he turned his dogs and sledded back until the wind was pounding against them. Within minutes, he had found the trail and the marker.

But was he going the right direction? If he and the dogs were mistakenly headed again for the ice shelf, they never would have the strength to get back. Siple stopped again. Scouting had taught him to be observant. He remembered: the wind always struck the left side of his face when driving toward the camp. It was doing that now: he still was headed in the right direction. Within minutes, to his relief, he had caught the other two sleds. Once again, the now-terrified young men agreed to stick closely together.

But it wasn't to be. A half-mile from Little America, just as the trail turned directly into the storm, Blackburn's dogs, believing they were almost home, took off from the trail in a straight line for the buildings. Blackburn couldn't hold them back, and he disappeared into the storm.

Siple and Thorne reached Little America at last. Siple, his eyes still nearly frozen shut, and with a ring of blisters around his wrists from snow getting under his gloves, was rushed to Dr. Coman. Assuming that Blackburn already had arrived, it was only then that he discovered that his friend was still lost in the storm.

They rushed to Byrd to mount a rescue—but the commander, worried he might lose more personnel, refuse to let anyone leave the buildings until the storm abated. The men waited, praying that the winds would slow before darkness fell.

The storm broke at last, with only a couple hours of light to spare, Thorne and Byrd himself went out in search. Siple begged to go along, but Byrd refused, telling him to recover from his hyperthermia instead.

Byrd and Thorne eventually returned: no sign of Quin Blackburn. Now there was only an hour of light left. There was one last chance: now Byrd sent out four teams, each in a different direction. This time Siple was allowed to go.

In the end, it was Thorne's team that found Blackburn. Overwhelmed by the storm, he had buried himself and his dogs in a hole in the snow, using the sled as a windbreak. He was carried back to Little America, where he joined Paul Siple—who had been ordered back into the dispensary—under the care of Dr. Coman. In the next few days, sharing their stories, the two young men became fast friends.

THE ENDLESS NIGHT

After these near-fatal experiences, the bigger adventure—wintering over in Antarctica—was something of an anticlimax.

Outside, in the perpetual darkness, the temperature fell below −40F and stayed there—bottoming on July 28, 1929, at −72F. Inside, in buildings almost buried completely in snow, life slid into a daily routine of meals, workouts, lectures, and reading time in the library, work shifts, and evening poker. As could be expected in such tight quarters, the occasional fight broke out to relieve the tension, and the men soon came to live for their Sunday night movie and the radio broadcasts from the USA carrying messages from wives and families. When the claustrophobia grew too great, the men would step outside, accepting the bitter cold in exchange for a few minutes of privacy.

Through all of the long weeks, Paul Siple's reputation grew among both the men and the leaders of the expedition. He had begun this journey as little more than a publicity exercise, a novelty. But he had proven himself over and over as a man upon whom others could depend. He was also a model of uprightness and perpetual cheerfulness. He helped break up fights, never started them. He spent long hours in the library improving his skills or watching the expedition's tailor and sail maker, Martin Ronne, creating custom clothes out of leather and reindeer skins. And, because he didn't smoke and ate his chocolate ration the moment he received it, Siple had nothing to bet in the endless poker games, so he never joined in, sparing himself the biggest source of team tension.

As always, Commander Byrd was watching. He saw the endless care with which Siple had dug out a tunnel for the dogs, how tenderly he cared for them, and how patiently he trained them. In reward, he gave the young man a second job of using his Scouting merit badge skills to perform the taxidermy of seals and other specimens promised for delivery to the American Museum of Natural History. Siple took to the work with his usual enthusiasm.

Finally, the sun reappeared on the horizon, and the weather began to improve. In surviving the winter, Byrd, and his crew had made history—though they were now too occupied to give it much thought. Siple was as busy as anyone in the crew. Byrd had given the 20-year-old another promotion—this time as the scientific researcher for the expedition. Now, often teaming up with Quin Blackburn, who had been named surveyor, the pair traveled to the unexplored regions of the Ross Ice Shelf. Blackburn mapped the area and Siple surveyed the birthrate of baby seals and their growth and behavior—a process that often led to unfriendly encounters with mother seals.

OVER THE POLE

At noon on November 28, 1930, the Ford TriMotor *Floyd Bennett* rose from the runway at Little America into a clear sky and headed toward the South Pole. In the camp's radio room, the rest of the expedition crew, minus the five men on the plane, gathered around the speaker to follow the flight.

At the last moment, Byrd had ordered an extra 100 gallons loaded onto the plane—a decision that proved to be another case of Byrd's Luck. The flight faced two huge challenges, one technical and the other geographic. The technical challenge was simple: the plane was so heavily loaded and so far from help that if anything went wrong with one of the three engines, the plane would have to make an emergency landing and its crew soon would die from exposure.

The geographic challenge was equally basic: two huge glaciers stood in the middle of the flight path to the South Pole. The flight crew knew the height of one, the Axel Heiberg, but not the other, the Liv. At 10,500 feet, the Axel Heiberg's summit, was near the TriMotor's flight ceiling. The Liv was believed to be shorter but no one knew for sure. The crew prayed that the sky would still be clear when they got there.

It wasn't. The Axel Heiberg Glacier was covered with a fog that obscured its summit. Byrd quickly shifted the route over to the Liv. But as the plane approached the glacier, it became obvious that the plane wouldn't be high enough to clear the pass. So Byrd ordered hundreds of pounds of food—their one chance of survival if the plane crashed—jettisoned. The *Floyd Bennett* just cleared the pass—so close that they saw the bags of food explode on the rocks below.

The South Pole was now 300 miles ahead—three hours—across a vast frozen plateau.

At midnight, the navigational instruments and compasses confirmed that they were now over the South Pole, a location they confirmed by criss-crossing over the site. Commander Byrd threw out an American flag, weighted with a rock found near Bennett's grave, and radioed the news back to Little America and the world.

On February 19, 1930, at 9:30 a.m., the *City of New York*, cast off lines from the barrier of the Ross Ice Shelf and made for open sea. Paul Siple, standing on the deck, just could make out the radio towers of Little America in the distance. His arm was in a sling from a chest muscle torn while trying to lift a frozen seal for study. Nevertheless, along with several other scientists on the expedition, Siple had lobbied Byrd for the chance to spend another year in Antarctica doing research. But the commander, sensing that the expedition already had tested its luck too many times, refused.

On June 18, 1930, the *City of New York* docked in its namesake city to a hero's welcome. Once again, the Scouts were there, as was Paul Siple's family, the sponsors, and the media. But the man who returned was very different from the young man who had left two years before. Paul Siple was now an American hero, the most famous Scout in the world, and known nationally as "Boy Scout #1." Now, after the most remarkable adventure of his generation to date, he had to figure out what to do with the rest of his life.

BETWEEN THE WARS

Statistics and probability suggest that if you create an organization of hundreds of thousands of teenage boys, self-selecting for character, ambition, and self-discipline, and you then train them for leadership and self-reliance, you are going to see some very successful and famous middle-aged men appear from this cohort a quarter-century later.

And that is precisely what happened with Eagle Scouts. By the late-1920s there were perhaps 50,000 Eagles in America, the very youngest in their mid-teens, the oldest in their mid-30s.

LEFT: Eagle Scout H. Loren Adams delivers a copy of the BSA's 5 millionth Handbook to President Calvin Coolidge at the White House in 1928. RIGHT: Fatyy LaBauve of Lake Charles, Louisiana, one of the most accomplished merit badge earners in the country at the time with 61, sits for his official Eagle Scout portrait in December 1925.

One individual who carried into the 21st century the memory of what it was like to be an Eagle Scout in the 1920s, was **Ron Neale**, who earned his Eagle with a Northern California troop on December 3, 1928, not long after Charles Lindbergh's solo transatlantic flight. Unlike many Scouts of the era, Neale's troop was blessed with a dedicated adult leadership—one that made a point of having a troop participate in local and regional jamborees.

Nearly ninety years later, Neale still fondly recalled these gatherings and credited them with changing his life: "They'd have a boy lying in a field, and on his arm would be a handkerchief saying 'broken leg' or 'knocked out' or something. I got interested in thinking, 'Now what should you do with that person?'"

President Calvin Coolidge poses with a group of cheering Eagle Scouts outside the White House in 1927.

That curiosity led Neale to Stanford Medical School, then to work at Highland Hospital in Oakland and the Mayo Clinic in Rochester, Minnesota—and then, as a surgeon with the U.S. forces in England supporting the Normandy invasion on D-Day. "In the morning," he recalled, I had 200 patients, and in the evening I had 2,000."

After practicing in several California hospitals, Dr. Neale retired in 1984. But the Eagle sense of duty never left him—and at 101 years old he still was volunteering at his local church and senior center. Said Dr. Neale, "I always have appreciated that my folks and the Scoutmaster and all those people devoted a lot of time to us" —and, now, in a new century, this centenarian was still paying them back with his own service.

THE QUIET YEARS

One reason that Paul Siple was so singular—beyond his obvious abilities— was that he rose to prominence so *early*. By being plucked out of near-anonymity while still a teen and allowed to participate in one of the famous, and daring, adventures of the era, Siple's very existence gave a prominence to Eagle Scouting that it normally wouldn't have enjoyed for another decade.

And, in fact, thanks to both demographics and the few career opportunities available in the strained economic circumstances of the Great Depression, only a handful of Eagles rose to prominence in the years after Siple's adventure—and most of them, like Paul, were comparatively young. But the young Eagles who had, symbolically, served as the honor guard for President Franklin Roosevelt at the first jamboree in 1937—would, in five more years, serve as real-life officers for Commander-in-Chief Roosevelt in World War II. And, at the same time, in the ranks of the Cub Scouts could be found the leaders of the second, more powerful, half of the American Century.

The best known of these 1930s Eagles was **Milt Caniff**, the celebrated cartoonist. He earned his Eagle in 1923 at age 16 in Hillsboro, Ohio. By age 23, he had landed a job as an illustrator for the *Columbus Dispatch*. But when the Depression arrived, he was laid off from the paper. He briefly considered an acting career until an older cartoonist, Billy Ireland, told him, "Stick to your inkpots, kid, actors don't eat regularly."[5]

He did stick with cartooning—and by 1934 he had found a job with the *New York Daily News*. There, he created one of the iconic comic strips of the twentieth century, *Terry and the Pirates*—its powerful images, strong plots, noir shading, and exotic locales inspiring generations of cartoonists that

Eagle Scout and Catholic Saint Francis J. Parater.

followed. At the beginning of World War II, Caniff created a hugely popular armed forces-only version of *Terry* called *Male Call* that still is noted for its realistic depiction of military life.

After the war, chafing at his lack of ownership of his creation, Caniff killed off *Terry* and replaced it with the Air Force-oriented *Steve Canyon*, which proved almost as popular as its predecessor. It only ended with Caniff's own death in 1988. At that time, the National Cartoonists Society named its lifetime achievement medal after him and he also was inducted into the Comic Book Hall of Fame.

The only known Eagle Scout to be nominated for sainthood was **Francis J. Parater**, who earned his Eagle in 1913 from a Virginia troop. Just a decade later, as a young seminarian, he was sent to study in Rome, where he contracted rheumatic fever and died at only 23. He was nominated for canonization in 2001.

The third celebrated young Eagle of the pre-war years—he earned the rank at age 13 in a troop from Ridgefield, New Jersey—was a musician whose first big hit, "And Then Some," hit number one on the pop charts in 1935. Later that year he married his duet partner, Harriet Hilliard, with whom he had two sons. When his music career began to fade, **Ozzie Nelson** tried films. And then, anxious to spend more time with his family, created a radio show-turned-television program that employed all of them. *The Adventures of Ozzie and Harriet*, which ran on radio and TV from 1944 to 1973, was one of the most enduring comedy shows in television history.

Band leader and television pioneer Ozzie Nelson.

The most famous Eagle Scout of the era was a fictional character, the product of Broadway and Hollywood. Henry Aldrich was the most minor, but also most interesting, character in the 1938 comedy *What a Life*, written

by Clifford Goldsmith and produced and directed by the legendary George Abbot. Audiences loved Henry (played by Ezra Stone), a cheerful, energetic, and consistently misdirected teenager who seemed to embody the whole "bobby soxer" ethos.

The next year, an Aldrich family radio show, again starring Stone, and with its iconic opening of Mrs. Aldrich calling her son's name—and Henry shouting back "*Com*-ing Mother!"—was an instant hit, joining Bob Hope and Jack Benny at the top of the radio ratings.

A promotional image of actor Jimmy Lydon as Henry Aldrich, Boy Scout in 1944.

Not surprisingly, the radio show in turn spawned a series of mid-budget films from Paramount revolving around the adventures of the increasingly more responsible and mature Henry. The first two Henry Aldrich films featured major child star Jackie Cooper, like Henry. For the rest of the nine films of the series, the role was assumed by Jimmy Lydon, who quickly became synonymous with the character.

Audiences always had known that Henry was a Boy Scout. But with the ninth film of the series, *Henry Aldrich, Boy Scout* (1944), this participation moved to the forefront. More than that, in a shorthand for Henry's growing maturity during wartime, the one-time troublemaker became an Eagle Scout and patrol leader, shouldering the responsibility for a troublesome Scout, who resembled his younger self. Henry's achievement quietly celebrated a milestone taking place in the larger society: in 1940, for the first time, ten thousand Scouts earned the Eagle rank.

Meanwhile, Jackie Cooper, having established the series, moved on to his own Scouting-related production, the hugely popular 12-part serial *Scouts to the Rescue* (1939). In it, Cooper played Eagle Scout Bruce Scott who, after his Scoutmaster has to leave a camping trip because of a family emergency, leads his troop into a series of wild adventures involving a ghost town, counterfeiters, and even a lost Inca tribe. Not only is this serial an interesting precursor to *Indiana Jones and the Last Crusade* a half-century later but it even takes place the same year.

Henry Aldrich and Bruce Scott, in their theatrical way, represent a last glimpse of the first era of Scouting. By the time these films appeared, the world already had changed, the young men who had filled theaters to watch them were gone, and like everything else in America, Scouting was being transformed into a very different organization.

EAGLES OF WAR

Pearl Harbor was attacked at the very moment the first generation of America's Eagle Scouts reached middle age and the second generation became old enough to fight. And since war elevates both heroes and natural leaders to prominence, it is not surprising that America's Eagles assumed high profile roles in the war and were recognized for some its most famous acts of heroism.

Among the thousands of highly decorated Eagle Scouts who fought in World War II, eight stand apart because their extraordinary heroism— some at the cost of their lives—earned them America's highest military award, the Congressional Medal of Honor.

Lt. Colonel Aquilla J. "Jimmy" Dyess earned his Eagle in 1925 with a troop in Andersonville, Georgia. In 1928, already showing his courage, Dyess was awarded the Carnegie Medal for saving the lives of two swimmers off the coast of Charleston, South California. He remains the only American to receive the nation's highest civilian and military awards for heroism. Joining the Marines in 1936, Dyess, a crack shot, quickly became a member of the Marine Corps Rifle Team.

In February 1944, during the brutal battle for Kwajalein Atoll in the Marshall Islands, Lt. Col. Dyess led a company of Marines in a flanking attack on the last Japanese position on Namur Island. As always he led from the front, driving his troops forward against withering enemy fire. As he stood atop the parapet of an antitank trench waving his men forward, he was cut down by a machine gun burst.

Today, the Georgia-Carolina Council of the BSA holds an annual Jimmy Dyess Day at Fort Gordon—and the four-lane highway the Scouts take from Augusta to the Fort is named after Dyess as well.

2nd Lt. Robert Edward Femoyer only had been in the European theater six weeks when he found himself, as the navigator of a crippled B-17 Flying Fortress in a raid over Merseburg, Germany, wounded and bleeding, with the pilot and co-pilot dead. Struggling to remain conscious in the face of massive blood loss, the West Virginian Eagle refused the morphine offered by crewmates—despite agonizing pain described as "almost beyond the realm of human endurance"—to keep his head clear enough to pilot the plane.

For the next two-and-a-half hours, Femoyer piloted the damaged plane through six-course corrections around anti-aircraft flack. It was only after the plane reached the English Channel that Femoyer finally accept a shot of morphine. He successfully landed the plane and died of his wounds just 30 minutes later. He was 23 years old.

Rear Admiral Eugene Fluckey earned his Eagle Scout in Washington, DC, but left for the U.S. Naval Academy before it could be awarded. After commissioning, he served on a battleship and a destroyer before finding his permanent home in the U.S. Navy submarine fleet. He assumed command of the *USS Barb* in April 1944 and embarked on what is often considered the greatest career of any submariner.

The *USS Barb*, under "Lucky" Fluckey, sank more tonnage than any other submarine in the war—including a carrier, a cruiser, a frigate, and 14 other ships. Fluckey also is credited with the only military landing on the home Japanese islands in World War II: when a *Barb* landing party blew up a 16-car train passing along the coast. For the raiding party, Fluckey specifically asked for former Boy Scouts because of their resourcefulness.

Fluckey already had earned the Navy Cross four times when he and the *Barb* crew embarked on their 11th—and most celebrated—mission. During this raid, Fluckey invented a new way to attack night convoys by sneaking into the line of escort ships. The *Barb* attacked two convoys of Japanese ships and then, while escaping and under attack, set a then world speed record for submarines.

In later years, Fluckey was commander of the United States Pacific Fleet's submarine force and Director of Naval Intelligence. He finally was awarded his Eagle in 1948.

Charles P. Murray, a 1st Lieutenant leading a patrol near the medieval town of Kayserburg on the border of France and Germany on December 16, 1944, came upon a 200-man German unit shelling a nearby American force.

Moving forward alone to get a better view, Murray called in artillery—but when its aim was off, and he tried to call in corrections, Murray found his radio was dead. The German force was too large to attack directly, so Murray decided instead to pin it down until he could get support.

Returning to his patrol, he gathered up automatic weapons and grenade launchers and went back alone to his outpost. There, despite drawing extensive fire, Murray attacked the Germans, killing ten, scattering the rest, and even destroying a truck loaded with three mortars. He then led his patrol forward, capturing its bridge objective and capturing ten more of the enemy. At that point, another German soldier, who was pretending to surrender, threw a grenade that seriously injured Murray, who refused aid until he had properly positioned his unit.

Murray would stay in the U.S. Army through the Vietnam War era, ultimately, as a Colonel, commanding the Old Guard that guards the Tomb of the Unknown Soldier. When it was learned in 1971 that Murray never had officially completed the paperwork for his Eagle, the BSA awarded him an honorary Distinguished Eagle Scout Award, one of the first ever given.

On October 13, 1943, **Captain Arlo L. Olson** performed feats of bravery that would seem unbelievable had they not been witnessed. Having led his company 30 miles into enemy territory in Northern Italy, Olson waded chest deep across the Volturno River under nearly point-blank machine gun fire, climbed the opposite bank and threw two hand grenades into the enemy gun position that killed its crew.

Soon after, a second enemy machine gun opened up 150 yards away. Olson, according to his Medal of Honor citation, "advanced upon the position in a slow, deliberate walk. Although five German soldiers threw hand grenades at him from a range of five yards, Capt. Olson dispatched them all, picked up a machine pistol and continued toward the enemy. Advancing to within 15 yards of the position he shot it out with the foe, killing nine and seizing the post."

For the next 13 days, Olson continued these superhuman feats, often leading attacks directly into machine gun fire, despite the fact that the enemy gunners were specifically targeting him. Finally, his luck ran out during an assault on Monte San Nicola. Grievously wounded, Captain Olson still finished his reconnaissance, put his men in position, and ordered that his wounded fellow soldiers be tended to first. He died of his wounds while being stretchered down the mountain.

In October 1942, **Colonel Mitchell Paige** was a 22-year-old platoon sergeant in the Battle of Guadalcanal when his unit came under heavy fire. Paige commanded the counterattack. Then, when all of the other Marines in his unit had been killed, Paige continued the fight himself—running from one machine gun to another to return fire. When reinforcements arrived, Paige organized them into a line and led a bayonet counterattack, driving the attackers back and punching a hole in the enemy's line.

Paige, the son of Croatian immigrants, had earned his Eagle in 1936 from a troop in Charleroi, Pennsylvania, but graduated high school and immediately joined the Marines. He finally received his Eagle medal just before his death in 2003. Paige also lived long enough to see a GI Joe modeled after his younger self.

Lt. Colonel Jay Zeamer Jr. earned his Eagle at age 13 with a troop in Orange, New Jersey. A year later, he left for military school and then went on to the Massachusetts Institute of Technology. In 1941, even before the war began, he earned his pilot's wings and officer's commission in the U.S. Army Air Corps. In April 1943, now a captain and a veteran of 46 missions,

Zeamer volunteered to pilot an unescorted B-17 on a reconnaissance mission of an island near Bougainville. The Japanese had assembled a force of an estimated 400 fighters in the region and Zeamer's assignment was to discover where they were.

Zeamer and his crew made the 600-mile flight to their target, took the photographs and quickly were set on by an estimated 20 fighters, five of which made a devastating first attack that severely damaged the bomber. The severely wounded bombardier, who also would win the Medal of Honor, managed to shoot down two of the fighters before bleeding to death while still manning his guns. Zeamer, covered with shrapnel wounds and with a broken leg, managed to shoot down another fighter even as he evaded the attackers.

For the next 45 minutes, Zeamer flew evasive maneuvers as his crew fought off 17 more fighters. Bleeding heavily and drifting into unconsciousness, Zeamer refused treatment until the bomber escaped the attack. Then, realizing the plane wouldn't clear a mountain pass in its path, his last order was to crash land the plane on a nearby runway.

When the rescue crew reached the crashed bomber, Zeamer had lost so much blood that he was at first believed dead. But he survived and lived a long life. When he died in 2007 at age 88, he was the last surviving Army Air Corps Medal of Honor recipient.

Captain Benjamin Salomon never expected to see combat. He was a dentist, assigned to frontline surgeon duty during the battle of Saipan in July 1944. An Eagle from Milwaukee, Wisconsin, he had graduated from the University of Southern California dental school in 1937 and opened a practice.

Drafted in 1940 as a private, he eventually was commissioned as an officer in 1942. Dr. Salomon saw his first combat two years later when he went ashore on Saipan with the 105th Infantry. With little need for his dental services, Salomon volunteered to replace the battalion's wounded doctor. His surgical station was just 50 yards behind the front foxhole line. And when that line was overrun, Salomon found his surgical tent filling with Japanese soldiers who had run in through the tent fly and crawled under the sides.

Salomon fought them off—kicking the knife out of one's hand, shooting another, bayoneting a third, and rifle butting at fourth—even as he ordered his staff to evacuate the wounded. Without a second thought, Dr. Salomon stayed behind to provide cover.

When Salomon's body was found the next day, it was slumped over a machine gun, with 98 dead enemy soldiers lying in front of him. Salomon's body had 76 bullets and multiple bayonet wounds—as many as two dozen of them received while Dr. Salomon was still alive.

Sadly, after this mind-boggling act of heroism, the War Department resisted awarding the Medal of Honor to Salomon. One reason was doubt regarding his eligibility as an official noncombatant. But just as important was institutional anti-Semitism: at this point in the war, only two other Jews had received the Medal of Honor (one of them the uncle of musician Lenny Kravitz), and none would again for the rest of World War II and Korea. Where Scouting hadn't hesitated to give Ben Salomon its highest award, the U.S. Army had failed in its duty.

In 1951, a nomination for the award was made but turned down. In 1969, the surgeon general of the U.S. Army made the nomination. and was turned down without explanation. The next year the secretary of the army made the same nomination—again without luck.

In 2002, 58 years after the death of Captain Ben Salomon DDS— thanks to a nomination by the USC Dental School, supported by a local Congressman—the nomination finally was accepted and the award signed by President George W. Bush. The Eagle Scout had earned his true honor at last.

COLOR BLINDNESS

Benjamin Salomon's story is a reminder of the prejudices that still divided America at the beginning of the World War II—and that would begin to crack at its end.

Though the Boy Scouts of America didn't entirely escape the racism and biases of early 20th century America, to its eternal credit, it set at the very core of its philosophy that *every* Scout of sufficient character, discipline, and ambition—no matter their race, intelligence, or physical ability—could earn the rank of Eagle. That meant the Eagle rank was, in the end, not just a measure of skill or competence or ability, but most of all, of *character*. And character had no prejudice.

Thus, from the very beginning, even when communities still demanded that Scout troops be segregated, young men of otherwise marginalized racial, religious, and ethnic groups could still make the run for Eagle. And they did just that.

THE AFRICAN AMERICAN EAGLE

There was one group of American Scouts whose entry into the ranks of Eagles was long overdue: African Americans. It took 16 years, but in mid-1926, in the face of enduring Jim Crow and the second rise of the Ku Klux Klan, a small group of black Scouts scattered around the country earned the rank at last.

Records have long been murky, but it is believed that the first African American Eagle Scout was **Edgar Cunningham Sr.** He earned his Eagle on June 8, 1926, as a member of Troop 12 Waterloo, Iowa, of the Wapsipinicon Area Council. As great as his achievement was, it was certainly equaled by his Scoutmaster, **James Lincoln Page**, a World War I veteran who had organized two all-black Boy Scout troops (Troops 9 and 12) in February, 1925. For his work, Page received a presidential citation from President Calvin Coolidge while Cunningham also received a handwritten letter from the president.

Scoutmaster Page spent the rest of his life in Scouting, mentoring numerous other Eagles. When asked by younger Scouts about his early Scouting experiences, Page replied, in words that can serve as his epitaph: "We were tough, we didn't give up."[6]

Francis "Tick" Coleman was the third African American Eagle Scout, earning the award in October, 1926. He joined Troop 181 at his local Episcopal Church in Philadelphia mainly because his mother insisted he do something to fill his afternoons after school. But Tick took to Scouting, just as he did the YMCA—the only other local organization that looked past his race—and, in thanks, he would stay loyal to both organizations for the next 80 years.

In the course of his long life (1911–2008), Coleman, even as he worked as an educator and school counselor, set a standard for community service that few have ever matched by working in the Boy Scouts, Peace Corps, YMCA, Boys Club, Salvation Army, the local Hebrew Center, and many others—all to help the disadvantaged youth of his city.

At his death, at age 97, Coleman was believed to be the oldest African American Eagle Scout. To honor his service, the BSA created the Coleman Service Award to honor Scouting paraprofessionals.

But like Paul Siple, Tick Coleman was a singular case: a man before (and indeed, after) his time. It would take World War II, and a social revolution, before America's black Eagles would begin to make their mark.

TUSKEGEE AIRMEN EAGLES

And that mark would first be made by the Tuskegee Airmen of the 332nd Fighter Group. The Airmen, with their historic fight against military prejudice, and a sterling record in their red-tailed P-51s in the skies over Germany, remain one of the most compelling stories of the war. What was rarely noticed—at least not until recent years—was the presence of at least three Eagle Scouts in their ranks.

Lt. Colonel Eugene C. Cheatham Jr. was born in Georgia but at a young age joined his Episcopal missionary father and family on trips to Africa and Europe. Eventually, the family settled in New York City, where Cheatham joined a troop and completed his Eagle requirements by age 15.

But his family was too poor ever to buy him an official Scout uniform. And so, when the time came for young Eugene to appear before an Eagle board of review, he was too embarrassed to go.

After flying with the Tuskegee Airmen in World War II, Cheatham went on to fly 150 more missions in the Korean War. The Air Force had been good to Cheatham and he returned the favor, remaining in the service and retiring as a Lieutenant Colonel in 1977.

In 2001, at a Veterans Day event where he was a guest of honor, Cheatham watched the Boy Scout honor guard and casually remarked that he regretted never having finished his Eagle. One of his companions, an organizer of the event who happened to be an Eagle, decided to rectify the situation. When a search found that Cheatham's Scouting records were long gone, the BSA decided to allow the 80-year-old to participate in an Eagle board of review that met the tough 1930 standards.

On September 18, 2004, just seven months before his death, Eugene Cheatham was awarded his Eagle medal at a Court of Honor held at the San Diego Air & Space Museum.

Colonel Charles E. McGee, who earned his Eagle in 1940, had a military career that extended almost three decades beyond the Tuskegee Airmen. A career officer in the USAF, he holds an Air Force record of 409 combat missions in three wars (World War II, Korea, and Vietnam)—136 of them with the Airmen. At the time this is being written; he remains deeply committed to the Air Force, even flying to Iraq at age 86 to meet with and inspire the current generation of fighter pilots.

Col. Charles E. McGee after the presentation of his Distinguished Eagle Scout Award at the BSA's 2010 Centennial Jamboree. Photo courtesy of NESA.

One distinction that separates McGee from his peers is that not only was he a Boy Scout—in a troop in Cleveland, Ohio—but he also has continued his affiliation with Scouting throughout his adult life, holding both district and regional positions with the BSA.

Like the other Tuskegee Eagles, McGee has been awarded the Distinguished Eagle Scout Award—in his case, appropriately enough, at the 2010 Centennial Boy Scouts of America Jamboree.

Percy Sutton may have had the most remarkable and varied life of the three Tuskegee Eagles.

Born in San Antonio, Texas, as the last of 15 children, Sutton's father had been born a slave and had become a farmer, entrepreneur, high school principal, and early civil rights activist.

Percy joined Scouting in San Antonio and at age 16, achieved the rank of Eagle. He later would say that Scouting played a key role in shaping his life.

All of the Sutton children, including Percy, who was the youngest and apparently the wildest, attended college. Once out in the world, Sutton took up stunt flying and barnstorming but quit after a friend crashed. The outbreak of war found him at the Tuskegee Institute and it was a natural next step for him to join the Airmen. He earned battle stars in both the Italian and Mediterranean theaters as the squadron's intelligence officer.

But for a many like Percy Sutton, a place in the Tuskegee Airmen was just a prelude to adult life for an ambitious 25-year-old.

With the war's end, Sutton set out to become a lawyer and attended both Columbia and Brooklyn Law Schools. Brilliant, black, and fearless, he soon was one the best-known civil rights lawyers in the country. His most famous client was Malcolm X, whose widow he supported after that leader's assassination. He also was jailed for his vigorous defense of black radical Stokely Carmichael.

Sutton used the credibility this work had gained for him in the African American community to enter politics. He co-founded the "Harlem Clubhouse," a Democrat power center that still dominates Harlem politics that over the years has produced such important African American politicians as New York Mayor David Dinkins, U.S. Congressman Charles Rangel, New York Secretary of State Basil Paterson and son New York Governor David Paterson.

In time, Sutton entered politics himself and served in the New York assembly and as Manhattan borough president. In 1977, he ran for mayor of New York but lost to Ed Koch. But that didn't stop the irrepressible Percy Sutton. He already had co-founded the Inner City Broadcasting Corporation and purchased New York's first African American radio station, WLIB. Now he expanded his media empire: after helping drive the restoration of Harlem's famed Apollo Theater, Sutton produced a popular syndicated television series, *Live at the Apollo*, originating from there.

Percy Sutton was a legendary figure in New York—especially in Harlem— when he died at 89 in 2007, leaving Leatrice, his wife of 66 years. But if New York City had been his stage, in the end the old Tuskegee Eagle went home to San Antonio. There he is buried, not far from where he had once camped as a Scout.

THE LAST EAGLE OF THE GREATEST GENERATION

Eighty-six year-old George Maher was a legend at the Pacific Skyline Council headquarters in Palo Alto, California. After having raised his children and served for years as a Scoutmaster, the long-retired engineer had found a job that seemed to suit him perfectly—devoting eight hours each week processing Eagle Scout applications—which, by 2013, numbered in the thousands. He also sat on hundreds of Eagle boards of review.

It wasn't until Mark Manchester, development director for the Council, happened one day to ask a casual question that Maher's secret came out: "George, when did you get your Eagle?"

Manchester, an Eagle himself, always had assumed that Maher was a fellow Eagle. "He just looked like an Eagle Scout to me," Manchester later would recall.

The answer he got was wholly unexpected. "I blurted out that it should have been March 10, 1944."

Confused by the old man's response, Manchester decided to pursue the story further. And what he found astonished him. On that March night in 1944, seventeen-year-old George Maher was in the middle of his board of review…when it was interrupted with the news that George's father was in the hospital, dying. The Board quickly adjourned and George raced off.

He never returned. There were other priorities now. With his father gone, George needed to help his family and within days, he joined the Navy and soon was shipped out to the Pacific. By the time he returned at war's end; George's Scouting days were long past as he now focused on family and career.

But Scouting still called to him. And when his youngest son became a Cub Scout in the early 1970s, Maher rejoined the program as a volunteer—and had remained so for four decades when he had that fateful conversation.

Haunted by the story, Manchester was determined that George Maher finally should be awarded his Eagle. Happily, over the intervening seven decades, Maher had managed to keep all of his Scouting records, including ranks and merit badges. All that was missing was his Life Scout card, which had been lost when George had been nearly swept off the deck of his ship by a giant wave during the infamous typhoon of December 1944.

The BSA hardly was going to penalize a war hero for over such a trifling detail. And so, on January 6, 2013, exactly 68 years, nine months, and 28 days after his fateful Eagle board of review, George Maher received his Eagle medal in a special Court of Honor. The event, filled with Eagles young and old from throughout the region, as well as news camera crews, received national attention. And what made the event especially moving was that George Maher's Eagle badge was presented to him by his grandson, Eagle Scout Marcus White.

HOME FRONT

Scouting during the Great Depression and World War II was a very different organization from that of the preceding boom years.

Massive unemployment and widespread poverty placed heavy pressure on families in the 1930s. The more elaborate troop activities and summer camping trips of the 1920s now were often replaced by weekend campouts nearby using improvised tents and bedding. As with Eugene Cheatham, many Scouts couldn't afford uniforms, much less the traditional accoutrements (knife, compass, and hatchet) of Scouting.

Moreover, many families were on the move, searching for work, which bedeviled unit cohesion. Many older Scouts, recognizing the economic burden they placed on their families, dropped out of school and hit the rails or roads searching for work. Others joined the Civilian Conservation Corps (CCC) or other government programs. Not surprisingly, the annual number of new Eagles, which had more than doubled from 4,500 in 1927 to 9,200 in 1932, slumped the next year to 7,000 and stayed there until the end of the decade.[7]

In 1934, President Roosevelt, recognizing in Scouting an established mechanism to organize young people to both get them off the streets and help contribute to the nation's rebuilding, publicly called on Scouting to help the distressed and needy. The result was a National Good Turn that ultimately netted 1.8 million items of clothing, food, household furnishings, and supplies.[8]

And if the number of new Eagles fell—underscoring the impact of the Depression on older teenaged boys—Scouting itself continued to grow, passing 1 million members in 1935, the BSA's silver jubilee year.[9] Even the two-year postponement of the first national jamboree in 1935 (due to an infantile paralysis or polio epidemic) failed to slow Scouting's growth.

Maj. Stanley C. Scott of the US Army's 17th Field Artillery Observation Battalion as an Eagle Scout in 1931. Maj. Scott died outside Saint-Lô, France, on an August 1944 reconnaissance mission during World War II.

The New Deal once again transformed the image of Scouting. Ever since the bond drives of World War I, Scouting largely had returned to its camping roots. But now it was back in the community—collecting clothes, visiting the needy, serving as a kind of de facto Youth Auxiliary of the national recovery effort. The BSA had long since become an institution identified with American life but now that image was sealed forever and immortalized in Frank Capra's *Mr. Smith Goes to Washington* (1939).

Tellingly, the Boy "Rangers" in that movie, organizing in support of a bill to create a national boy's camp—proposed by their old leader, now a U.S. senator—is largely led by older boys, the movie's surrogate Eagles. To a Depression audience, this scenario, with a troop led by older Scouts while the grown-ups are off trying to save the country, would have seen far less unlikely than it does today.

As for the national boy's camp, that idea too was one of the moment: even as the movie was opening, oil baron Waite Phillips was in the process of donating 128,000 acres in New Mexico's Sangre de Christo mountains to create Philturn (later Philmont) Scout Ranch, still Scouting's premiere summer camp and a source of employment for generations of young Eagles.

By the time Philmont opened, the Eagles were there to fill its many counselor and ranger positions. With the economy improving, older boys were able to stay home and, inevitably, the number of new Eagles again rose to 10,000 in 1939.[10]

President Franklin D. Roosevelt receives a special edition of the Boy Scout Handbook *celebrating the BSA's 5 millionth member in 1935.*

Needless to say, when war came two years later, Scouting again was challenged and found a vital role. Once again, President Roosevelt called on Boy Scouts to serve as a homefront auxiliary.

By war's end, the federal government had made 69 specific requests for assistance from the BSA for the war effort. They included the collection of rubber in the form of spare tires and other consumer products—in a two-week drive Scouts collected 30 million pounds; Victory gardens—20,000 Scouts earned the General Douglas MacArthur Victory Garden medal; the distribution of pledge cards for war bonds and war savings stamps; the distribution of stamp and Victory posters; the collection of aluminum, waste paper, and salvage; the management of defense housing surveys; and the distribution of air raid posters. Scouts also served as firewatchers, emergency medical personnel, messengers, and dispatch bearers.[11]

If mainstream Scouting became a kind of pre-boot camp for future soldiers in World War II America; the process of becoming an Eagle Scout served as a prep for Officer Candidate School. Uncelebrated, because largely unnoticed, the great Scouting service initiatives of the early 1940s largely were managed by Eagles and other Scouts in senior leadership roles, because most of the fathers who normally would have led Scout troops had gone off to war. This presented a tremendous challenge, as even the Eagles typically had only a year or two to lead the younger Scouts before they too went off to war.

Even the BSA itself was suffering a shortage of senior

Scouts collect rubber (top) and metals (bottom) during special World War II material drives in 1942.

leadership. An aging James E. West, the only chief Scout executive that Scouting ever had known, retired in 1942. National Scout Commissioner Dan Beard died at age 90 in 1941. Ernest Seton would die in 1946. And, most traumatic of all, Lord Baden-Powell, Scouting's founder, died in Kenya at age 83 in 1941. The men who had built Scouting and led it for three decades suddenly were gone from the scene.

It was inevitable now that dramatic changes were in store for Scouting— and its Eagles—in the postwar world. There would be new leaders, new priorities, and most of all, a gigantic new wave of postwar baby boomer boys heading in Scouting's direction. Scouting soon would have to reinvent itself several times to keep up with this new, and rapidly changing, America.

THE ARCTIC EAGLE

And what of Paul Siple, the "Eagle on Ice" as his biographers would call him?

Home from the Byrd Expedition in June 1930, he was feted in both New York and at home in Erie, Pennsylvania. Within three months, he returned to the life he once had led as if nothing had happened. In September, he went back to Alleghany College to complete his degree.

But everything *had* changed. Siple had left an America kicking up its heels at the height of the Roaring Twenties and had returned to a stunned nation sinking ever deeper into the Great Depression. America, especially young people. was facing an uncertain future and needed heroes. And Paul Siple, having been part of one of the great adventures of the century while still a teenager, fit the bill. Soon, he found himself giving speeches—three years' worth—to Scouting organizations and other groups throughout the Northeast, often sharing the stage with (now Rear-Admiral) Byrd himself.

And despite appearances, Paul Siple had been changed by his experiences. He now seemed a young man in a hurry. Even as he was touring and giving speeches, he raced through the remaining three years of his bachelor of science degree in biology, with a minor in geology. At the same time, he *also* managed to author two best-selling books on his experiences. Then, soon after graduation, Siple took off on a two-year backpacking tour of the world, traveling to England, Western Europe, Russia, the Middle East, and North Africa. Erie, Pennsylvania, had grown too small to keep him.

He returned from his travels to an invitation by Byrd to join a second Antarctic expedition. Byrd, who in the years to come would show that he had boundless trust and faith in the young man, asked Siple to join him on his personal staff and help him plan the voyage—then, once it was underway, made him the expedition's chief biologist. During this expedition's two years in Antarctica (1933–1935), Siple led the Marie Byrd Land Sledging Party that identified and cataloged 90 new species of moss and lichen.

Siple returned to the States to two more years of lectures (hundreds of them now) around the country. He also found time to write his third book.

In 1936, he enrolled in graduate school at Clark University in Worcester, Massachusetts. He had found his life's work now: the adaptation of human beings to their physical environment and would earn a PhD in geography and climatology three years later. Also in 1936, he married Ruth Ida Johannesmeyer, and between 1940 and 1946 they would have three daughters.

It's amazing they had the time. Between 1939 and 1941, now-Admiral Byrd was named head of the U.S. Antarctic Service and embarked on yet another expedition. He asked Paul Siple to be his assistant. Ultimately, Siple became supervisor of all Antarctic expedition logistics and supply, senior geographer of the Service, leader of the west base of Little America III and—again putting his Scouting training to good use—official navigator on all Antarctic exploratory flights.

With the outbreak of war, Siple was hired by the U.S. Army to help design cold weather clothing and gear, as well as develop maps. Within a year, he was commissioned as a captain in the U.S. Army Quartermaster Corps, where he directed research on clothing and environmental protection for troops in all climates. He had come a long way from those days in Little America I watching Martin Ronne sew reindeer skins.

Ultimately, Siple founded the U.S. Quartermaster Corps' Climate Research Laboratory. The revolutionary clothing the Laboratory invented (notably the cold weather parka and the thermal barrier boot) saved thousands of lives and earned Siple both the Legion of Merit medal and an honorary knighthood (MBE) from the king of England. Those designs still define outdoor clothing to this day.

With the war's end, Siple did field research in the Arctic and Greenland and then traveled to Little America IV as the scientific advisor to the War Department. In 1946, he left the army as a Lt. Colonel and immediately rejoined the army's general staff as a civilian expert in science and geography. He was the acknowledged world's expert on human adaptation to all of the Earth's diverse climates.

One of the most celebrated feats of U.S. military leadership is General Matthew Ridgeway's command of the NATO and United Nations forces during the Korean War. Ridgeway arrived to find his troops demoralized, in retreat, and freezing to death. One of his first command decisions (one which both saved lives and restored morale) was to order new winter clothing for the troops. Siple and his design would travel twice to Korea during those years, traveling into combat zones to test and perfect the technology. There, he also would put to use a scientific discovery he had made with a colleague in 1946: "wind chill", a term now used casually by the general public.

In 1953, now generally recognized as the greatest of all polar scientists, Siple was named director of scientific projects and environmental living for the task force preparing for Operation Deep Freeze I that would begin the construction of research facilities across the Antarctic. This initiative was in turn the kickoff for 1958's Deep Freeze II (67 nations at 40 stations)—the first great international exploration of the Antarctic and South Pole. Soon, he was named deputy to the rapidly fading Admiral Byrd—after 30 years, this would be their final partnership.

Paul Siple inspects the winter parka of Eagle Scout Richard L. Chappell, who will become the second Eagle Scout to travel to Little America, Antarctica in 1956.

On December 31, 1956, Eagle Scout Paul Siple appeared on the cover of *Time* magazine as part of a larger story about Deep Freeze II, the first-ever attempt to winter-over at the South Pole. Siple had been named scientific leader of the 18-man expedition that would spend six months at Amundsen-Scott South Pole Station.

In late September 1956, they emerged to great acclaim as the first Scott expedition. In the months that followed, Siple would receive five honorary doctorates, medals from the U.S. Army and Defense Department, and most prized of all (because he now joined the ranks of the most famous Polar explorers) the *National Geographic* Hubbard Medal.

In making the award, Chief Justice Earl Warren, after listing such names as Peary, Amundsen, Scott, and Byrd, said, "Our Hubbard medalist today is of the same stature as the great explorers I have just mentioned. Six times he has journeyed to the forbidding continent of Antarctica, the first time with Admiral Byrd as a young Eagle Scout."

Now, Justice Warren continued, Paul Siple had led the team that survived "the longest, darkest and coldest winter yet endured by man."[12]

Paul Siple accepted the medal with typical humility, "on behalf of all those who have taken part in the exploration and uncovering of a continent."[13]

In his final years, Siple continued to work with little thought to retirement. Like his beloved sled dogs, he remained in harness to the very end. In 1966, while serving as the first scientific attaché to the U.S. embassies in New Zealand and Australia, he suffered a stroke. He was only 58, but after the physical stresses of living in the most inhospitable places on the planet, Paul Siple's body had begun to wear out. He returned to Washington as special scientific advisor to the army's research & development office. And there on November 25, 1968, he died at his desk, hard at work on his next adventure. In his memory, the U.S. Army created the Paul A. Siple Award, a silver medallion awarded biannually to an Army scientist or scientific team for excellence in scientific research.

But Paul Siple's greatest legacy is Antarctica. Today, travelers to that frozen continent can visit Mount Siple, Siple Island, Siple Ridge, and Siple Station (and even the Siple Coast of New Zealand) all honoring a great explorer, a great scientist, and the most famous young Eagle of Scouting's first century.

The author thanks Dr. Neil Armstrong for his assistance—in what would prove to be the last days of his life—in correcting many long-standing factual errors in his standard biography.

CHAPTER FIVE

SHOOTING THE MOON

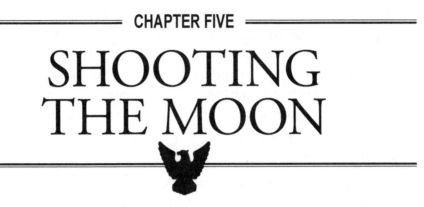

They only would get one Chance.

T he targeted landing area was on the southwest edge of the Sea of Tranquility. After saying goodbye to Michael Collins in the command module, the two men had climbed through the tight passage into the lunar excursion module (LEM), sealed the hatches, and readied the LEM for separation.

That was almost an hour ago now. Collins was now 70 miles above them, listening intently to the radio, and hundreds of NASA employees were monitoring their progress back on Earth from the Houston control room. And—almost impossible as it was to imagine—all over the surface of that little blue marble hovering above them, a billion or more people were listening as well in living rooms and auditoriums and public marketplaces.[1] None of that mattered now. All that counted was a successful touch down.

At 6,000 feet, a yellow caution light flared on the console. **Neil Armstrong** and Edwin "Buzz" Aldrin glanced at each other. "Program alarm," said

Armstrong brusquely, "It's a 1202." Twenty miles above, Collins dove for his checklist and began thumbing through its pages. But before he could find the designation, he heard a voice from Houston—it was fellow astronaut and designated capsule communicator Charlie Duke—saying, "Roger, we're GO on the alarm."

Collins found the listing: "1202: Executive overflow." It meant that the onboard computer, little more powerful than an electric adding machine, now was being overwhelmed with so much input from so many sources that it was postponing some of the calculations for later.

What calculations? When? Was the computer now putting off calculating a critical piece of information?

At 3,000 feet above the surface, another yellow caution light appeared. The computer now read "1201," yet another kind of program overflow alarm.

Recalled Aldrin later: "Back in Houston, not to mention on board the Eagle, our hearts shot up into throats while we waited to learn what would happen. We had received two of the caution lights when Steve Bales, the flight controller responsible for LM [lunar module] computer activity, told us to proceed, through Charlie … We received three or four more warnings but kept on going."

The Apollo 11 lunar module now was fully committed to a landing—and with little extra fuel on the descent engine, Armstrong knew he had to pick the final landing site quickly and commit to it. There would be no time to change his mind.

Hands on the controls and looking out the LEM's window, Armstrong began bringing the LEM down, adjusting the descent rate to make minute course corrections. He checked the landscape off to his starboard—good; they are on track.

Armstrong looked out ahead. To his horror, he saw "an NFL stadium- sized crater, with a large number of big boulders and rocks for about one or two- crater diameters around it." That is exactly where they didn't want to land. And the LEM's autotargeting landing system was taking them right for it. The LEM risked landing at an angle on the crater's wall and perhaps tipping. Worse, on the rippled surface at the edge of the crater, Armstrong risked the worst nightmare of all: *stubbing a toe*, as he called it—catching one of the legs of the LEM on the ground or on one of the many boulders that strewed the area while the lander still was moving sideways—a potentially fatal mistake.

Without a second thought, Armstrong switched off the autotargeting system and grabbed the controls. He'd have to land the craft manually. But at only a couple hundred feet up now, there seemed to be no safe place to go. He scanned the horizon for a better landing spot that he could reach with the 60 seconds of fuel that remained, working the rockets to slowly bring the craft closer to the lunar surface. To use a modern analogy, it was like a computer game playing four different variables at once—only this time the cost of failure was everything:

> *540 feet, down at 30 [feet per second]... down at 15... 400 feet down at 9... forward... 350 feet, down at 4... 300 feet, down 3½... 47 forward... 1½ down... 13 forward... 11 forward? coming down nicely... 200 feet, 4½ down... 5½ down... 5 percent... 75 feet... 6 forward... lights on... down 2½... 40 feet? down 2½, kicking up some dust... 30 feet, 2½ down... faint shadow... 4 forward... 4 forward... drifting to right a little...* [2]

LIFTOFF

At that moment—July 20, 1969, at the controls, hovering a dozen feet off the surface of the moon in the lunar excursion module with just seconds of fuel left—no human being was better suited for the task at hand than 39-year-old Neil A. Armstrong, a former test pilot and aerospace engineer from Wapakoneta, Ohio.

Armstrong was born on August 5, 1930, just five weeks after Paul Siple's return from the Antarctic. He was the oldest of three children born to Stephen Koenig Armstrong and the former Viola Louise Engel. Because his father worked for the state of Ohio and was transferred regularly to a new town, the Armstrongs lived an itinerant existence for most of Neil's childhood—living in 20 different places in his first 15 years.

Such a childhood teaches a young man to adapt quickly to new surroundings, immerse himself immediately into daily life, and to be prepared to move on with little advance notice. And so, somewhere in the middle of those moves, Neil Armstrong at age 13 joined a newly-formed Boy Scout troop in his town. And, because his father made his last forced move to Wapakoneta when Neil was 14, the young man finally got the stability he needed to stay with a troop and complete his Eagle at age 17.

Neil left for college at Purdue that August. He also had been accepted to MIT but chose to stay in the Midwest. He proved to be a merely average student those first two years, no doubt in part because he fully enjoyed campus life (including being a member of the Marching and Concert Bands) and perhaps because he also knew that a job already was waiting for him: he'd gone to Purdue on the Holloway Plan, which meant he now was also an apprentice seaman and owed the U.S. Navy three years on active duty and two more, during his final years in college, in the Naval Air Reserve. It was an interesting career choice because Armstrong had a history of motion sickness.

TOP: Eagle Scout Neil Armstrong (left) is celebrated along with President Dwight D. Eisenhower on a commemorative stamp for the 13th World Jamboree in Japan in 1971. BOTTOM: Neil Armstrong as a young Scout with his patrol.

Fulfilling that commitment, Neil Armstrong joined the Navy in 1947 as a midshipman. Eighteen months later, a week after his 20th birthday—after he had made six carrier landings in a propeller trainer and six more landings in a propeller fighter aircraft—he received his wings. Six months after that, in June 1951, now an Ensign, he made his first carrier landing in a jet. And three months after that, just weeks after his 21st birthday, Ensign Neil Armstrong saw his first action over Korea as an escort on a reconnaissance mission.

Five days later, on a low-altitude bombing attack in a valley, Armstrong's F9F Panther was hit by anti-aircraft fire. The damaged plane, flying at 350 mph, headed directly toward a cable the North Koreans had strung between the walls of the valley 500 feet above the floor. As Armstrong struggled to regain control of the plane, it clipped the cable, slicing off six feet of one wing.

The young pilot somehow still managed to regain control of the plane before it crashed and then fly out of the valley for home. But now he realized that, because the wing's aileron was gone, it would be impossible to land. And so, after Armstrong limped his plane to the nearest friendly airfield— he flew directly over it, aimed the plane for the nearby ocean, and hit the ejection seat.

Neil's plan was to parachute into the water and wait to get picked up by rescue helicopters. Instead, as he ejected, Armstrong ran into an onshore wind, and his parachute was blown back over land. Amusingly, he found himself picked up by a Marine officer, sent out in a jeep to find the parachuting pilot and who just happened to be his old flight school roommate.

Ensign Neil Armstrong left the Navy in August 1952, having flown 78 combat missions, which earned him an Air Medal with two gold stars. He went home to finish his degree at Purdue. Like Paul Siple before him, Armstrong was a changed man. This time he hit the books, becoming an honors student, yet still finding time to join a fraternity.

He finished his aeronautical engineering degree in 1955. Two years later, he was a married man with the first of three children on the way. He was working for NACA (soon to be NASA) at Edwards Air Force Base in the Southern California desert. Edwards, of course, was the home of the nation's best test pilots including Chuck Yeager, the first man to break the sound barrier.

Armstrong flew on his very first day at Edwards and soon was piloting chase planes and co-piloting the B-29 Superfortress assigned to perform high-altitude drops of the new jet-powered experimental planes. As co-pilot on the B-29, Armstrong's job was to fly the airplane while the pilot supervised the drop sequence activities. Armstrong flew as pilot and sometimes co-pilot on more than 100 of these launch flights.

He quickly learned the dangers of his new profession. During one of his first flights, one of the B-29's engine propellers went out of control and cut through both the engine nacelles and the fuselage—severing the pilot's control cables. It was up to Armstrong now to save his plane and crew.

Nosing the plane down to pick up speed, Armstrong managed to launch the test plane attached to the B-29's belly. Then, cutting one more engine to keep the plane flyable, Armstrong, with only his controls intact, brought the big bomber down from 30,000 feet in a series of slow circles and landed it safely—despite having lost three engines and landing on the sole remaining, outer left-hand engine.

Within a few years, Armstrong was flying the premiere experimental plane of the pre-space age: the X-15. In April, 1962, in a famous flight, he pushed the X-15 to 207,000 feet—the brink of space, and the highest Armstrong would fly until he joined the Gemini program. But on the descent, he left the nose of the craft high for too long and suffered the singular experience of literally bouncing off the outer edge of the lower, thicker atmosphere. The X-15 was reportedly flung back up to 140,000 feet (though Armstrong isn't sure it reached quite that height), where he had to attempt a second re-entry.

By now, Armstrong was already over Edwards Air Base, rocketing along at 2,000 mph. Legend has it he was all the way to the Rose Bowl in Pasadena (a bit of an exaggeration, according to Armstrong) when he finally banked the X-15 back around to land at Edwards.

Neil Armstrong's career reached a turning point in 1962. After seven flights in the X-15—and ultimately having tested more than 50 different aircraft—Neil's career as an experimental test pilot was nearing its end. He had been named one of the six engineer-pilots chosen to fly a proposed new space plane.

His life also was marked by tragedy. In late January that year, his only daughter, Karen, died from complications from brain cancer. That may have been why, when NASA announced that it would recruit a second group of astronauts (after the Mercury group) for the planned Apollo missions to the moon, Armstrong's letter of application arrived a week after the June 1, 1962, deadline. Luckily, Dick Day, who had worked with Neil at Edwards before joining NASA, spotted Armstrong's letter and slipped it into the applicant pile.

In March 1966, Neil Armstrong was the commander of Gemini VIII. It was to be a flight of firsts—not least that Armstrong himself was the first American civilian in orbit. Gemini VIII also would be the first spacecraft to ever dock with another—in this case, an unmanned Agena target vehicle—and the third to feature a spacewalk.

However, it wasn't a flight without controversy. Soon after the successful docking—and out of contact with ground stations—the joined pair of spacecraft began to roll. Armstrong decided the only solution was to undock and try to get the capsule under control. But it only got worse until the capsule was rolling once per *second*.

In the end, because the craft was out of radio/telemetry contact with Houston, Mission Control was unable to assist the crew in diagnosing the system failure. So, left to his own devices, Armstrong executed an emergency maneuver that stopped the rolling but that also required the mission to end before his co-pilot, David Scott, could take his spacewalk.

Afterward, Armstrong was depressed because the spacecraft failure had prevented the crew from doing all of the things it had planned. Still, he consoled himself with the knowledge that had he not taken the decisive action he did, none of them might have survived. NASA ultimately concluded that the error had been its own and that Armstrong had made the right decision.

And so, at age 36, Neil Armstrong found himself assigned to the Apollo program. On December 23, 1968, even as Apollo 8 (for which he had been backup commander) was circling the moon, Armstrong was offered command of Apollo 11.

The entire world watched as Apollo 11, atop a gigantic Saturn V rocket, lifted off from Cape Kennedy on the morning of July 16, 1969. Millions had watched the three astronauts, looking cool and confident, walk from the control center to the special vehicle that would carry them to the launch pad. Millions of viewers also knew that the previous May, in a test run of the LEM landing process, Armstrong had ejected from a failing system just 100 feet from the ground—and scientists had determined that if he'd ejected *one-half second* later, he would have been killed. It was just one more close call in a career filled with near-death experiences.

Apollo 11 crewmen Edwin "Buzz" Aldrin (left), Michael Collins (center), and Neil Armstrong (right) wave to the press and NASA engineers before traveling to the moon in July 1969.

The Saturn V, bearing its tiny capsule, roared into the sky. In the next few days, the world would learn more about the three men in that capsule, especially the command pilot, Neil Armstrong. It also would learn the name of the lunar excursion module—the "Eagle"—a name chosen for the symbol of the United States of America. But for millions of Americans who knew Armstrong's Scouting history, the LEM's name took on a second meaning.

Now, at 20:17 UDT, Neil Armstrong, manually directing the controls of the LEM as it hovered over the surface of the moon, needed every one of the skills he had learned in his remarkable career—Boy Scouts, fighter pilot, test pilot, and astronaut—to touch down safely. With the fuel indicator saying the tanks were nearly empty, Armstrong knew he had just seconds left.

At last, Neil found his spot and cut the engines. Would, as some feared, the moon dust prove so fine and deep that the spacecraft just sink beneath the surface? The two astronauts held their breaths.

A sensor on one of the lunar module's legs registered contact with the lunar surface. In turn, a panel light on the control panel lit up.

"Contact light," said an excited Aldrin, "OK, engine stop ... descent engine command overrides off ..."

"Houston," said Neil Armstrong, "Tranquility Base here. The Eagle has landed."

MAKING UP FOR LOST TIME

In 1946, America's dads—current and near-future—came home from the war. Armed with their GI Bills, and exhibiting unusual maturity and worldliness for men of their age, several million former American soldiers hit the States running and ready to make up for lost time. They wanted college degrees, a career, marriage, and a house full of kids—and they wanted them in a hurry.

And even more than most American institutions, the Boy Scouts of America was anxious for their return. For a quarter century, Scouting had been suffering a shortage of adult leadership. From 1911 to 1929, the BSA's explosive growth had outstripped the number of available volunteers— which is why many troops, like Arthur Eldred's, had been largely created and run by boys. In the 1930s and during the Depression, as fathers searched for work, they had little free time to contribute. And in the 1940s, almost every able-bodied adult male was either off at war or working extra shifts in war-related industries—leaving Scouts to be led by old men and young Eagles who soon would themselves head off to boot camp.

But now America was suddenly awash in men aged 20 to 50 and, even as these members of the Greatest Generation raced to turn themselves into organization men, they also were committed (to an unprecedented degree) to making sure their children wouldn't suffer the same deprivations and abandonment they had. And if they couldn't be on hand to do so, they would hire surrogates to take their place. It didn't take a prophet to recognize that Scouting (and every other youth organization in America from the Little League to Campfire Girls) was about to be overrun with a vast demographic wave of new young members—the baby boomers—led by an army of anxious and engaged parents.

To its great credit, and perhaps better than at any other time in its history, the BSA exhibited considerable prescience as it prepared for the postwar world. With its new generation of leaders, the organization seemed to intuitively recognize that not only would the new world be very different from what came before—the Atomic Age, the Information Age, the Space Age, and an economy increasingly defined by a giant demographic bulge of children—but that for Scouting to maintain its presence at the heart of boyhood, it too must radically transform itself. Scouting, for the first time, also had the funds to implement these changes, in part because of Irving Berlin's stipulation in 1940 that the royalties from "God Bless America" be divided between the Girl and Boy Scouts.[3]

That transformation already had begun during World War II. The 1943 *Handbook* saw a burst in the number of merit badges, as Scouting recognized that the Trail to Eagle now needed much more than just perfecting outdoor skills (though there were still the "required" merit badges); it needed adult and professional skill development.

The result was an explosion in the number of merit badges: 100 by 1948, including 23 related to agriculture (a vital skill during this era of national rationing and home gardens) and four dealing with aviation, the most exciting new technology of the war.[4]

Then, as if in recognition that the future now truly belonged to the young, the BSA also made plans to remove adults from the rank process—a new rule it officially announced in 1952. No longer would an adult Scouter be able to continue to work toward the Eagle rank; from now on the cutoff would be the

Scout's 18th birthday (resulting in generations of scrambling 17½-year-old Life Scouts). However, in a later codicil to that new rule, Scouting made one of the most enlightened— and ultimately, as we will see, the most moving— decisions in its history: it waived the 18-year-old retirement rule for mentally, and otherwise permanently, disabled Scouts.

Americans also were beginning their great migration to the suburbs. And Scouting followed, moving its New York City headquarters to New Brunswick, New Jersey, in 1954.

Finally, in 1948 Scouting made what one of its historians called "a seemingly innocuous change that foreshadowed the next major step in the Eagle Scout award's evolution."[5] It was simply an elaboration of the long standing requirement for Eagle that the Life Scout perform six months of "satisfactory service."

The new rule stipulated that the Life Scout spend those six months actively working:

> As a leader in his troop's meetings, outdoor activities, and projects; his best to help in his home, school, places of worship, and community; and take care of things that belonged to him and respect the property of others.[6]

Practically speaking, for a Life Scout in an active Boy Scout troop working on various merit badges such as Citizenship, the precise words of this requirement were all but superfluous as the boy likely was performing this sort of work already. But philosophically, it was a major step: for the first time, the BSA was unequivocally stating that its vision of what constituted a true Eagle Scout now included a deep engagement with his community— family, school, church, and neighborhood. It established a position from which Scouting has not deviated for more than 70 years.

Less than two decades later, Scouting would refine that requirement one more time and in doing so, give itself a brand new purpose.

SECOND LIFE

Appropriately enough, Scouting launched its second era in 1950, at the midpoint of the century and Scouting's 40th anniversary. The kickoff was a second national jamboree to be held at Valley Forge, Pennsylvania, in mid-June. The site selection was brilliant: Scouting underscored its status as an iconic American institution by placing itself at one of the most inspiring of American locations—one with particular resonance for millions of new American veterans.

This second jamboree drew an astounding 47,000 Scouts, nearly twice that of its 1937 DC, predecessor—and in the process attracted considerable national attention.[7] Its official theme (casting back to the famous Leyendecker poster) was "Strengthening the Arm of Liberty," which the BSA promoted by donating 200 eight-foot copies of Lady Liberty to organizations around the country. But the implicit message of the event was: *Scouting is back, and it is bigger and more important than ever.*

But what kind of Scouting? Young Scouting. The Knights of Dunamis, Exploring, Air Cadets and all of the other older Scouting programs were busy reconstituting themselves and enjoying impressive growth. But really the attention—as with every other part of American society—was focused on the boomers and the first of that cohort was just now entering elementary school.

Not surprisingly then, Cub Scouting got most of the attention from both the BSA and the general public. In fact, seeing what was coming, Scouting had spent much of the 1940s restructuring Cubbing, most notably added the Webelos rank—that critical, hybrid transition rank for 11- (later 10-) year-olds between Cub Scouts and Boy Scouts. The Webelos "Arrow of Light" bridging ceremony smoothly transferred boys between the two programs, minimizing dropouts. At the same time, Den mothers, who had been allowed as optional leaders beginning in 1936, were allowed to be registered officially after 1949.

But in terms of capturing the imagination of both boys and their dads, Cub Scouting's greatest recruitment tool would be invented in 1953: the Pinewood Derby. This annual race of small wooden cars, constructed by the boys themselves, was the brainstorm of Cubmaster Don Murphy of Pack 280 in Manhattan Beach, California. Quickly adopted nationally, it would go on to become one of the most famous annual events of American boyhood.

President Harry S. Truman addresses Scouts at the 2nd National Jamboree held at Valley Forge, Pennsylvania, in June 1950.

Cub Scouting enjoyed explosive growth throughout the 1950s and, inevitably, the image of the Cub Scout in his blue uniform, yellow neckerchief, and baseball cap, became ubiquitous in the culture. As for Boy Scouts, their profile was much lower except during the jamborees. The third such jamboree, held in 1953 at Irvine Ranch, California, managed to draw more than 45,000 Scouts despite being held on the West Coast—underscoring that Scouting, if anyone still wondered, was now a continental phenomenon. In 1957, it was back at Valley Forge and this time drew nearly 53,000 Scouts.[8]

Where were the Eagles? Anyone who was looking saw more of them than ever. Throughout the mid-1950s, more than 14,000 Scouts each year earned their Eagle awards—double that of both the 1930s and the war years. And they were busy: providing leadership for inexperienced new troops, and swollen older ones, through the Knights of Dunamis, helping build new campgrounds with the Order of the Arrow, spending a season in the Antarctic with the National Science Foundation (and sometimes meeting Paul Siple), presenting BSA's *Annual Report* to the president of the United States, and working on the staff of the Philmont Scout Ranch. Others were helping to build the new Explorer program for older Scouts, which earned official backing from the BSA in 1959 as the official Senior Scouting organization. Exploring also offered (until 1972) a back door to Scouts to continue to pursue their Eagle until age 21. That was one reason why Exploring's membership more than tripled from 1949 to 1958 to 220,000.[9] It could be said that any great adventure or initiative—mountain climbing, hiking in the wilderness, helping with disaster relief—by a team of Americans in this era, if it included teenage boys, inevitably featured an Eagle Scout.

THE NEW ARISTOCRACY

Meanwhile, adult Eagle Scouts continued their march through American life. With the war over, it was time for other older Eagles in the civilian world to make their way into the limelight.

Barber Conable, an Eagle Scout from Warsaw, New York, and a veteran of Iwo Jima embarked on a political career that would make him an 11-term Republican congressman. A close friend of Richard Nixon, he broke from that president because of Watergate—in the process adding the indelible phrase "smoking gun" to the political lexicon. In 1984, President Reagan named him president of the World Bank.

John Creighton not only served as CEO of Weyerhauser and United Airlines, but also as the national president of the Boy Scouts of America. Commenting on the last, Creighton said: "Scouting always has reflected the expectations of the American family. That so many American parents have chosen to involve their children in Scouting is a powerful testament to Scouting's effectiveness in building character in American youth."[10]

James Daughdrill resigned as president of a successful carpet and textile company to study to become a Presbyterian minister. He ended up as secretary of stewardship for the Presbyterian Church, USA. Then he successfully took on the challenge of saving struggling Rhodes College in Memphis, raising the endowment from $6 million to more than $200 million during his quarter-century tenure there.

Tom C. Clark, who earned his Eagle at the dawn of the BSA (1914) in Dallas, Texas, was named U.S. Attorney General in 1945 by President Harry S. Truman. Four years later, Truman nominated him to the United States Supreme Court, where he served—voting on such landmark cases

Supreme Court Associate Justice Tom C. Clark as a young Boy Scout in Dallas in 1914.

as B*rown v. Board of Education*—until 1967, when he resigned due to the nomination of his son, Ramsey, as U.S. Attorney General that posed a potential conflict of interest.

Distinguished Eagle Scout H. Ross Perot in 1968.

.**Ross Perot** was one of those extraordinary young men who earned his Eagle medal at age 12. After attending Annapolis and serving his time in the U.S. Navy, Perot went to work at IBM, becoming a top salesman. Leaving Big Blue in 1962, Perot founded Electronic Data Systems (EDS). The company initially only survived because of Perot's sheer tenacity—he finally landed the company's first contract after 77 turndowns. By 1984, when General Motors bought EDS, Ross Perot was a billionaire. By then Perot already was becoming famous for his swashbuckling patriotism—including organizing a raid into Iran to free two imprisoned EDS employees. By then, he was involved deeply in politics—culminating in his 1992 and 1996 runs for president of the United States. The former was the most successful third-party presidential run in 70 years. He garnered 18.9 percent of the popular vote.

Michael Dukakis, an Eagle from Brookline, Massachusetts, served twice as governor of Massachusetts, as a U.S. congressman, and most famously, was the Democratic candidate for the U.S. presidency in 1988. His running mate was another Eagle, **Lloyd Bentsen**, four-term U.S. senator from Texas and later secretary of the treasury. **Murphy Foster** was governor of Louisiana; **Lamar Alexander** was governor of Tennessee and secretary of education; **Richard Lugar** was elected senator from Indiana; **Jack Murtha** was a 27-year congressman from Pennsylvania; **Sam Nunn** served four terms as senator from Georgia; **Samuel Pierce** was President Reagan's secretary of Housing and Urban Development. **Warren Rudman** was a two-term senator for New Hampshire. And **Donald Rumsfeld** was a two-time secretary of defense.

Terry Sanford was governor of South Carolina, senator from that state and president of Duke University.

William S. Sessions, who earned his Eagle in Arkansas in 1947, went on to become director of the FBI (1987–1993). His son **Pete Sessions**, a Texas congressman, also became an Eagle, as did Bill Sessions' grandsons. Bill Session's father was the author of the *God and Country* religious medal program for the BSA.

Eagle Scout Terry Sanford (right) with President John F. Kennedy in 1962.

John Caldwell became chancellor of North Carolina State; financier **John Anderson** funded the UCLA School of Management that bears his name; **Norman R. Augustine** was CEO of Martin Marietta; **Stephen Bechtel** became chairman of his family's giant corporation, as was **J.W. Marriott**; **Daniel Evans** was governor of Washington and a U.S. senator; Washington Congressman **Tom Foley** became Speaker of the House and U.S. ambassador to Japan; **Howard Hunter** and **John Groberg** were leaders of the Mormon Church; attorney **William Gates Sr.** became CEO of the giant foundation created by his son, Bill, and daughter-in-law Melinda; **General Robert Herres** was chairman of USAA and first commander of the United States Space Command.

Dudley Herschbach, who earned his Eagle in Campbell, California, in 1946, became a noted science professor at Harvard. In 1986, he won the Nobel Prize in Chemistry for his experiments with crossed molecular beams. **Frederick Reines**, the son of Russian Jewish immigrants, earned his Eagle at age 16—and the Nobel Prize in Physics six decades later for his co-discovery of the neutrino. **Robert Richardson** wrote about his Scouting experiences in the biography he submitted to the Nobel Committee after receiving the 1996 Nobel Prize in Physics for his discoveries in the behavior of Helium-3 at supercold temperatures.

Ewing Kauffman founded Marion Laboratories and owned the Kansas City Royals. The wonderfully named General **Charles H. Bonesteel III** commanded the U.S. Army in South Korea in the late 1960s. Oklahoman **Glen McLaughlin** became a noted Silicon Valley venture capitalist and head of the 1,000-year-old Catholic Order of Knights of St. John. **Major Gen. Charles Metcalfe**, who earned his Eagle in 1949, became director of the National Air Force Museum while also serving as vice president of the BSA central region. **Jim Mora** became a much-traveled NFL head coach and sportscaster. **Walter Wriston** became chairman of Citicorp and an influential business writer.

Not all Eagle Scouts of that (or this) era lived out the stereotype of the upright and culturally mainstream Scout. As with any group of superachievers, Eagle Scouting also produced its share of mavericks and revolutionaries. **Clive Cussler**, who grew up in Alhambra, California, and earned his Eagle in 1946 at just 14, went on to become a best-selling adventure novelist and marine archeologist. **James "Red" Duke** became a successful surgeon and founder of Houston's Life Flight helicopter emergency medical service program. **Lawrence Ferlinghetti** became a noted poet of the Beat era and was co-owner of that most famous of Beat publishers and gathering places, City Lights Bookstore. **"Big Daddy" Don Garlitz** earned his Eagle in 1946. He invented the rear-engine, top fuel eliminator dragster on his way to becoming the "Father of Drag Racing." Saturday morning television featured **Dick "The Destroyer" Beyer**, a masked wrestler and Eagle Scout, class of 1946. **Admiral Elmo Zumwalt** commanded Swift boats in the Vietnam War, then became chief of naval operations in 1970 and embarked on a series of radical changes—including improved racial relations—that were loved by enlisted men but often drew criticism from his fellow officers.

Famed cartoonist and Eagle Scout William Hanna.

William Hanna, who earned his Eagle in 1924, teamed with Joseph Barbera to found one of the most successful of all animation companies. Hanna-Barbera earned seven Oscars and eight Emmies in the course of creating *Tom and Jerry, The Flintstones, The Jetsons, Scooby-Doo, Yogi Bear*, and the *Smurfs*. Through all of this, he also managed to serve as a Scoutmaster to a local Culver City troop. Another animator, who earned his Eagle the same year, was **Alfred Harvey**, founder of Harvey Comics.

Philo Farnsworth, born in a log cabin in Utah, earned his Eagle medal in 1932. By then he already had scratched on a piece of notebook paper the design for one of the most influential inventions in human history: the television. In the course of earning more than 300 patents, Farnsworth also made seminal contributions to the electron microscope, the telescope, gastro scope, baby incubators, and nuclear fusion. Despite being one of the greatest inventors of the 20th century, his name remains almost unknown. Farnsworth never received his Eagle in his lifetime; it was only in 2006, after Farnsworth's widow asked her great-nephew to investigate, that Scouting determined that Philo was indeed eligible. In December 2005, local BSA Council officials visited Pem Farnsworth in a Salt Lake City nursing home to inform her of her late husband's award. She died four months later. Said her great-nephew Daniel Farnsworth, "It's actually kind of remarkable because it was the last bit of recognition she was able to get for her husband, who received very little recognition during his lifetime."

A young L. Ron Hubbard as a Boy Scout in 1922.

L. Ron Hubbard earned his Eagle in 1924 with a Puget Sound troop. He would not be remembered solely for his work as a pioneering science fiction writer because he also founded a controversial new religion, Scientology, with its self-help system, Dianetics. Scientology claims to have several million adherents around the world.

Along with Hubbard, probably the most controversial Eagle Scout to enter the public eye in the 1950s was **Dr. Alfred Kinsey**, the pioneering researcher into human sexuality. The child of devout parents and a fan of the outdoors, Kinsey was active as a boy in the YMCA until a Scout troop was founded in his community. Supported by his parents, and despite a weak heart, Kinsey earned his Eagle in 1913—making him one of the very first Eagle Scouts—and continued to be an active hiker for the rest of his life. Scouting was even the source of Kinsey's college senior undergraduate thesis, which was on the group dynamics of boys. Surprisingly, given his later notoriety, Kinsey first gained fame for his research into gall wasps, and as the author of a hugely popular high school biology textbook and (again based on his Scouting experiences) a classic on edible plants. **Wallace Stegner**, the "Dean of Western Writers", earned his Eagle about 1925 as a Presbyterian boy who joined a Mormon troop in Utah. His great love of the outdoors, begun with Scouting, filled both his writing (he won the Pulitzer Prize for Fiction in 1972 for *Angle of Repose* and the National Book Award in 1977 for *The Spectator Bird*) and his environmental work. Stegner also founded and ran for many years the influential creative writing program at Stanford University.

E.O. Wilson, a 1944 Eagle from Alabama, not only became one of the premiere biologists of his generation with his research into the social behavior of ants, but the often-controversial Harvard professor then went on to become one of the great writers about natural science, earning two Pulitzer Prizes for nonfiction.

Sam Walton, who earned his Eagle with a troop in Kingfisher, Oklahoma, in 1934—the youngest in the state's history—was one of the greatest entrepreneurs of the 20th century. Walton worked through much of his childhood to help his family make ends meet; then went on and worked his way through the University of Missouri. After leaving the military in 1945, Walton took $5,000 of his military pay, combined with a $20,000 loan from his father-in-law and bought a small variety store in Arkansas. There he experimented with many of the innovations that would make him a retailing legend. By 1962, having turned this store into a chain, Walton opened the first true Wal-Mart. By the time of his death in 1992, Wal-Mart had 2,000 stores and was on its way to becoming the largest retailer in the world.[11]

There also were Eagles who achieved national fame while still young. Perhaps the most notable example in the 1950s was **Ernest Green**. He earned his Eagle from a troop in Little Rock, Arkansas, in 1956. A year later, at age

17, he received national attention as a member of the "Little Rock Nine": African American students who tried to attend the segregated Little Rock Central High School. When the Nine attempted to integrate the high school, they were attacked by students, and their way was blocked by the Arkansas National Guard. In the end, President Dwight D. Eisenhower called in

Eagle Scout Ernest Green at the National Scouting Museum in Irving, Texas, for the presentation of his Distinguished Eagle Scout Award in August 2009. Photo courtesy of NESA.

the Army's 101st Airborne Division to escort Green and the others. Ernest Green, who received a Congressional Gold Medal, went on to be the first black graduate of Little Rock Central. Martin Luther King Jr. attended his graduation. He later was assistant secretary of Housing and Urban Affairs in the Jimmy Carter Administration.

AMERICA'S ARTIST

As impressive as these real-life figures were, none better personified the Eagle Scout more in the public eye than those anonymous Eagle Scouts who appeared in the works of the most famous illustrator—and most popular American painter—of the century.

Norman Rockwell was 18 years old when he walked into the offices of *Boys' Life* magazine, in his native New York City, looking for work. Having left public high school to bounce around the city's art schools—Chase Art

School at age 14, then the National Academy of Design, and finally the Art Students League (the last, ironically, given Rockwell's intense realism, would become the heart of American abstract expressionism)—young Rockwell had proven himself to be something of a prodigy at illustration.

Boys' Life itself was just a couple years old and only had been purchased (for $6,000—or $1 per subscriber) the year before by the Boy Scouts of America.[12] The magazine still was edited partially by boys, so it was not surprising that Rockwell, with his portfolio of sketches, was not only hired, but named art director—a position he held for three years. It was the beginning of his relationship with the magazine and with Scouting, which would last six decades.

During his time on the *Boys' Life* staff, Rockwell painted several covers for the magazine. The first, a grisaille (black & white) image for the September 1913 issue, showed a Scout in captain's hat standing at the large wheel of a ship. Interestingly, unlike Leyendecker's Scouting images of the same era that Rockwell admired and often emulated—this Scout is much older, almost an adult. And

Legendary American artist Norman Rockwell working in his Stockbridge, Massachusetts studio.

though, as with many Rockwell images of Scouts over the next 60 years, the boy's rank badge is hidden, given his age and position of authority—perhaps not coincidentally, there is a photograph of Paul Siple in the same pose taken 15 years later. This painting might be seen as the first public image of an Eagle Scout.

Anxious for action, turned down when he first tried to enlist in World War I, the underweight Rockwell gorged himself on food until he was accepted and still ended up spending the war stateside as a military illustrator. He used the time to perfect his craft (which now had begun to reflect the patriotic values that would characterize his art), move with his family to New Rochelle, New York, and get married two years later. Rockwell was given an early discharge in exchange for painting a portrait of his commanding officer.

It was during this period, thanks to an introduction by his studio mate, that Rockwell began to work for the *Saturday Evening Post*. Between the *Post* and *Boys' Life*, Rockwell ultimately would publish more than 400 covers—as well as, through the latter, produce 50 years of hugely popular Scouting calendars. And it was with this pair of magazines (and later *Life* magazine) that Norman Rockwell would cement his reputation as the most beloved illustrator of American life.

Part of the appeal of Rockwell's paintings—and what distinguishes them from more mawkish imitators—is that their sentimentality usually is checked by superb technique and absolute precision in the details. Vladimir Nabokov famously complained that Rockwell wasted his great technique on "banal" subjects but he didn't appreciate the artist's extraordinary understanding of the world he painted. His Scouts always *look* like real Boy Scouts: their uniforms always have the correct color and badges, they wrinkle like real cotton twill, and they hang just right on skinny young frames. The same is true for the tents, backpacks, and cooking gear. In the late (1969), famous self-portrait of Rockwell standing before an easel in the field being watched by older Scouts, the boys themselves stand like real teenagers: slumped, hands in pockets, with neckerchiefs slightly askew.

This same discernment enabled Rockwell to see Scouts essentially as they saw themselves. Looking over his scores of images of Scouts over the six decades, it is apparent that Rockwell divided Scouts into three general categories. The first are the little ones: the young Tenderfeet, distinguishable from Rockwell's Cub Scouts mostly by their oversized khaki uniforms. In these images (the most famous being "Can't Wait"—the little boy trying on his older brother's Scout uniform and saluting into a mirror), the theme is inevitably excitement, bewilderment, and earnest effort.

Next are the "middle-aged" boys. These are the First Class and Star Scouts who do the day-to-day heavy lifting in Rockwell's paintings, just as they do in Scouting. In Scouting, they lead the patrols, manage the meetings, and teach the basic Scout skills to the little ones. In Rockwell's paintings they demonstrate how to tie knots; put bandages on injured children and pets; manifest the 12 tenets of the Scout Law, Oath, motto, and slogan; and promote the next big Scouting event or initiative. Most of these images, being instructional, usually are also far less memorable. And in this area, Rockwell's early images are usually better than the later. The painter himself used to complain, "The Boy Scouts simply are going to have to devise some new deeds or Brown & Bigelow [the calendar printer] will be in a stew."

Finally, there are the Eagles. Often they aren't identified as such— Rockwell liked to position his subjects to hide the rank patch on their breast pockets— but it's usually quite evident who they are. The messages in these paintings are almost always inspirational: the older Scout is presented as noble, heroic, and confident. Most of the time—and unlike the other two types of Scouts— these older Scouts are looking off into the distance, typically upward as if being called to glory.

The most iconic image in this last group is "We, Too, Have a Job to Do" in which a stern-faced older Scout in a campaign hat, stands before an American flag and salutes directly toward the viewer. This image, painted for a

Norman Rockwell's "We, Too, Have a Job to Do." Photo courtesy of NESA.

World War II campaign poster, regularly has reappeared in Scouting, most recently on the patch for U.S. Scouts attending the 2008 World Jamboree in Chelmsford, England. But there are many other memorable images, some nearly as famous: the older Scout striding across the cover of the 1960 *Scout Handbook*; the young Eagle receiving his medal from his mother, father, and Scoutmaster in 1965's "A Great Moment"; the older Scout being pointed in the right direction by George Washington in "A Scout is Loyal" (1962); and in 1929's "Spirit of America" of an older Scout in profile in campaign hat and red neckerchief standing with half-toned images of Washington, Lincoln, Theodore Roosevelt, and other heroes.

In the words of the Rockwell Museum in Stockbridge, Massachusetts, Norman Rockwell became the "visual spokesperson for Scouting." But that only captures part of his appeal. Boy Scouting is an organization built on ideals—none more than its idealized image of itself. Norman Rockwell began his career by painting this idea of Scouting. But as the years passed and his understanding of Scouting grew, Rockwell came to realize that there was another, equally real, ideal of Scouting: the one of young men struggling—often humorously, sometimes foolishly, and always movingly—to make themselves into something better. At his best, Rockwell caught these moments with breathtaking technique and gave Scouting a mirror from which to view itself.

But when it came to Scouting's elite, its Eagles, Rockwell's early perspective never changed. Here, the old ideal was very much real— and the artist seems to imply that to pursue the Eagle was to choose the same path taken by the greatest of American heroes. In his Eagle paintings, Rockwell offers not a mirror to Scouting but a telescope to see the loftiest vistas. If Norman Rockwell's Scouting paintings amuse and entertain both Scouts and the general public, his Eagle paintings quietly haunt them. *This is what it is possible to become*, they whisper.

In the early 1950s, Rockwell was treated by the legendary German psychologist Erik Erikson, the man who first defined "identity crisis." Erikson reportedly told Rockwell that he painted his happiness but did not live it. It is not difficult to conclude that, in painting his Eagles so nobly, Norman Rockwell secretly dreamed of being among their ranks.

FATED TO SUCCEED

Demography is destiny—especially if you are an institution with strictly defined age limits.

It was easy to predict that the explosion of Cub Scouts in the 1950s would lead to a massive expansion in the rolls of Boy Scouting in the Sixties as the great baby boom bulge passed through American life. What wasn't so apparent was that that the sheer size of this generational cohort not only would begin by giving American Scouting its Golden Age but end by so transforming American culture that Scouting would find itself alienated from (even an enemy to) large segments of the population.

Former Boy Scout and Senator John F. Kennedy repeats the Scout Oath with an Eagle Scout in 1959.

Scouting hit the 1960s running. By 1954, Scouting already had passed 20 million total members in its history, 4 million current members, 1 million volunteers, and 100,000 units. *Boys Life's* subscription level crossed 1 million that year.[13]

Three years later, the 4th National Jamboree—again at Valley Forge—drew more than 50,000 Scouts and leaders. By then, 15 million copies of the *Handbook* were in print.[14]

And so, as the 1950s ended, the BSA—rich, swollen with members, increasingly synonymous with American youth—was ready to break out. The election of John F. Kennedy, the first former Scout ever to be president of the United States, seemed prophetic: this was going to be Scouting's decade.

Norman Rockwell, as usual, led the way. His cover for the new *Handbook* was a tall, waving—implicitly Eagle—Scout striding into the future. His more melodramatic than usual February 1960 cover for *Boys' Life* showed a Scout in a 1910 BSA uniform handing an open scroll bearing the words of the Scout Oath to a modern Scout—this time the Eagle medal is explicit—who has his other hand on the shoulder of a Cub Scout, who in turn is looking down at a globe.

That year, American Scouting's Jubilee, the BSA also began the process of formally looking back, and archiving and preserving its past by opening the Johnston Historical Museum at its headquarters in New Brunswick, New Jersey. In time, earning pride of place would be Arthur Eldred's battered Eagle medal. The 5th National Jamboree ("For God and Country"), held in Colorado Springs, would—despite its less accessible location—draw more Scouts and Scouters than ever: 53,400.[15] It would never be so large again.

This was Scouting at its most triumphant: an American institution thriving in the heart of the American Century. And it only could get better, at every level. Cub Scouting was still growing; and Exploring, now capturing the vanguard of the boomers, was seeing record growth. And, most important for the future of Scouting—because from its ranks would come many of the adults who would lead the BSA into the new century. The number of new Eagle Scouts continued to climb. By 1963, 27,000 Eagle medals were being awarded each year; reaching 30,000 by decade's end.[16]

But 1965—coincidentally the year when the 40 millionth Scout would join the BSA[17]—was the year that would prove to be the most important of the decade for Scouting. And the BSA would make the one decision, seemingly minor at the time that would prove among the most important in its history and may well have saved the organization.

Confident organizations make confident moves and that is what the BSA did at its zenith: it rewrote the requirements of its ranks.

The first print runs of the new 1965 *Handbook* contained two sets of requirements for Scouting advancement; one set that had been in effect with few changes since just after the war; the other that made changes to almost every rank, but most of all to the top ranks of Star, Life, and Eagle. Scouts who were completing a rank were allowed to finish it according to the old rules but then had to switch to the new requirements for all future ranks.

For Tenderfoot, Second Class, and First Class, this was an almost invisible transition. The most notable change dealt with a requirement at each rank for a "Scoutmaster Conference": a final meeting with the leader of the troop to make sure the Scout truly had met the requirements and learned the skills, of that rank. This gave Scouting a "product" quality control that it never had before—yet still did so within the troop itself, where it belonged. Over the next three decades, though occasionally abused by overzealous Scoutmasters, the conference would profoundly improve the overall quality and consistency of Scouting across its thousands of troops.

The second change, also at all ranks, dealt with participation and essentially formalized what was already a de facto characteristic of most Scout troops: all Scouts, Second Class and above, were required to hold a "warrant" position—that is, a role of responsibility in the troop (patrol leader, senior patrol leader, instructor, and so on). If the Scoutmaster Conference was designed to codify and improve the quality of the skills and ranks, the goal of the participation requirement was to underscore that leadership and management skill training were an inextricable part of the Scouting experience.

This second requirement also had the planned secondary effect of forcing high school-aged Life Scouts to stay engaged with their troops — even though they already were distracted by the larger world, not to mention the demands of working on their Eagle. The result was that, after a decade of having adults running the show, many troops again enjoyed the salutary improvement of a cadre of senior Scouts in charge.

The third change dealt with merit badges. In the 1948 *Handbook*, the BSA took the hundred merit badges available at the time and grouped them into 15 subject areas: animal husbandry, aquatics, arts, building, campcraft, citizenship, communication, conservation, crafts and collections, nature, outdoor sports, personal development, plant cultivation, public service, and transportation.[18]

These categories may seem a bit arbitrary and overlapping but they served a larger purpose. Eagle candidates still had to earn the traditional core of ten required merit badges—Camping, Swimming, Nature, Public Health, Firemanship, Cooking, Lifesaving, Personal Fitness, Safety, and First Aid—that had been in place for decades (and would be for decades more); but they also had to earn one badge from conservation, three from citizenship, one from outdoor sports, and one from animal husbandry, plant cultivation, communication, transportation or building categories as well as five more merit badges of their choice to reach the traditional total of 21.

One half-million Scouts had earned their Eagle medal along this path (the 500,000[th] Eagle medal was awarded in 1965).[19] But, to the innocent eye, it was the obvious product of a half-century of modifications, edits, and bolted-on ideas. Shockingly, but shrewdly, the BSA swept it all away. Henceforth, there would be no more merit badge categories: just 11 required badges (Firemanship disappeared, Citizenship became four badges for Home, Community, Nation, and World) and ten that each Life Scout chose. With over 110 merit badges then available, it rightly was felt that the ten optional badges would be sufficient to give any Eagle a broad range of life skills and career experiences.

But if that change simplified the path to Eagle, the addition of one new requirement made that path much, much more difficult—and changed Scouting forever. This fourth change added a service component to all of the ranks. At the lower ranks, this requirement was just for a few hours of contribution to the community. For Star and Life, this requirement had two components: a conservation project and a community service project. Both remained comparatively general in subject and brief.

But the Eagle service project was a whole different matter. It returned to a single requirement and it was unlike anything Scouting (or any other American youth group) ever had seen before.

In the words of the 1965 *Handbook*, the Life Scout had to:

> ...*plan, develop, and carry out a service project helpful to [his] church or synagogue, school or community approved in advance by [his] Scoutmaster.*

The Eagle Scout service project had begun.

Over the next few decades, as the details of its scope, duration, magnitude, and approval were teased out through the iterative process of hundreds of thousands of examples, the "Eagle project" came to stand as not just the last requirement but the culminating achievement of a Scout's career. In time, it even began to stand outside of the rest of Scouting as the great transitional experience from youth to adulthood. And if earning the Eagle Scout rank was indeed "the PhD of Boyhood," then the service project was now its dissertation.

Over time, the Eagle project would transform Scouting. But literally in a million small ways, it also would change the face of America.

Still, in 1965, as they read this new requirement and scratched their heads over its implications, only America's Life Scouts had even a glimmering of what was to come.

EAGLE AT THE TOP

Of all of the Eagle Scouts who rose to prominence in the postwar world, probably none cherished his Eagle rank more than the boy born in Michigan in April 1913 named Leslie Lynch King Jr.

Leslie Jr.'s early childhood was, by any measure, a nightmare. His paternal grandfather was a significant individual in early 1900's America: Charles Henry King was an Omaha banker and entrepreneur who had founded several cities in Nebraska and Wyoming in the course of making money off the railroads. He was a very rich man for the era and lived in a famous Omaha mansion. King's wealth at its peak was estimated at nearly a quarter-billion in today's dollars.[20]

One of the businesses King created was a wool brokerage and he brought his son Leslie (Sr.) into the business with him, probably to launch him on a career. This might seem like your typical tycoon setting up his ne'er do well son but Leslie King Sr. was much more than that—he was a monster.

In 1912, Leslie Sr. married Dorothy Gardner, the daughter of a small town mayor. He had been visiting his sister at college and Dorothy, the girl's roommate, found the young man smooth and charming.

However, the marriage went bad almost from the first day. On their honeymoon, Leslie reportedly thought he saw his new wife smiling at another man—and promptly beat her. Upon returning to their new home in Omaha, Dorothy quickly realized that her new husband was also an alcoholic and inveterate liar. Unfortunately, by then she was already pregnant. Little Leslie Jr. arrived eight months after their wedding day. And the beatings returned immediately after that. Leslie Sr. even threatened his new bride with a knife.

That explains why, just 16 days after Leslie Jr. was born, Dorothy took her baby and fled for the safety of her parents' home in Grand Rapids, Michigan. Leslie Sr. didn't pursue her; nor, before or after the subsequent divorce—and despite his family's great wealth—did he ever support his child or the boy's mother.

The resulting scandal not only engulfed Leslie Sr., but also his parents, who had been pillars of Omaha society. In their shame, they sold out and moved to California. But always, until his death in 1930, little Leslie's grandfather sent his ex-daughter-in-law money in support of the boy. Unlike his son, Charles Henry King had remained a man of honor and integrity through the entire mess yet he never would see his name attached to that of his famous grandson.

Three years later, Dorothy Gardner King married Grand Rapids businessman Gerald Rudolff Ford. Severing all links to her terrible past, Dorothy named her son, now three, Gerald Rudolff Ford Jr. The boy didn't officially change his name, to **Gerald R. Ford** until he was 22—and he did so then to honor the man he considered his real father. In this close-knit family (he would

LEFT: President Gerald R. Ford as a First Class Scout in 1926.
RIGHT: Ford as an Eagle Scout (right) in 1929.

have three younger brothers), Jerry Ford learned the decency and integrity that characterized his adult career, and taught him to control the fiery temper he had inherited from his natural father.

Jerry Ford only learned his real family history when he was 17—and, by coincidence, that same year, while he was waiting tables in a restaurant, he first encountered Leslie King Sr., who had sought him out. Ford would later describe his father as a "carefree, well-to-do man who didn't really give a damn about the hopes and dreams of his firstborn son."[21] They only would be in contact a few more times before King's death.

Gerald R. Ford as the center of the University of Michigan Wolverines' football team in 1934.

By then, Jerry Ford had grown to be a large, hugely athletic young man—captain of his high school football team and headed for college as a star varsity athlete. Even more than sports, the single-most important activity in young Jerry's life was Boy Scouting. He seemed to take to the outdoors, the skills, the ranks, and leadership responsibilities like few before or since. Whereas for many famous old Eagles there is often little more than a date and a memory, for Gerald Ford there is a wealth of photographs of him as a Scout: visiting the governor of Michigan, serving on camp staff, standing with his troop, and in each shot, he is unmistakable: burly, blonde, and radiating confidence like a Rockwell painting. Ford seems the ultimate Eagle Scout—which he was, earning the rank at age 14 in 1927, then staying involved in the program until he left for college.

It would be hard to exaggerate just how important Scouting was to Jerry Ford. He often treated it—as much as the presidency of the United States—as the emblematic achievement of his life. Interviewed during his time in the White House about his Scouting experiences, Ford said, "One of the proudest moments of my life came in the court of honor when I was awarded the Eagle Scout badge. I still have that badge. It is a treasured possession."[22]

He would show that love not only throughout his long life, but also in death.

As high school graduation approached, Jerry Ford was approached by numerous college recruiters. In the end, he chose the University of Michigan, where, playing center and linebacker in his sophomore and junior years, he helped lead the football to back-to-back undefeated seasons and national championships.

Ford was a superb football player but not a great one. And in his senior year, all of his efforts weren't enough to keep the team from suffering a miserable season in which it won only a single game. However, it was, in retrospect, Jerry Ford's most important season. Besides unwittingly making a bit of historic trivia—in a game against the University of Chicago, he became the only future president to tackle a future Heisman Trophy winner (Jay Berwanger, and Ford carried a scar from that tackle for the rest of his life)— the long, frustrating run of games tested his character far more than any of the winning seasons. So inspiring was Ford and teammate Cedric Sweet's performance in one lost-cause game that their coach wept at halftime.

Ford later would recall about that effort: "Remembering [that game] has helped me many times to face a tough situation, take action, and make every effort possible despite adverse odds."[23] At the end of the season, Ford's teammates voted him Most Valuable Player—because, said one assistant coach, "They felt Jerry was one guy who would stay and fight in a losing cause."[24] Ford was selected for the East-West Shrine game and was named to the Collegiate All-Star team.

That spring, Jerry was recruited by the Detroit Lions and Green Bay Packers but turned them down for a coaching job at Yale in hopes of also being accepted to the Law School there. Unfortunately, the plan backfired, as the Law School concluded that Ford would be too busy with his coaching work, so instead he spent a summer at the University of Michigan Law School and then in the spring of 1938 transferred at last to Yale.

He earned his law degree in 1941. By then, Ford already had had his first taste of politics by working on the Wendell Willkie presidential campaign. He even signed an antiwar/neutrality petition. But after Pearl Harbor, Ford left his newly created law partnership and enlisted in the U.S. Navy.

Commissioned as an ensign, Jerry Ford spent the war in the Pacific as assistant navigator and anti-aircraft battery officer on the carrier *USS Monterey*. He saw considerable combat, including the Battle of the Philippine Sea, the landings at Leyte, and the fighting in the Marshall Islands. But the most dangerous moment for the young officer came during a devastating typhoon (named Cobra) that battered the Third Fleet in December 1944. Ford was racing to his battle station on the *Monterey*'s bridge when the ship rolled 25 degrees, sending him sliding across the deck. Only his athletic skills saved him; Jerry caught the lip of the deck and swung himself down to the catwalk below—instead of being flung overboard.

Like many young men of the era, Lt. Commander Jerry Ford left the war as a man in a hurry to make up for lost time. In 1948, he not only decided to run for Congress, but also to marry Elizabeth Warren. Worried about possible bad publicity—Betty was both divorced and a former dancer—the two postponed their wedding to just before the election. In the end, Jerry won on both counts: he would go on to serve 13 terms in Congress, and Betty, to whom he would be married for 58 years, would prove to be among the most admired of all First Ladies.

So it might have remained, with the couple raising their four children, and Jerry serving out a long and comparatively undistinguished career as a middle-of-the-road congressman slowly working his way up into the Republican Party leadership—perhaps even fulfilling his dream of becoming Speaker of the House. Indeed, if there was anything in Ford's long House career that was memorable it was, first, his participation as a junior member of the Warren Commission; second, the general opinion (driven by an angry Lyndon B. Johnson) that Ford was merely a dumb jock; and, finally, his reputation for honor and integrity. Congresswoman Martha Griffiths would say of him, "In all the years I sat in the House, I never knew Mr. Ford to make a dishonest statement nor a statement part-true and part-false. He never attempted to shade a statement, and I never heard him utter an unkind word."[25]

Then, in October 1973, destiny called on Gerald Ford, who was happily ensconced in his eighth year as House Minority Leader. Vice President Spiro Agnew resigned in scandal, and his position needed to be filled. President Richard Nixon called on the Republican leadership to offer candidates. The recommendations were unanimous. "We gave Nixon no choice but Ford," recalled House Speaker Carl Albert.[26]

In December 1973, Gerald R. Ford became the first vice president to assume the job under the vacancy provisions of the 25th Amendment. He barely had time to settle into his new role when, nine months later, buried in the Watergate scandals, Richard Nixon became the first person to resign from the U.S. presidency.

President Gerald Ford receives the Scouter of the Year award in 1974.

Taking the oath of office, President Gerald Ford said that he was "acutely aware that you have not elected me as your president by your ballots and so I ask you to confirm me as your president with your prayers."[27] He knew that his task was to heal a nation torn by scandal, an unfinished war, racial strife, and cultural divisions and with that first speech, President Ford made a memorable start: "My fellow Americans," he announced, "our long national nightmare is over. Our constitution works. Our great republic is a government of laws and not of men. Here, the people rule."[28]

For the next three years, Ford presided over one of the most tumultuous periods in modern American history. Despite Ford's last-ditch attempt to help South Vietnam, he was overruled by Congress and the Vietnam War was lost. At home, the country suffered the economic body-blows of rampant inflation, a potential swine flu epidemic, and the near-bankruptcy of New York City. Internationally, Cambodian collapsed into genocide and the

United States, and the Soviet Union signed the Helsinki Accords.

Ford himself was the target of two failed assassination attempts, occurring within three weeks of each other.

But in terms of scandal and public debate, all of these events paled in comparison to one single act of President Ford's: the pardoning of Richard Nixon. Though he would be accused of numerous underhanded motives in making the pardon, Ford always would claim that he did it to heal the nation's open wound and put Watergate behind them. That decision likely lost Ford the election in 1976.

But as the years passed, Ford's greatest opponents eventually came to believe that he had made the right decision. Even Senator Edward Kennedy, who had excoriated Ford at the time, admitted—as he honored his old enemy with the John F. Kennedy Profile in Courage Award in 2001—that history had shown that Ford had made the right decision.

But his successor understood immediately. In his inaugural address, President Carter said, "For myself and for our Nation, I want to thank my predecessor for all he has done to heal our land."[29]

In the long aftermath—Jerry Ford would live to age 93, the longest life of any president—the ex-president filled his life with speeches, commissions, occasional acts of diplomacy ... and golf. In the intervening years, all of the controversies had fallen away and what remained was the memory of those bitter years, and how President Ford had healed the nation even at the cost of his career. He finished his life among the most beloved of modern presidents.

Thanks to his long life, Jerry Ford had time to design his own funeral. It, of course, included his casket lying in state in the Capitol rotunda but the rest, including the ceremonies in Michigan, would be the former president's choice. Looking back on his life, choosing the experience that most defined him, Gerald Ford chose the Boy Scouts.

He died on December 26, 2006. In both Washington, DC, and in Grand Rapids, Michigan, calls went out for Scouts. For former President Ford's funeral service at Washington's National Cathedral, 125 Scouts helped with the preparations and Eagle Scouts served as ushers for the honored guests.

In Michigan, the scene was even more extraordinary. Fulfilling Eagle Scout Gerald Ford's final wishes, 200 Eagle Scouts were requested to serve in the honor guard for his casket. It was an easy request to fulfill. "I could have had a thousand Eagle Scouts there," said Scout Executive Michael D. Sulgrove of BSA's Gerald R. Ford Council.[30]

Eagle Scouts pay their last respect to their fallen Eagle brother in 2006.

It was an indelible sight and among the most moving in the history of American Scouting. Four hundred Eagle Scouts, aged 15 to 85, some having driven hundreds of miles, lined the Grand Rapids road leading to the Presidential Museum & Library and saluted as the funeral cortege passed.

That night at the Gerald R. Ford Library, the chosen 200 Eagles served as the President's honor guard. In the single most affecting image of the funeral ceremonies, the Eagles, without prompting, lined up in three columns and, in turn, marched up to the flag covered casket and silently saluted their fallen brother.

"I can say without hesitation," Gerald Ford once stated, "because of Scouting principles, I know I was a better athlete, I was a better naval officer, I was a better congressman, and I was a better-prepared president."[31]

BOOMER EAGLES

In 1966, the first of the baby boom Boy Scouts, along with hundreds of thousands of other 18-year-old American boys, signed up with the U.S. Selective Service. Within months, many were fighting in the Vietnam War.

A classic Army brat, **Phil Gioia** joined Cub Scouts while his father was an instructor at West Point and became a Boy Scout when his father was transferred to Italy. In Livorno, he joined Troop 76 of the Transatlantic Council, along with other sons of Cold Warriors from around Europe, North Africa, and the Middle East. Every summer, Troop 76 would go to Camp "Passalacqua" (Camp Waterfall) in Northern Italy, at a beautiful old chalet near Lake Garda and there would compete against the Scouts from the other American Scout Troops in Italy from Verona and Vicenza.

When his father was again transferred, to Fort Rucker, Alabama, Life Scout Phil Gioia joined Troop 49. He joined the Order of the Arrow, earned the *Ad Altare Dei* Catholic religious medal, and taught in the NRA marksmanship program for Scouts. And, in early 1961, he completed his Eagle Scout.When Phil Gioia entered the Virginia Military Institute (VMI) in September 1963, it was still a time of optimism—but just three months later, Gioia found himself part of the VMI honor guard at the funeral of John F. Kennedy. When he graduated four years later, the Vietnam War was in full force—"a gigantic engine pulling millions into it and dividing the nation,"[32] he recalled. After a year of airborne and ranger training, in February 1968 he was sent to Vietnam.

He arrived in the middle of the Tet Offensive and immediately was sent to fight in the siege of Hue, one of the most savage battles of the entire war. His unit discovered the mass graves of the local citizenry slaughtered by the Viet Cong—an experience that haunted him for decades.

That April, Gioia was wounded and was sent back to the United States for surgery and recuperation. A year later, he was back in Vietnam, commanding an infantry company patrolling near the Cambodian border and regularly clashing with North Vietnamese Army units. "The NVA were good soldiers," he says, "We were better."[33]

In November 1969, now a captain and unit commander, Gioia was wounded again, this time by shrapnel. It was the end of his war. He returned to the United States "a wiser and more experienced man," wearing two Silver Stars, a Bronze Star with a V for valor, and two Purple Hearts. He went on to become a successful investment banker and noted military historian. But he has never fully shaken off the memories of combat—nor ever stopped being thankful for Scouting:

Scouting stood me in good stead—I had slept on the ground as a Scout, hiked and camped in unfamiliar terrain, knew how to use a map and compass before I ever saw one at VMI or in the Army. I could build a fire. I could endure rain and snow without complaining. The self-confidence I gained as a Scout was priceless. And the friends I made in Scouting were terrific. I still know the Twelve Points of the Scout Law; I still have all my handbooks and all my uniforms, from Cub through Explorer, right down to the hand-carved neckerchief slides. I wouldn't have swapped it for anything.[34]

Phil Gioia, along with all of the other Fighting Eagles of the Vietnam era, came home to an America torn in two by Vietnam, a cultural war between young and old, assassinations, and race riots. The late 1960s was a time of choosing sides and many American boys found themselves on the opposite side from the Boy Scouts of America. The BSA had, from the beginning, tied itself to patriotism, the military, and the American way of life—and it had paid off handsomely both for Scouting and the country.

The Eagle Scout portrait of General William Westmoreland at age 15 in 1929.

But now all of those beliefs were under attack and an organization of boys and adults in "paramilitary" uniforms, saluting the flag, and advocating traditional values—that produced military officers like **General William Westmoreland** (Eagle Scout, 1930), an army commander in Vietnam, who reviled Presidents Johnson and Nixon as BSA's honorary head—seemed to many young Americans to be not only anachronistic, but an outright enemy.

As in World War II, the Vietnam War produced its own Eagle Scout heroes— none of them more famous than **Thomas R. Norris.** In April 1972, Lt. JG Norris, one of the last remaining Navy Seals in Vietnam, in one of the most harrowing missions of the war, led a team of Vietnamese Navy commandos behind enemy lines to rescue a downed Air Force officer Lt. Col. Iceal Hambleton.

The desperate rescue attempt to keep Hambleton, an intelligence officer, out of enemy hands, already had cost five aircraft and 11 lives. Now Norris led his team in on the ground, hoping to rescue both Hambleton and any surviving downed airmen. The successful rescue of the colonel and one of the airmen has become part of Seals' legend and was the subject of the popular movie *Bat 21*.

Six months later, while protecting the evacuation of troops to his rear, Lt. Norris suffered such a grievous head wound that he was left for dead. But a fellow Seal, Michael E. Thornton, refused to accept that news, went back under fire, and found Norris, now barely alive, and rescued him.

For the Bat 21 mission, Norris initially refused the Medal of Honor but eventually accepted it from fellow Eagle, President Gerald Ford, in 1975. For his rescue of Norris, Michael Thornton also was awarded the Medal of Honor—the only time in American history that one Medal of Honor recipient was honored for saving another Medal of Honor recipient.

Despite the loss of an eye and part of his skull, Norris not only recovered from his wounds but went on to a distinguished 20-year career with the FBI, where, appropriately, he was a founding member of the agency's Hostage Rescue Team.

Eagle Scouting's other Medal of Honor recipient during the Vietnam War was Major (later **Colonel) Leo K. Thorsness**. On April 19, 1967, Thorsness led four F-101 fighters on an attack on surface-to-air missile installations outside Hanoi, Vietnam. Dividing his forces to confuse the enemy, Thorsness found his plane and his wingman under attack. The second plane was hit, and the two crewmen parachuted out. Thorsness circled the drifting parachutes to spot their landing—not knowing that the other two fighters had been attacked and returned to base. This left Thorsness' plane alone over Hanoi.

Spotting a North Vietnamese MIG-17 heading toward the parachutes, and though the F-101 wasn't designed for air-to-air combat, he attacked, shooting down the enemy plane with his cannon. Now, Thorsness and his crewman,

Captain Harold Johnson, came under attack both from ground missiles and two more MIGs coming up on their tail. Thorsness went to afterburner, dove to treetop level, and outran the two attackers through narrow canyons.

By now, the pair had called in a rescue on the downed fliers and were heading for a tanker refueling, when Thorsness learned that the rescue team of slow-flying planes and helicopters was under attack. With less than 500 rounds of ammunition left, Thorsness and Johnson raced back to try to draw off the attackers. Finally, after 50 minutes of aerial combat, Thorsness and Johnson were relieved by other fighters and left the combat zone. Then, as they approached the tanker once again, the pair learned that a lost U.S. fighter, nearly without fuel, had spotted the tanker and was limping in. Thorsness decided to give away and, though hiswn plane was also low on fuel, attempt a dangerous trip to a ground base at Udorn, nearly 200 miles away. Sixty miles out, and in growing darkness, Thorsness cut the engines on the F-101 to idle and glided to the runway, landing on empty tanks.

Just eleven days later, Thorsness was shot down and taken prisoner by the North Vietnamese. Despite continuous pain from a back injured on ejection, as well as torture by his captors, Thorsness refused to cooperate— an act of heroism that earned him a year in solitary confinement. Six years later, in 1973, Colonel Thorsness was released from captivity—and learned for the first time that he had been awarded the Medal of Honor.

Like many institutions, Scouting had thrived on the fickle attentions of the baby boom; now it would wither as those attentions turned elsewhere. After 60 years of working to find its place at the heart of American culture, Scouting now found itself facing a counterculture for which it seemed to have nothing to offer. The BSA continued to produce more Eagles than ever but that was a trailing indicator, drawn from the ranks of boys who had joined Scouting early in the decade. The real measure was further down in the ranks—and there, membership was falling. The 7th National Jamboree drew just 35,000 Scouts and leaders (a 40 percent drop in attendance)[35] that was blamed in part on the site's isolation. But it was, in fact, an omen.

Even as the Boy Scouts of America rushed to hire outside consultants to produce reports with titles (in psychedelic font) like *Is Scouting in Tune with the Times?* Scouting lost 65,000 members in 1969.[36] And the numbers looked even worse indefinitely into the future as the culture wars combined with the end of the baby boom to continuously shrink the pool of available new Scouts.

In just five years, Scouting had fallen from the zenith of the most successful era in its history into a nightmare of declining membership, with a society that seemed to be turning against it. And worst of all, it seemed to have serious doubt about its mission and core philosophy. It would take most of the next decade for the Boy Scouts of America to regain its confidence and footing.

In the meantime, it would fall to the Eagles, even as they struggled to understand the dimensions of the Service Project now facing them, to maintain Scouting's image in the public eye until Scouting once again rediscovered itself.

THE EAGLE HAS LANDED

Though it didn't seem so at the time, with the nation wracked by protests, riots, war, and domestic terrorism, 1969 was, in retrospect, an *annus mirabilis* in modern American history. Scouting, like many other established American institutions, may have seemed to be sliding into the abyss but elsewhere miracles were taking place that would give new meaning and purpose to everything. The microprocessor was being invented in a laboratory at Intel Corporation in Northern California. Meanwhile, just up the road in Menlo Park the first network connection that would lead to the Internet was under construction. In New York, a vast crowd gathered for a rock concert on the Yasgur farm in Woodstock.

And, on July 21, the entire world—including the Scouts at the national jamboree in Idaho—watched as, on the moon, Neil Armstrong and Edwin "Buzz" Aldrin prepared for the extravehicular activity (EVA)—humanity's first steps on another world. After landing on the evening of July 20, the two astronauts were supposed to sleep for five hours, as they already had been up for more than 15. But they were too excited and decided to spend the time preparing.

At the 2½ hour mark during this interval, Aldrin, an elder in his Presbyterian Church, radioed down to Houston and fellow astronaut/chief communicator **Charlie Duke** (Eagle Scout, 1946) to say, "This is the LM pilot. I'd like to take this opportunity to ask every person listening in, whoever and wherever they may be, to pause for a moment and contemplate the events of the past few hours and to give thanks in his or her own way." Then, turning off the microphone, he performed a quiet communion with a kit he'd brought with him.

At 2:39 UTC on Monday, July 21, 1969, Armstrong opened the hatch of the lunar excursion module and slowly made his way down the ladder attached to one of the LEM's legs. Because of the remote control device on his chest, he couldn't see his own feet, so he made the descent very slowly, using the low-gravity to help him "feel" his way to the next rung. Along the way, he reached out and pulled a D-ring that activated the external television camera and beamed the now-historic images to Earth.

Pausing on the LEM's footpad, Armstrong described the dust on the moon's surface as "fine-grained … almost like a powder."[37] Then, as a billion people collectively caught their breaths, Neil Armstrong stepped off the footpad onto the lunar surface—the first human being to step on to another world. As he did, Armstrong, the most famous person—the most famous Eagle Scout—in the world, said over the crackling radio the immortal words, "That's one small step for [a] man, one giant leap for mankind."[38]

CHAPTER SIX

LOST AND FOUND

In the 1970s, Boy Scouting experienced a crisis that shook it to its foundation. At the same time, Eagle Scouting embarked on the greatest youth community service initiative in History.

I n 1965, as part of that milestone year, the BSA set out to address an underserved segment of American youth and in the process make amends for past sins. As the stories of the Tuskegee Eagles tell, poverty had been a limiting factor to the Scouting experience from the beginning. Any poor boy could join Scouting and some communities and sponsoring organizations even helped with the comparatively low BSA annual dues. But real-life Scouting also was about uniforms, patches, camping equipment, and summer camp. And they all cost money.

Poor boys, even if they were able to obtain the funds for uniforms and events, typically faced a shortage of leaders (dads often held multiple jobs or were looking for work) and a lack of sponsoring groups and places to meet. This was true in low-income communities from the hills of West Virginia to migrant worker camps in the Southwest to the inner-city neighborhoods of Northeastern cities.

But it also went deeper than that. Like many venerable organizations, and despite considerable vigilance, Scouting had not escaped enitrely the subtle threat of *de facto* segregation. The BSA had shown admirable inclusiveness in its early years, allowing African American, Native American, and Jewish boys (among other minorities) to join the organization even as Jim Crow, reservations, and quotas still ruled in the rest of American life. Indeed, black and Jewish Scouts were part of Scouting almost from the start, and one of the very first Scout troops in the Midwest was founded on an Oklahoma Indian reservation. Santee Sioux Charles Eastman (nee Ohiyesa), a physician, advised both Chief Scout Ernest Thompson Seton and National Scout Commissioner Dan Beard in the early days of the BSA.

But Scouting headquarters couldn't control the day-to-day operations of individual troops. As the organization spread across the country, some troops, especially in South, were segregated unofficially. Unfortunately, this trend continued well into the 1950s and beyond.

And so, in 1965, enjoying a level of success it never had before known (and never would again), Scouting set out to make amends. It embarked on a major new initiative it called the Inner-City Rural Program (ICRP). Though this project was presented to the public as an update to the previously racially oriented programs of the BSA—the Inter-Racial Service (1927) and the Urban Relationship Service (1961)—it represented a very different level of commitment. And though ostensibly it was targeted at all low-income boys in America, its primary target was inner-city minorities, especially African American boys, whose participation in Scouting was near zero.

This time the BSA went all out. It essentially gave the ICRP carte blanche to change whatever it deemed necessary in order to successfully recruit and keep low-income boys in 18 urban and rural locations. In practice, this often meant bypassing traditional troop meeting sites such as churches and schools, and instead gathering in private homes or (in the case of Cincinnati) aboard a van that moved through the city. Where there weren't traditional sponsors, some troops tried "Block Scouting," in which they were supported by neighborhoods in exchange for community service projects. And where camping trips to the countryside were all but impossible, ICRP substituted tree planting, sidewalk hiking, street or park camping, and other alternative activities.

The biggest supporter of the Inner-City Rural Program was Alden G. Barber, who assumed the title of Chief Scout Executive in 1967. Barber, whom the reader will remember as the young leader of the Knights of Dunamis a quarter century before, was a man of his time—confident, media savvy, and eternally optimistic—and he saw the ICRP not only as a way to reach "at risk" boys in America, but also as a superb promotion for Scouting. As time passed, and Scouting's membership began to fall, Barber also saw in the program a source of new recruits to the organization. Said Barber at the time, "The boy in the ghetto had no real basis for many of the things we [the BSA] talked about ... so we had to make the program acceptable to him."[1] But dedicated and brave as were both its volunteers and Scouts—and it often took real heroism to wear a Scout uniform on the same streets as urban gang members who saw Scouting as a threat—the ICRP ultimately proved to be little more than a *succès d'estime*. While hundreds of young men in America's inner cities (and to a lesser degree in impoverished rural areas) did enjoy an experience they might never have known otherwise, in terms of results, the time, energy, and money spent by the BSA on this initiative probably could have been invested better elsewhere.

Unfortunately, the lesson Scouting learned from the ICRP was the wrong one. It saw a noble failure in the face of almost intractable social and economic obstacles. But on closer inspection, the real lesson of the ICRP was that even boys trapped in the depths of ghetto life were drawn to Scouting for the same reason as their middle-class suburban and country brothers: camping, ranks, leadership experience, and skills training. Scouting's real strength and appeal lay in its traditions dating back to Seton, Beard, and Baden-Powell, not in its attempts to stay relevant to the latest cultural fads.

Scouting was hardly alone. Across the country, organizations and institutions walked away from long-standing practices and traditions in a desperate attempt to adapt themselves to the reigning youth culture. And the desperation only grew greater as the vast youth population bulge reached adulthood and the ranks of youth organizations began to fall.

It is a tragic, but widespread, behavior pattern of mature and especially of successful enterprises that, when faced with a cultural shift and declining numbers (i.e. in membership, customers, revenues, profits, and market share), they almost always will choose to change their operations (even abandon their core philosophy) in an attempt to shore up those numbers in the short term, at the cost of the long-term. It almost never works.

What usually *does* work also is counterintuitive: fall back on your core business, participants, and philosophy, take the hit in the numbers while you regroup, and then implement your comeback strategy when the marketplace is ready. The primary reason most institutions don't take this path, even when the evidence is right before their eyes, is that careers are short, and nobody gets rewarded for presiding over decline.

And so, as the 1960s ended and Scouting found itself both on the far side of the cultural divide from many of its prospective members *and* with falling membership numbers—and with an entrepreneurial character in charge—it decided to roll the dice.

The result, seemingly appropriate for those difficult times, was a radical, top-to-bottom reorganization of Scouting—the most sweeping in its history—called the Improved Scouting Program.

The final catalyst for this initiative was a 1969 report by market researcher Daniel Yankelovich, Inc. investigating why (and why not) boys joined and stayed in Scouting. The results were both sobering and, ultimately, compelling. Yankelovich discovered that a growing number of teenaged boys found Scouting to be out-of-date, overly structured, and even socially embarrassing. This was particularly true with older Scouts.[2]

None of these results were in dispute. But what was missing from the Yankelovich report was *context*. Scouting, after all, always had been anachronistic—those city boys heading out into the woods in 1908 with the Woodcraft Indians and Sons of Daniel Boone already were living out an experience whose age had passed. And older Scouts always had chafed at the same structured experience in which younger Scouts thrived. That was why they had filled the ranks of Exploring, the Order of the Arrow, and the Knights of Dunamis, and why many Scouts left the program after earning their Eagle. As for wearing the uniform in public places, that had been at least a mild embarrassment for many boys since Armistice Day 1918.

Still, Scouting had thrived in spite of—and in important ways because of—these "weaknesses" for 62 years. But now after its first real setback, the BSA felt it needed to be saved from itself.

NEW AND IMPROVED

The official launch of Improved Scouting, as usually was the case with a revision in the program, came with the publication of a new *Scouting Handbook*, the eighth edition, in 1972. And it was only the *Scouting Handbook* because the BSA decided to drop the word "Boy" from the title.

And that was only the start. Inside, the text about camping, first aid, and woodcraft that had changed the lives of 27 million readers over the previous six decades now almost was entirely thrown out, and was replaced by a new narrative that emphasized more "modern" and largely urban and suburban topics.

As one commentator later wrote: "Gone were signaling, map-making, canoeing, tracking, and fire-by-friction. In their place were sections on drug abuse, family finances, child care, community problems, and current events."[3]

The first aid section of this new edition dealt with urban problems such as rat bites, bringing along money for pay toilets, and the proper etiquette for long-distance hikes on city streets.

Troops themselves also were reorganized. Older Scouts, who had traditionally made up a quasi-patrol of "Senior Scouts," now were divided into multiple groups. Fourteen- and 15-year-olds, who traditionally had led the troops' patrols, now were placed into a "Leadership Corps" with their own forest-green uniforms and separate activities. Sixteen- and 17-year-olds, who traditionally had run the troops and provided their institutional continuity, now were expected to either move up to a title called "Junior Assistant Scoutmaster" or to leave the troop entirely and join an Explorer post. It was an inspired strategy for keeping Scouting relevant to individual boys at each age level but was hugely destructive to the long-standing principle of the "boy-run troop": the boys who were supposed to be running the troop now were busy elsewhere.

That now put the onus on the adults: the Scoutmasters and Assistant Scoutmasters. But here the incentives were changed as well. In the words of the BSA's official history:

> Scoutmasters now were expected to be 'managers of learning' and to hold 'personal growth agreement conferences' with Scouts before they moved up a rank, and they were encouraged to master a 'Cornerstone' leadership program based on eleven 'competencies.' Many Scoutmasters felt that they hadn't volunteered to become 'counselors' instead of leaders and they weren't comfortable with their new responsibilities.[4]

Thus, at a time of enormous change, Scouting managed to alienate much of its unit leadership—the heart of the organization—and the very people it depended on to execute its new philosophy.

But that only was the beginning. The biggest change in the new *Handbook* dealt with that most defining feature of Scouting: the ranks and their requirements. Here, in an effort to clarify the process of advancement, Scouting managed only to sow confusion.

The starting point for this confusion was the establishment of a whole new set of "skill awards"—camping, citizenship, communications, community living, conservation, cooking, environment, family living, first aid, hiking, physical fitness, and swimming—essentially all the things that used to be the stuff of Scouting that a young Scout had to earn as part of the trail from Tenderfoot to First Class. Painted brass loops were worn on the Scout's web belt to show attainment of these skills. The notion behind these skill awards was that they provided more immediate recognition of a Scout's advancement in competence. But the reality, writes Scouting historian Robert W. Peterson trenchantly, was that up until 1989 when they were abandoned: "[It] was possible to become a First Class Scout without ever going hiking or camping or cooking over an open fire."[5]

It only got stranger with the higher ranks. In terms of requirements, the Eagle award looked about the same, notably in continuing the new service project concept. But now to become an Eagle, a Scout had to earn 24 merit badges—three more than ever before in Scouting history—but with only ten, instead of 11, required.

The good news in this was that Scouting also expanded the number of optional merit badges to include the likes of Environmental Science and Computers. The bad news was that, once again, the experience for the individual Scout on his Trail to Eagle now was a long away from the original vision of Scoutcraft. The official history records the complaint of one veteran Scoutmaster from New York:

> [The Eagle] rank, respected throughout the country as a top-notch achievement for youth, has been cheapened drastically. By the elimination of Camping, Cooking, Nature and other [merit] badges heretofore required, a Scout may become an Eagle virtually without ever setting foot past his city line.[6]

As if to drive home this notion of the new "Pop Culture" Eagle, even the historic Eagle Scout uniform badge was changed radically. Though it had gone through some minor modifications over the years (mostly to take advantage of improved embroidery equipment) the badge always had consisted of an Eagle, in the upward wing formulation of the medal, clutching the Be Prepared scroll from the Boy Scout Insignia, atop red, white, and blue stripes, within a red ring bearing the words "Eagle Scout Boy Scouts of America" in silvery-white thread.

The new badge featured simply a small, silver Eagle silhouette against two broad red and blue stripes, and a narrow white stripe in the center. No detailing. No words. No hint of the meaning of the image. It was, in almost every way, a cruder image than the Tenderfoot badge—as if recognizing that the Eagle Scout, spending much of his time in the public eye, might not want to be associated with the Boy Scouts of America. Not surprisingly, there soon were reports from around the country that troops and new Eagles were custom-ordering the previous, 1956-version, of the badge from private vendors.

The new Eagle patch, shocking as it may have seemed, was in fact a part of the overall new "look" of Scouting: the Oscar de la Renta-designed uniforms, skill awards on the belt, streamlined and simplified badges, and most infamously, red berets.

These last came to symbolize this era of Scouting. Scouts had long worn very American headgear, from Army campaign caps to World War

II-type garrison flat caps. Now, reflecting its own identity crisis as it was torn between the two sides of divided nation, Scouts were asked to wear a piece of European headwear, impractical against the sun and weather while camping, and being most associated with two groups on opposites sides of the ideological spectrum: United States Army special forces and the Black Panther party.

By the mid-1970s, the Boy Scouts of America had lost an estimated one-third of its membership. Ironically, even as Scouting had scrambled to keep up with the cultural changes taking place around it, those changes already had begun to come full circle. The vanguard of the New Age had left the cities, psychedelia, and revolution and now had gone back to the land and to traditional skills. Even as the new *Handbook* diminished the role of Scout craft, *The Whole Earth Catalog*—dubbed "the Boy Scout *Handbook* of the counterculture" by *Time* magazine—was extolling its earlier edition as a key text of the back-to-earth movement.[7]

Remarkably, in the face of all of this confusion, radical change, and obstruction, the one part of Boy Scouting that continued to grow was Eagle Scouts. Though the total number of new Eagles per year fell in the 1970s—to an average of 29,306—the ratio of Eagles to total Scouts maintained its climb: from the historic 2 percent of all Scouts who joined the organization, to 4 percent—and climbing starting in 1991.

In other words, Scouts were continuing to pursue their Eagle rank as they always had, accepting whatever new obstacles as merely a new set of requirements to overcome. Even the service project, whose unwritten demands seem to grow by the decade, wasn't enough to slow their progress.

ABOVE AND BEYOND

For some, even earning the Eagle wasn't enough. Some Eagles chose to pursue goals, such as having every member of a single patrol achieve the award. No records have been kept on this competition but no doubt several hundred patrols reached that goal over the decades. Perhaps the most remarkable of these efforts was undertaken by the Coyote patrol of Troop 16 in Texarkana, Texas.

In late 2011, the twelve members of the patrol set a goal of earning their Eagles in 2012 as their contribution to the Eagle Centennial year. Time was short, so the Scouts went into overdrive, dedicating nearly every moment of the new year to the program—in the process earning at total of 321 merit badges, camping 687 nights, hiking just short of one thousand miles, and devoting three out of every four weeks during the year to working on their own or others' service projects. They made it, celebrating their achievement in a group Court of Honor in December 2012.

The most popular pathway for ambitious Scouts to compete and continue their accomplishments after earning their Eagles was through the earning of merit badge palms. A sizable percentage of Eagles earned at least a bronze, gold or silver palm device to pin to their Eagle ribbon for 5, 10 or 15 extra merit badges, respectively, beyond the required 21. This often happened because most Scouts accumulated extra optional merit badges while working on their required ones. It also was much easier when palms were awarded for earning increments of five badges; once a three-month service requirement was added in September 1965, many Eagles ran out of time before their 18th birthday and were denied the one-upmanship of festooning their medal's ribbon with an array of shiny silver palms.[8]

But throughout the history of Scouting there always has been a small subgroup of Eagles for whom only the ultimate achievement—earning *every single merit badge*—is acceptable. Then and now, such an accomplishment almost always has guaranteed local (and sometimes national) media coverage, endless looks of awe at a merit sash covered front and back (and sometimes on a second, crossing sash) with an impossible number of merit badges, an impressive resume entry in later life—

Eagle Scout Peter Blum of Salem, Oregon, earned all 123 merit badges available at the time by June 1982.

and, in theory, proof of highly-developed skills in organization and time management.

Over the last century, there have been enough of these ultimate merit badge earners actually to produce category winners within the group. Thus, the youngest all-merit badge winner is likely **Christopher Haskell** of Elk Ridge, Utah, who did it in 2003 at the tender age of 13. And then there are the brother all-merit badge winners **Chad and Craig Carson** of Ogden, Utah, who each had earned 127 by 1975—which, not coincidentally, also happened to be the year that the most merit badges ever were offered.

James Calderwood's completion of his 122 merit badge in 2008 became a national story. The Chevy Chase, Maryland, Eagle's achievement earned stories on National Public Radio and in the *Washington Post*, dozens of radio interviews, and coverage on all three major television networks. ABC's World News Tonight even named Calderwood its "Person of the Week."

Bryce, **Taylor**, and **Alex Kunz** of San Diego were likely the record holders for siblings. The three brothers, born two years apart, earned every merit badge available while they still were Scouts: Bryce earned 121, Taylor earned 122, and Alex, who completed all available as well as the four historic merit badges offered in Scouting's 2010 centennial year (Scouting Heritage and Scuba Diving), earned 129. Because the boys were so close in age, they often worked together on their badges. The family spent Sunday nights planning the next week's requirements to be passed.

Merit badges, it seems is a Kunz family tradition: the boy's father earned 69 merit badges on his way to Eagle; their uncle earned 70. As Sewing never has been a merit badge, it fell to the boy's mother to sew on all 372 badges.

But among all the Eagle Scouts who have earned every available merit badge—and the entire group would probably just fill an average high school classroom—only one Eagle can claim to have earned the *most* merit badges. As already noted, Scouting began with just a handful of merit badges and climbed to more than 100 during World War II. In the 1950s and 1960s—and again today—the number has hovered around 130 badges, give or take about five and the BSA has been vigilant about retiring obsolete badges as often as it creates them.

But, thanks to the distortion created by the Improved Scouting program, there was a seam that briefly opened between 1970 and 1972 in which a Scout might earn one group of merit badges and then also earn the second set of the badges that replaced them, often merely with the substitution of a new name (e.g., Textile and Textiles). And that appears to be what Eagle Scout **John Stanford** from Limestone, New York, did. By his 18th birthday, he had earned his 142nd merit badge and eighth silver palm—the most ever. Unless the BSA decides to upend itself a second time, his is likely to be a Scouting record that stands forever.[9]

At various times in its history, Scouting had contemplated answering this hyper-competitiveness with an award *above* the Eagle. Happily none of those plans have come to fruition because it likely would have resulted in an open-ended Scout rank arms race. And for most Scouts, the Eagle medal, much less a palm or two, was more than enough of a challenge.

Still, in 1969, the BSA (largely for promotional reasons to show the importance of adult Eagles in American life and to maintain contact with its most successful alumni) created what is Scouting's highest, most exclusive, and least known, rank. The award derives, at least officially, from a special gold Eagle Scout medal awarded to **Dan Beard** in 1922.

It is called the Distinguished Eagle Scout Award (DESA) and consists of the BSA Eagle, now in gold, suspended from a red, white, and blue neck ribbon. It is not a rank you can earn—at least not intentionally—but rather, it is awarded only to adult Eagles after at least 25 years of distinguished service in their lives, profession or avocational field. Most of the Eagle Scouts named in this book, if they were still alive in 1969, have been recipients. This award is so exclusive most Scouts never have heard of the DESA. Of the 2 million Eagle Scouts in the BSA's history, less than 2,000—that is, 1 in 1,000—have been honored with the Distinguished Eagle Scout Award.[10]

But what about those adult Eagles who had made their career contributions in their own communities and not on the national stage?

As the ranks of Distinguished Eagle Scout recipients grew over the decade, with all of the attendant honors and publicity, this oversight at the local level became increasingly obvious. Was the mayor of a large city or a major local philanthropist or the head of a community charity any less worthy of recognition than a member of the military or a member of Congress?

It took more than four decades, but at last, in 2011, Scouting announced the NESA Outstanding Eagle Scout Award. Taking the form of a large silver medallion showing an Eagle in flight and suspended from a bright blue ribbon, the NOESA award maintained the high standards of the Distinguished Eagle at the community level. In some respects, however, it differed. The NOESA required only an important contribution to the community and not at a quarter-century remove. Selection, properly, was to be made at the council level (not by a secret community at the national headquarters) and based on a ratio of awards to the annual number of new council Eagles (approximately one per hundred). Finally, existing DESA recipients were not eligible for the NOESA award but the reverse was possible. (The first NOESA/DESA awardee didn't appear until January 2015).

Given these different requirements, the ranks of NOESA recipients grew quickly. In the inaugural year of 2011, the NESA Outstanding Eagle was awarded to 152 adult Eagles. Two years later, the number reached 582 suggesting that the number of NOESA recipients might overtake the number of Distinguished Eagles by the end of the decade.

GREEN BAR BILL

The man who saved American Scouting in the late 1970s was an elderly gentleman who recently had retired from the BSA after 60 years as the most important Scouter in the organization's history.

The climax of Improved Scouting came in 1976, which also was the same year it died. Chief Scout Executive Alden Barber had done what mavericks always do: he had shaken up the organization and made the BSA rethink all of its assumptions and revisit every one of its long-standing practices.

Many of the results had been restorative. Scouting now was fairer than it ever had been in its history: disabled boys, minority boys in the inner city, poor boys living in rural areas—all now had an equal chance to experience Scouting fully. The BSA now, at last, lived up to what it had always claimed to be: the ultimate experience for *all* boys.

And if the Boy Scouts was seeing declining membership, Barber could point to the huge success of Exploring, which not only was thriving, but also creating such enduring initiatives as the High Adventure program—an outdoor program that had all of the exciting characteristics that Boy Scouting now seemed to lack.

At the same time, Scouting now was more engaged with the communities it served than at any previous time (other than during war). Part of this was the massive expansion—and greater delineation—of the community and environmental service requirements at each rank, especially so for Eagle Scout. But beyond that, Scouting also embarked on a series of high-profile service initiatives during this era, most notably *Operation REACH*, an anti-drug campaign; and *Project SOAR*, a National Good Turn event, held on June 5, 1971, that engaged 2 million Scouts and Scouters cleaning up an estimated 1 million tons of litter across the country.[11]

After the dark days of the late 1960s, America began to see Scouting in a new, and more positive, light. This was an opinion that continued to improve when the nation experienced its first Eagle Scout president. It was a timely coincidence that 750 Scouts camped on the U.S. Capitol Mall to celebrate the nation's Bicentennial.[12] But for all of the extraordinary accomplishments of Scouting under Alden Barber, the BSA ultimately paid for that other side of mavericks: their indifference to tradition. Not only was the Boy Scouts continuing to lose members, but also many troops were in open revolt: wearing older uniforms and patches, teaching Scoutcraft, and even bending requirements.

Scouts themselves chafed at the increasing aggrandizement of troop leadership by the adults; while the adults, who had little choice but to lead in the face of the new national initiatives and rules, wondered how they had become neighborhood organizers and child counselors when they had signed on to lead campouts.

There were no real objections to the cultural changes made by national headquarters—Scouting's widespread acceptance and support of disabled, disadvantaged, and minority Scouts was one of the greatest achievements of its long story. But Scouts and Scouters wanted Scouting's *soul* back. They just wanted to go camping again. At first these dissidents were dismissed as a reactionary minority obsessed with an imagined better past, but in time, they became the majority—at least among Scouting veterans.

In 1973, the BSA held its eighth national jamboree, this time at two different sites: Moraine State Park in Pennsylvania and Farragut State Park in Idaho. The combined attendance of 73,610 Scouts and Scouters disguised the fact that each event drew less than 37,000 attendees, fewer than any before.[13]

However, at the 1973 jamborees, an announcement was made that would point toward the future of Scouting. At public gatherings of hundreds of Eagles, fellow young Eagles—several of them having been Knights of Dunamis—took the stage and announced the creation of a new entity designed to bring together all Eagles, new and old: the National Eagle Scout Association (NESA).

In 1976, even as Scouting was putting on a good face for the U.S. Bicentennial and preparing for the next year's ninth jamboree, the BSA's leadership decided to cut its losses. Alden Barber, the great innovator of Scouting's modern era, was pushed quietly into retirement before the normal age. Scouting, after nearly a decade of experimentation, had decided to hit the "reset" switch and it turned to the one person who knew how to lead the BSA back to its core principles.

That person was **William "Green Bar Bill" Hillcourt.** He was 77 years old and happily retired with his wife, Grace Brown, former secretary of Chief Executive Scout James E. West, in their home just outside the Schiff Scout Reservation in Mendham Borough, New Jersey.

William Hillcourt (left) and Robert Baden-Powell outside Hillcourt's cottage at the Schiff Scout Reservation on July 15, 1935.

Hillcourt already had enjoyed a fabled Scouting career—one that was, in the words of historian Robert Peterson, "the foremost influence on the development of the Boy Scouting program."[14] Now, he would be given his greatest challenge.

He was born Vilhelm Hans Bjerregaard Jensen in Aarhus, Denmark, in 1900. When he was ten, Vilhelm's older brother gave him a copy of the newly printed Danish language version of Baden-Powell's *Scouting for Boys* and the boy found his life's work. Joining Danish Scouting two years later, Vilhelm earned his Knight-Scout award (the equivalent of Eagle) at age 18.

Three years later, in 1920, he attended the First World Jamboree, in Olympia, Greece, and there met his hero, Lord Baden-Powell, for the first time.

By this point, Vilhelm was studying to become a pharmacist. But he also was getting more deeply involved in Scouting as well—serving as a Scoutmaster, a national instructor, and the editor of the *Danish Scouting Journal*. He even published a book about his early Scouting experiences.

While preparing his troop to attend the Second World Jamboree, this one in their own backyard of Ermelunden, Denmark, Vilhelm also managed to obtain press credentials to cover the event. This led to a journalism career—and in time a decision by Vilhelm, probably for a book, to tour the world studying the best Scouting practices in different countries. Toward that end, he traveled throughout Europe, then visited the UK, and finally in February 1926, he arrived in New York City at the offices of the Boy Scouts of America. He stayed for the rest of his life.

Thanks to a friendship he'd made at the World Jamboree in Ermelunden with an American Scouter (and future head of Cub Scouting), William Wessel, Vilhelm soon found a job at the National Scout Headquarters and, in a foreshadowing of the future, he soon found himself teaching American Indian dances to a group of American Boy Scouts from Brooklyn.

After working briefly at a Scout camp, Vilhelm landed a job at Scout headquarters in the Supply Division. There, in a fortuitous turn of events, his leg was broken by a falling crate. A week after this accident, he hobbled on crutches into headquarters. As he recalled, "I was walking into the elevator when an astonishing coincidence changed my life completely"—he ran into Chief Scout Executive James E. West. Here is his account of that meeting:

He knew of my accident. He stopped to greet me, and then said, 'Well, my young man, what do you think of American Scouting?' The elevator came. We went down together, chatting.

His words may have been just a casual remark. But I took them seriously. I wrote an eighteen-page report and sent it to him. It was complimentary in spots, critical in others. But for each criticism I offered a suggestion for remedying the situation.[15]

Within days, Vilhelm was called to West's office. "While I don't agree with everything in your report," West said, "I am interested in what you have to say about the Boy Scouts of America not using the patrol method effectively. You suggest that we should have a *Handbook for Patrol Leaders*. What should it contain?"[16]

As he did throughout his life, Vilhelm answered with the written word. With West's blessing, and despite deep doubts about his facility with English, he set to writing the BSA's *Handbook for Patrol Leaders*. First published in 1929 (and now having gone through numerous editions with three of them by Vilhelm himself), it remains the classic text on small unit organization and leadership—not only for Boy Scouts but also for adults as well.

The *Handbook for Patrol Leaders* changed Scouting. It also represented a turning point in Vilhelm's life. In 1930, he Anglicized his name to Bill Hillcourt, an almost direct translation. Two years later, he began working for *Boys' Life*—and for the next 33 years, each issue carried a page dedicated to Scoutcraft, advancement, and outdoor skills, written by and signed by Hillcourt. The signature, superimposed over the two green bars of the Patrol Leader badge, quickly earned Hillcourt the nickname "Green Bar Bill."

In 1934, the newly-wed Hillcourt was asked by E. Urner Goodman—the BSA National Scouting Director and co-founder of the Order of the Arrow—to write the new version of the *Boy Scout Handbook*. With his typical attention to detail, Bill moved with Grace to a renovated barn on the grounds of the 500-acre Mortimer L. Schiff Scout Reservation in Mendham. There, he formed and served as Scoutmaster to Troop 1—a troop of local boys that was uniquely chartered by the BSA National Council—and set off to discover how Scouting *really* worked.

With the run of the entire camp, the boys of Troop 1 remembered it as one of the greatest experiences of their lives. But for Bill Hillcourt, it was the ultimate test bed, his beta site, for his theories about Scouting. Over time, this research became increasingly sophisticated and codified. Even the family of IBM founder Thomas J. Watson donated a complete film studio at Schiff to help create training materials for Scouting. Meanwhile, Hillcourt reported on his discoveries both in *Boys' Life* and in other Scouting publications.

Hillcourt's most important finding—and one for which he became the passionate advocate—was that Baden-Powell had, intuitively, been right from the start: the heart of all Scouting was the *patrol*. Everything great about Scouting—teamwork, camaraderie, learning to follow and to lead, mastering new skills, a sense of duty, and responsibility—all emanated from those small groups of six to eight boys. Everything else, Hillcourt concluded, from adult leadership to jamborees to the BSA itself, merely existed to empower and enrich these tens of thousands of patrols and their young leaders.

The "patrol method" was a vision of Scouting that, though often observed in the breach, has defined the BSA ever since—not least because "Green Bar Bill" (the name had proven prophetic) expounded it on the pages of *Boys' Life* every month. It also colored every critical Scouting text Hillcourt authored: three editions of the *Handbook for Patrol Leaders* (1929, 1952, and 1967), the *Scout Fieldbook* (1948, with West; generally acknowledged as the greatest text on outdoor craft ever written), the *Handbook for Scoutmasters* (1936), and three editions of the *Boy Scout Handbook* (most famously, the 1959 sixth edition that Hillcourt considered his masterpiece and one of the best-selling children's books of all time; the 1965 seventh edition; and the 1979 ninth edition). The patrol method also lay at the philosophical heart of the BSA's Wood Badge adult leader training program that Hillcourt tested at the Schiff Scout Training Center and at the Philmont Scout Ranch, both in 1948.

Hillcourt retired from Scouting in 1965, having earned every honor and award that U.S. and World Scouting could give. Green Bar Bill even was unofficially designated "Scoutmaster to the World." The first thing he did after retiring was to travel with Grace to the World Jamboree in Japan—thus, 40 years later, finishing the Scouting tour he had begun years before.

Bill Hillcourt was a dozen years retired and a widower when Scouting called on him one final time. Improved Scouting now was generally acknowledged as a failure, the BSA was in crisis, the 1977 National Jamboree had drawn less than 29,000 attendees[17]—and there was no solution to which everyone agreed. What was obvious was that many Scout troops were reverting to older uniforms, a renewed focus on patrols, and most visibly, to dog-eared old *Scout Handbooks*, with Norman Rockwell's smiling, striding Eagle Scout on its cover.

William Hillcourt signing his new edition of the BSA's Handbook *at the 1981 National Jamboree at Fort A.P. Hill in Virginia.*

The new Chief Scout Executive Harvey L. Price approached Hillcourt and asked him to come out of retirement to write a new edition of the *Handbook*—one that retained the best of Improved Scouting but that still restored "the 'outing' to Scouting."[18]

Hillcourt agreed. Perhaps sensing the BSA's desperation, he delivered the ninth edition (1979) of the *Boy Scout Handbook*, complete with a (1970) cover painting by his old friend Norman Rockwell, showing a Scoutmaster and group of Scouts camping, cooking, and canoeing in the woods. Inside, with a deftness unexpected from an octogenarian author, Hillcourt brilliantly wove together the two great threads of Scouting at the end of the 20th century: the power of traditional camp craft and outdoor skills, with the lure of modern life and technology.

If the ninth edition of the *Handbook* didn't quite rank with Hillcourt's other masterworks, this valedictory might have been the single most important contribution of his distinguished career with the BSA. This version of the *Handbook* was universally acclaimed as Scouting's return to its roots; and as a timely reassertion of the patrol method. It pulled Scouting back from the brink and set it again on a path to health. In the words of the BSA in promoting the new *Handbook*:

This edition places greater emphasis on fun and adventure and uses Scout skills as a method to achieve the aims of Scouting. Strengthening the family and broadening the outdoor experience also are major objectives of th[is] new handbook.[19]

Green Bar Bill Hillcourt lived to age 92, long enough to see the profound impact of his last work. He died as he lived, while on a Scouting trip to Stockholm, Sweden, in 1992. And his work still is widely read: his columns are regularly reprinted in *Boys' Life*, his editions of the *Handbook* have sold more than 12 million copies,[20] and his immortal *Fieldbook* likely will remain the standard text for outdoorsmen— and outdoorswomen—for generations to come. The Danish "Eagle" who saved Scouting is buried alongside his wife Grace near the Schiff Scout Training Center.

William Hillcourt sitting for his official BSA portrait prior to the 1985 National Jamboree.

THE LIST

Very little survived the transition from the Improved Scouting eighth edition *Handbook* to the restorative ninth edition *Scouting Handbook*.

But Green Bar Bill Hillcourt, in exorcising the BSA's brief fling with trendiness, decided to retain one piece of the old book in the new. It was the section on the Eagle Scout service project. And in keeping it, Hillcourt unconsciously established one of the most enduring and influential documents in Scouting history.

The section had just three pages of large print in the eighth edition (and even less in Hillcourt's ninth edition) but it was read by tens of thousands of Scouts who dreamed of earning their Eagle. Indeed, it quickly became *the* text for Eagle project planners. It remained so for almost 40 years: not the text itself, but the attached list of model Eagle service projects.

There are just nine projects on The List; two more were added quietly in later years. But, after it was perpetuated in the ninth edition of the *Handbook*, The List took on a life of its own. That same list of Eagle projects not only has appeared in subsequent issues of the *Handbook*, but also become enshrined in the official *Eagle Scout Workbook* that 21st century Eagle candidates use to organize and track their progress.

Whether The List was recycled on its own merit, or was merely the result of a lazy copy editor, it proved so venerable and so influential as the gold standard to more than a million Eagle Scout candidates (half of all of them in Scouting history) that it too is now an important chapter in the Scouting story.

Here is The List of exemplary Eagle service projects:

- Made trays to fasten to wheelchairs for veterans with disabilities at a Veterans Administration hospital.

- Collected used books and distributed them to people in the community who wanted and needed, but could not afford, books.

- Built a sturdy footbridge across a brook to make a safe shortcut for children between their homes and school.

- Collected and repaired used toys and gave them to a home for children with disabilities.

- Organized and operated a bicycle safety campaign. This involved a written safety test, equipment safety check, and a skills contest in a bike rodeo.

- Surveyed the remains of an old Spanish mission and prepared an accurate map relating it to the present church.

- Built a "tot lot" in a big city neighborhood and set up a schedule for Boy Scouts to help run it.

- Set up a community study center for children who needed a place to do schoolwork.

- Trained fellow students as audiovisual aides for their school. Arranged for more than 200 hours of audiovisual work.

- Prepared plans for a footbridge on a trail in a national forest. Worked with rangers to learn the skills necessary to build the structure, gathered materials and tools, and then directed a Scout work group to do the construction.[21]

Why were these particular activities (the first nine at least) chosen to be the exemplary Eagle projects of the early years of the new service requirement?

And why did they remain as the touchstone for thousands of Eagle projects and millions of hours of service in the subsequent four decades?

One answer is that they do a pretty serviceable job of setting both boundary conditions and acceptable complexity for a good Eagle service project. On closer inspection, certain themes emerge. One is need: several of the projects deal with improving the lives of the disabled, the impoverished, and the at-risk. Others—such as the "tot lot," the footbridge to school, and the bicycle rodeo—deal with issues of safety. One, the footbridge at the park (the double appearance of footbridges probably was appealing because of the use of knots, lashings, and other Scouting skills) represents an improvement in a community's quality of life.

As for the audiovisual training, it suggests opportunities for a boy, within his daily milieu of school life, to make an important contribution. And the last, the most unusual of the group, the mapping of the mission, points not only to contributions to religious organizations, but also to Scouting's long-standing commitment to history and preservation.

If, in some ways, it is an odd list because it ignores 99 percent of all Eagle projects of that era that typically consisted of cleaning up a schoolyard or vacant lot, painting a neighborhood building, or working on a trail. It also is an interesting list because its very oddness forced Scouts to think beyond the usual prosaic projects and to ponder the real definition of "service."

Each of The List's projects also shows, if only implicitly, that a true Eagle service project requires not only heavy participation by the Eagle candidate himself (planning, execution, and follow-up), but also extensive interaction with adults, institutions, and the management of other people.

At a time when the still-new Eagle project requirement was largely seen as an extended solo effort by a Life Scout, The List pointed toward something much more sophisticated in its scope and purpose—the next step beyond the career and management training of the merit badges and troop leadership roles. Seen in this light, the Eagle project was to be not only a boy's last great act in Scouting, but also his first real experience of adult life. He was to devise, plan, and execute a major project for a nonprofit "customer," and then assemble and manage the project team needed to pull it off. Finally (as later refinements of the project required), he was to conduct a postmortem on the project, reporting on what worked and what did not, how he coped with unanticipated events, and what he had learned from the experience.

The List shows all of these things. And ultimately, that may be why it still endures after the Scouts who performed these projects have grown middle-aged and gray-haired; it lasted because it works. It is telling that when The List first appeared, its examples were considered to be model service projects that Eagle Scouts should aspire to; while today, largely because they helped propel 40 years of service projects to become ever-more ambitious, The List now represents a baseline for all good Eagle projects. The best modern projects *start* with The List—and then set the bar far higher than any Eagle Scout in 1972 ever could have imagined.

LEGEND AND REALITY

There is a second reason The List is important. Until 2005, when NESA took on the job, the national BSA office did not keep records of Eagle service projects. (The name of the Eagle project and the number of hours spent only was added to the application in August 2008.)

Until then, any record keeping of this kind occurred at the local council office, where most Eagle boards of review took place as well. And, whereas all Eagle applications eventually were sent to the national office, any reports and other documentation about the projects themselves typically were treated as ephemera and either returned to the new Eagle or trashed. Of what little remained, much soon would be lost to a conflagration.

As a result, other than anecdote and the occasional line in a newspaper story of the era, we have little record of what it was like to be a Life Scout pioneering the Eagle service project in the late 1960s and early 1970s. Through sheer serendipity, we *do* have a complete record of two of the projects enumerated in The List. That's because I happened to participate in one of those projects—the bicycle rodeo. And the other—the mission mapping and exploration project—was my Eagle project.

The fact that I was involved in two of the most well-known Eagle projects of all time is a mystery of its own. Both projects took place within weeks of each other in the early spring of 1967 and both were the work of two Life Scouts from a single troop: Troop 480, based at Mango Junior High School (now Sunnyvale Middle School) in Sunnyvale, California.

How these two projects from the same troop, taking place almost simultaneously at a local public school in a suburban city in the San Francisco Bay Area, managed to join The List—the bicycle rodeo even was illustrated in the 1972 *Handbook*—and become a mainstay of Scouting for decades, is a question that may never be answered. Perhaps some anonymous copywriter, desperate for some case studies for the *Handbook's* new Eagle Service Project section, stumbled across a cache of aging reports from the Santa Clara County Council and grabbed the two that best fit his narrative.

What I do know is that the now-famous Bicycle Rodeo was the project of Fremont High School student **Mark Habermeyer**, now a respected dentist nearing retirement in Southern California. Mark's father, John Habermeyer, was our Scoutmaster and had inspired the troop's older boys to strive for what would ultimately become more than a dozen Eagles. John also was director of safety at NASA's Ames Research Center, where in the early 1970s an electronics-dedicated Explorer post was formed that would ultimately provide many members to the Homebrew Computer Club and spark both the birth of Apple Computer and the personal computer revolution.

Mark's bicycle rodeo took place on the asphalt basketball courts and exercise area at the back of Mango Junior High. Mark had met with the Sunnyvale Safety Department and together with a police officer there had come up with a plan for the riding events to teach bicycle safety, a quiz, and even some awards.

The event took place early one Saturday afternoon. It was a small affair. For the Scouts of subsequent generations who would read the description and imagine an arena replete with crowds, flags, and professional bicyclists, they would have been disappointed. In fact, the illustrator of the *Handbook* got it about right: a bunch of little kids on Schwinn Stingrays riding a small course complete with traffic signs, being monitored by Boy Scouts with clipboards and stopwatches. We older Scouts arrived early to set things up, do some test runs on the course (which led to a lot of good-natured competition), and then safety-checked the bikes and managed the courses when the kids started to arrive. We were done before dinner.

In retrospect, it was a perfect Eagle project: carefully prepared, organized, and executed; it served an important purpose; and it educated a bunch of children, Scouts, and even adults about an important life skill. But I suspect few of those hundreds of thousands of prospective Eagles who read its entry on The List quite imagined the reality of Mark Habermeyer's Bicycle Rodeo.

But if the gap between reality and the mental image produced by the text was wide for Mark's project, it surely was a vast gulf for mine, the most exotic project on the list.

SUBURBAN EXPLORER

Over the years, I've often imagined what a 16-year-old Life Scout must have imagined as he read: *Surveyed the remains of an old Spanish mission and prepared an accurate map relating it to the present church.* Did he picture me in some crumbling desert village in the Southwest, dressed in khakis, and directing a crew of surveyors armed with transits and levels as they marked out the ruins of some long-abandoned 18th century Franciscan mission? Did they imagine some young Howard Carter ordering around the workers in an archeological dig for golden artifacts from the age of conquistadors? And if so, did they wonder how I ever managed to find such a project? Or did they simply conclude that such an unusual project was impossible for them—and move on to the more realistic "tot lot" and footbridge?

They might have thought differently had they known just how prosaic my

Eagle project was. I did survey the remains of an old Spanish mission but it was Mission Santa Clara, at the center of Santa Clara University and in the heart of busy Santa Clara (soon to be Silicon) Valley, just a few miles from my home. And I did prepare a map (though it was a far more complicated process than the description presented). The surveying was simple and almost an afterthought.

Here's what happened. I was just 13 years old, young for an Eagle candidate even then, when I heard that there might be a potential Eagle project idea available from the venerable archivist at Santa Clara—Father Arthur Spearman, SJ. I made a nervous telephone call. Being a suburban Presbyterian boy, I had never had an extended conversation before with a Catholic priest, much less a Jesuit academic. But Father Spearman was pleasant enough, patient with my obvious nerves, and invited me down to the university.

A week later my father drove me down to Santa Clara, helped me find my way to the Jesuit residence building, and then left me in the lobby. The dark lobby and ringing marble floor combined for an intimidating experience, but I managed to find the telephone and call upstairs.

In time, Fr. Spearman came down to meet me. He was an elderly man wearing very thick glasses, in black trousers, shirt, and collar. I didn't even know what to call him but eventually settled on "Father."

I didn't know at the time that Fr. Spearman had a reputation for being a crusty and difficult man. He once had been something of a firebrand and his stubbornness only now was being credited for having saved many of the mission's greatest artifacts. But he was kind enough to take me over to the basement of the nearby campus museum and show me some of those artifacts, some dating to the 18th century.

But what Fr. Spearman wanted to show me was a small stack of old maps, some of them on vellum that he carefully pulled from a drawer. "This is how you can help me if you are interested," he said. "These maps are of each of the five different Missions of Santa Clara, beginning with the first one in 1777, all of the way up to the present one built in 1928 after the previous one burned."

"No one," he continued, "ever has combined all of these missions into a single map. And that is because none of them are drawn in the same scale. Perhaps you'd like to try to put them all together?"

I didn't know enough to say no. And so, for the next three months, to my family's growing chagrin, I taped a large sheet of paper, covered with maps and smaller sheets of paper, to one end of our dining room table. This being well before the personal computer age, my father, who also worked at NASA Ames, arranged for me to visit the art department there and get some rudimentary instruction in using a rapidograph pen, overlay transparencies, and handling an Exacto knife to cut out forms in red mylar.

My goal was to create five overlaying transparencies, each showing the buildings of one of the missions, and each in the same scale and in the proper location.

But I quickly ran into a major problem: not only were the maps not in the same scale, as Fr. Spearman had said, they weren't even in the same *units of measurement*. The modern ones were in yards and meters, but the older ones were in such obsolete measures as rods, chains, and links. And in one, they were indecipherable.

The result was weeks spent in a nightmare of pocket calculator and hand calculations, followed by a clumsy attempt to act like a professional graphic artist and cartographer. Eventually, 80 hours into the project, I hit a wall: I simply couldn't reconcile one of the older maps to the modern city of Santa Clara.

Desperate, I went back to the men in the NASA art department. Being right in the middle of the transition from the Gemini to Apollo programs, they no doubt had better things to do but they still found time to both show me how to improve my work to date and, more important, suggested I visit a blueprinter and see if they would blow up portions of the two maps until one or two key features could be made congruent.

That led me to yet another meeting with an adult professional, the manager of a Sunnyvale blueprint firm. He managed to puzzle out my confused request, nodded brusquely, and told me to come back in a couple days.

I did as I was told and found that the man had created a series of blowups, both on paper and transparencies that put all of my missions and their outbuildings in a common scale. He had saved my project.

It had not been a simple job, nor an inexpensive one. I pulled out the blank check, signed by my mother (who waited in the car outside), and asked how much it would be. The man never smiled. Instead, he handed me the big prints and said, "There's no charge, son. Just remember today. And when you grow up, I want you to do the same thing for some young man working on his Eagle project."

I thanked him quickly and clutching the prints, raced home to get back to work.

Twelve weeks after I began, I finished the five maps, all of them properly aligned atop one another.

It looked great, especially considering that it had been created by rookie mapmaker. But was it accurate? There only was one way to know for sure. And so, late one Saturday afternoon that spring, I led of group of a half-dozen fellow Scouts from Troop 480 down to Santa Clara University and the bright green lawns around the Mission.

There, armed with hammers, we drove three stainless steel rods into the ground at scores of different locations, testing to see if they hit buried foundation rocks and stone floor, or just compressed dirt. We used stakes and strings to delineate the overall dimensions of the long-lost buildings.

We must have been an incongruous sight: seven young boys in Scout uniforms inching across a wide lawn beneath a tall campus dormitory building which, from almost every window—many of them draped with peace symbols and North Vietnamese and Cuban flags—blared acid rock-n-roll music. Certainly the students passing by found us amusing (when they weren't dismissing us as tools of the military industrial complex). We tried to ignore them by focusing on our work.

In the end, we confirmed as best we could that my maps were accurate. I wrote up the report on my project and delivered the results to a pleased Father Spearman, who took the maps and immediately stuck them in a drawer. I never saw them again.

A month later, I survived an Eagle board of review before adult strangers held in one of the chambers of a courthouse in San Jose (today's Eagle boards are typically held by the troops themselves). Finally, in July 1967, in the gymnasium of a local elementary school, I was part of a triple Eagle Court of Honor, along with Mark Habermeyer and **Chris Henry**, now a Silicon Valley senior executive.

It goes without saying that the reality of my Eagle service project was a long way from the mental image created by the description of that same project on The List. And yet, looking back over more than 40 years, I am struck that my real project was just as remarkable as any imagined one.

Four years later, I came limping home from the Air Force Academy with pneumonia and needing surgery on both knees. I had less than a week to find a college before classes started. Among those that I had turned down months before was Santa Clara. And so, armed with a recommendation letter from the mayor of Sunnyvale, I raced down to SCU and met with the academic vice president. I was accepted, thanks in part to his remembering my Eagle project. (This is my version of the adage that an Eagle is the ultimate college application tie-breaker.) I went on to earn two degrees from SCU, teach in its law school and English department, sit on numerous boards, and deliver the President's Lecture—all at a university I first visited for my Eagle project.

Meanwhile, Father Spearman, after a few years, took my map out of the drawer, and it became the basis for all subsequent maps of the university in brochures, tour guides, and other publications. I often passed a sign bearing a descendent of my map as I raced to teach one of my classes—one of which I taught in a temporary building atop one of the lawns where my little team had traced out old foundations.

But, membership on The List aside, the most enduring impact of my Eagle service project was on my life. I long ago forgot the name of the man at the blueprint company, and the shop itself is long gone. But I never forgot what he said to me. And four decades after he told me to pass on his contribution, I did just that: taking on the job of Assistant Scoutmaster, mentoring the next generation of Eagles. As I write this, there now have been more than 25 of these Scouts. All have read The List, of course, but few know of their historic connection to it or of the anonymous businessman of a half-century ago who still plays a role in helping them earn their Eagle.

A NEW GENERATION

Scouting had begun the 1970s convinced it had found a radical solution to both its declining rolls and its alienation from large segments of American society. It ended the decade turning to an octogenarian in a last-ditch effort to save itself. Green Bar Bill had delivered more than anyone could ever have expected.

But it would take more than a new *Handbook* to turn Scouting around. And even then, the iron rule of demographics almost guaranteed that Scouting likely would not see a return to its membership levels of the 1950s and 1960s for decades. And though in 1980 the BSA cheered as it showed its first membership growth (to 4.3 million youth members) in nearly a decade; it was obvious that most of that growth had come from member retention due to the restoration of traditional Scouting, not from a sudden burst of brand new members. That was good news, of course, but it hadn't changed the reality of a declining pool of potential new members.

So the challenge now was one that the BSA never had faced before: could it make Scouting a dynamic, engaging experience for American boys without depending on the built-in advantages of continuous growth?

Here too, Bill Hillcourt pointed the way: go small, go local, and go back to the patrol model. And, to drive that message home, for his final great contribution to Scouting he prepared a third edition of the Handbook for Patrol Leaders—*The Official Patrol Leader Handbook*—in 1980.

The old guard now had done all it could. It was time for a new generation of Scouting leaders to take Boy Scouting into its next era—one defined by fewer young people; a technology and communications revolution that soon would deliver the personal computer, Internet and wireless telephony; a greater emphasis on awards and other college application assets; a complete transformation in outdoor equipment; an explosion in immigration; the greatest period of wealth creation in U.S. history; and a return to more traditional values.

Scouting now had a new look, new texts, and a new/old philosophy with which to meet this new world and to complete its renaissance. And, on the eve of the 1990s, Scouting took one final step to show its commitment to the future: it moved BSA headquarters from New Jersey to Irving, Texas, into the heart of the fast-growing Sunbelt.

But if Scouting was going to become more traditional *and* diminished in size, how would it continue to gain the attention of the general public it needed to continue to recruit young Cub and Boy Scouts? Scouting had managed, in 1980, to mobilize millions of its Cubs, Boy Scouts, and Explorers to assist in making the U.S. Census that year the most accurate on record.[22] But the great national BSA initiatives now would be few and far between. How would Scouting continue to maintain its hard-earned role as an American institution, as a vital part of American boyhood, and as a critical part of the American way of life?

The answer would come, as if often had over the years, from Eagle Scouts.

By the 1980s, a new generation of Eagles, boys who had earned the rank in the 1950s and 1960s, now were coming into their own on the national stage.

An extraordinary number of these postwar Eagles were astronauts; including Neil Armstrong and Charlie Duke. They were the two Apollo astronaut moonwalkers (with a staggering 11 of 12 moonwalkers having been former Scouts). In total, as this book is being written, *40* Mercury, Gemini, Apollo, Skylab, and Shuttle astronauts have been Eagles—an extraordinary percentage that seems to underscore the unique balance of physical and mental acumen that is almost unique to the process of earning the Eagle rank.

Several of these Space Eagles are of particular note. Tragically, the best known is **Col. Ellison Onizuka**. Onizuka, the first Asian American in space was born in Kealakekua, Hawaii, and earned his Eagle with a Scout troop there. A veteran test pilot, he was selected for the NASA Space Shuttle program in January 1978. His first space flight was aboard the Shuttle *Discovery* six years later.

On January 28, 1986, Onizuka was a member of the crew of the Shuttle *Challenger* and was killed when the ship exploded soon after takeoff. An investigation after the disaster found that Onizuka likely had survived the explosion and had fought to save the *Challenger* until it crashed into the ocean. He was posthumously promoted to Colonel and the U.S. satellite facility in Sunnyvale, California—near where he trained at NASA Ames Research Center—now bears his name, as do a number of sites in Hawaii.

In late 1986, **Colonel Guion Bluford**, who participated in four Shuttle flights and was the first African American in space, was tasked by the federal government to visit Troop 514 of Monument, Colorado. The troop had successfully submitted the flag, which had flown over the U.S. Capitol, to be flown on the *Challenger* flight. When the wreckage of the shuttle finally was recovered, the flag still was miraculously intact, while the medallions with which it had been stowed had melted. Col. Bluford returned "the *Challenger* flag," as it was now called, to the troop in an emotional ceremony at nearby Falcon Air Station.

A year later, Chief Justice Earl Warren designated the *Challenger* flag as the official flag of the U.S. Constitution Bicentennial celebration. It has since been reflown over the Capitol (the first flag to ever fly twice there), at the 2002 Winter Olympics in Salt Lake City, and at the 25th anniversary memorial ceremonies for the *Challenger* crew.

Other notable Space Eagles include **Sonny Carter**, who had stellar careers as an astronaut, a doctor, a test pilot, and a professional soccer player; **Lt. Col. Roger Chaffee**, who died in the Apollo 1 fire during a ground test; **Col. Richard O. Covey** helped lead the commission that led NASA back into space after the *Challenger* disaster. He then piloted *Discovery*, the first Shuttle mission in NASA's "Return to Space" program in September 1988. **General Robert T. Herres** was slated to be an astronaut aboard the Manned Orbiting Laboratory but when it was cancelled, he became the first commander-in-chief of the Air Force Space Command, then the first vice chairman of the Joint Chiefs of Staff. Upon retirement from the USAF, he served as the BSA's president as well as the chairman and CEO of the USAA Group, where he took the insurance giant into the Internet age. **Vice Admiral Richard Truly** flew twice on Space Shuttles. His first flight into space in 1981 was as pilot of the Space Shuttle *Columbia*, which was significant as it was the first manned spacecraft to be reflown in space. His second flight in 1983 was as commander of the Space Shuttle *Challenger*, which was the first night launch and landing in the Shuttle program. He became the first former astronaut to lead NASA and served as NASA Administrator from 1989–1992.[23]

James Lovell, who earned his Eagle in 1943, had one of the most memorable of all careers as an astronaut, flying on Gemini 7 and 12, Apollo 8, and as commander of Apollo 13 (the role played by actor Tom Hanks in the movie)—one of the great human adventure stories of the 20th century. After retirement, Lovell served as president of the National Eagle Scout Association in the 1990s.

Baby boom Eagles also were showing up in leadership roles across American society. Medical doctor and biologist **Peter Agre** (Eagle 1964—Northfield, Minnesota) shared the 2003 Nobel Prize in Chemistry for his discovery of aquaporins, the proteins that channel water into cells. His two physician brothers, as well as Agre's son, also are Eagles. **Lamar Alexander** (Eagle 1954) served as U.S. senator and governor of Tennessee, as well as secretary of education. **Norman Augustine** was CEO of Martin-Marietta Corporation and led its acquisition of Lockheed Corp. He also was under secretary of the army and the president of numerous nonprofit organizations, including the Red Cross and Boy Scouts of America (1994–1996). **John W. Creighton Jr.** was president of Weyerhauser and Boeing and served as president of the BSA from 1996–1998.

Academia also saw it share of Eagles during this era, including **Lawrence Bacow**, chancellor of MIT; **Charles Bayless**, president of West Virginia Tech; paleoanthropologist **Lee Berger**; **John Caldwell**, chancellor of North Carolina State; **Kim Clark**, dean of faculty at Harvard Business School and president of Brigham Young; **James Daughdrill Jr.**, president of Rhodes College for 26 years; **Richard Herman**, chancellor of the University of Illinois, Urbana-Champaign; and **David Leebron**, president of Rice University. Noted oceanic engineer **J. Kim Vandiver** was dean of undergraduate research at MIT.

Famed investigative reporter **Michael Dunne** of the *Baton Rouge Morning Advocate* also volunteered with his local Scouting council. Brothers **Roy** and **Walter Menninger**, both Eagles, would start the foundation that bears their family name. **James Rogers** was CEO of Kampgrounds of America; while his brother **Gary** was CEO of Dreyer's Ice Cream. **Chuck Smith** became chairman of AT&T West. **Rex Tillerson** served as chairman and CEO of ExxonMobil beginning in 2006; he served as BSA president from

2010 - 2012. **Howard Lincoln**, CEO of the Seattle Mariners and Nintendo America, was also one of the sleeping boys who posed for Norman Rockwell's famous painting "The Scoutmaster."

Steve Fossett's official BSA portrait as the president of NESA in 2007. Photo courtesy of NESA.

Among the most famous adventurers of modern times was **Steve Fossett**, who as aviator, sailor, and balloonist, set 116 records in five different sports—60 of which still stood at the time of Fossett's untimely death in a plane crash in September 2007. Fossett grew up in Garden Grove, California. His father was an Eagle Scout, and Steve joined Troop 170 in the city of Orange, where he earned his Eagle at age 13. He later credited the trips he took with Scouts into the nearby San Jacinto Mountains as having changed his life: "When I was 12 years old I climbed my first mountain, and I just kept going, taking on more diverse and grander projects."[24] Fossett eventually joined the Order of the Arrow and served on the staff at the Philmont Scout Ranch. As an adult, he credited Scouting with having the most impact on his youth.

After a short corporate career, Fossett made his fortune as a commodities trader and later, renting floor trading privileges to new traders. This freed him to pursue a life as an adventurer and explorer. He trained himself to become perhaps the finest glider, small plane, and balloon pilot of his generation, as well as a world-class sailor, and then Fossett set out to break every record possible.

Thanks to his skill, technological acumen, and careful preparation, he did just that. In 1992, on his sixth attempt, he became the first person to fly a balloon solo around the world. In 2005, piloting the single engine jet *Virgin Atlantic Global Flyer*, he became the first person to circumnavigate the world solo, nonstop, and unrefueled. A year later, he did it again, setting the record for the longest plane flight in history. That same year, Fossett set the world altitude record for gliders. Meanwhile, between 1993 and 2004, Fossett also was the world's greatest speed sailor, breaking every known record—including, in 2004, the faster circumnavigation of the world by water.

In his amazing career, Fossett also ran in the Boston Marathon, drove a dog team in the Alaskan Iditarod, raced cars in Le Mans and in the Paris to Dakar Rally, and swam the English Channel. Along the way, he earned every award for adventure and achievement possible. But the one he continued to cherish the most was his Eagle. He remained deeply involved with Scouting his entire life and at his death was president of the National Eagle Scout Association.

The number of baby boom-era Eagles who entered politics and government would overwhelm this chapter. But here is a brief selection: Rep. **Gary Ackerman**, New York; Rep. **William Alexander**, Arkansas; Sen. **Jeff Bingaman**, New Mexico; Rep. **Sanford Bishop**, Georgia; Mayor (and noted businessman) **Michael Bloomberg** of New York City; Sen. **Sherrod Brown**, Ohio; Rep. **Russ Carnahan**, Missouri; Sen. **Thad Cochran**, Mississippi; Rep. **Jim Cooper**, Tennessee; Sen. **Mike Crapo**, Idaho; Sen. **Mike Enzi**, Wyoming; Rep. **Mike Fitzpatrick**, Pennsylvania; **Louis Freeh**, FBI director; Rep. **Daniel Frisa**, New York; Lt. Gov. **John Garamendi**, California; Majority Leader Rep. **Dick Gephardt**, Missouri; Rep. **Louie Gohmert**, Texas; Rep. **J.D. Hayworth**, Arizona; Rep. **Jeb Hensarling**, Texas; Lt. Gov. **Peter Kinder**, Missouri; Gov. **Gary Locke**, Washington; Rep. **Michael McNulty**, New York; Gov. and Sen. **Ben Nelson**, Nebraska; Gov. **Jay Nixon**, Missouri; Sen. **Sam Nunn**, Georgia; Rep. **Edward A. Pease**, Indiana (also chairman of the Order of the Arrow); Gov. **Rick Perry**, Texas; Rep. **J.J. Pickle**, Texas; Rep. **Dana Rohrabacher**, California; Sen. **Warren Rudman**, New Hampshire; Rep. and Gov. **Mark Sanford**, South Carolina; White House Chief of Staff **Samuel Skinner**; Rep. **Steve Stivers**, Ohio; Rep. Bart Stupak, Michigan; and Gov. **John Waihee**, first Native Hawaiian governor of Hawaii.

Togo West Jr. not only was secretary of the Army and the second African American to be named secretary of Veterans Affairs, he also maintained a lifelong relationship with Scouting, serving as the president of the National Capital Area Council and then on the executive board of the BSA.

Whatever the stereotypes attached to Scouting, you would be hard-pressed to find a common political position among all of these Eagle-politicians. The same is true in the judiciary, where hundreds of Eagles have achieved important positions as state supreme court justices, federal judges, and state attorneys general. Of this legal-Eagles generation, the best known is **Stephen Breyer**, associate justice of the United States Supreme Court. Breyer earned his Eagle with Troop 14 in San Francisco. Before his nomination to the Supreme Court, Breyer served as United States assistant attorney general and as an assistant special prosecutor during the Watergate investigation.

What may be surprising is the number of Eagle Scouts from this era involved in sports. Most of them were head coaches: **Chan Gailey**, Dallas Cowboys and Georgia Tech Yellow Jackets; **Ray Malavasi**, Denver Broncos and Los Angeles Rams; **Jim Mora**, Baltimore Stars, New Orleans Saints, and Indianapolis Colts; and **Ken Whisenhunt**, Arizona Cardinals. There were also a number of Eagles who became professional athletes, the best known probably being **Albert Belle**, the hard-slugging (and often combative) outfielder for the Cleveland Indians, Chicago White Sox, and Baltimore Orioles.

But perhaps no athlete Eagle ever has had a more remarkable career than **Bill Bradley**. Exactly how he managed to earn his Eagle in the middle of his famously rigorous basketball training schedule is a measure of both his intelligence and discipline. The most famous high school basketball player of his era, Bradley was offered 75 college scholarships. He chose Princeton, was

Promotional images for Sen. Bill Bradley while a member of the New York Knicks.

NCAA player of the year, and earned an Olympic gold medal. Then, after spending two years at Oxford as a Rhodes scholar, Bradley returned to the United States and joined the NBA's New York Knicks. He spent his decade-long career with the Knicks, which retired his number.

Bradley was elected to the basketball hall of fame in 1982. By then, he had been elected to the U.S. Senate (D-NJ) and held public office for three terms. In 1997, he retired from politics but then returned in 2000 with an unsuccessful run for president of the United States. He still holds the NCAA free throw percentage record, which he set between 1962 and 1965.

On April 29, 1975, in a tragic postscript to a painful era, Marine **Lance Corporal Darwin Judge**, who had earned his Eagle just four years before, became one of the last two U.S. servicemen to die in the Vietnam War. A member of the Marine security guard at the U.S. Embassy in Saigon he was killed by a North Vietnamese rocket attack. A year later, Senator Edward Kennedy used diplomatic channels to secure the return of Judge's remains to the United States. But it would be 25 more years, until 2000, before he would receive a full military funeral. The Fall of Saigon Marines Association sponsors two scholarships each year for Eagle Scouts attending Iowa's Marshalltown High School, Judge's alma mater.

Needless to say given the times, this generation of Eagle Scouts produced more than its share of outsiders and controversial figures.

Probably the most notorious was **Marion Barry**. Born in Leflore, Mississippi, the third of 10 children, Barry's father died when he was a child, forcing him to take work as a cotton picker, grocery bagger, and American Legion hall waiter. Despite this, he joined a Boy Scout troop and earned his Eagle just before his 18th birthday. Barry earned degrees from LeMoyn and Fisk University. And in 1978, he was elected as the second mayor of Washington, DC.

Barry's first tenure in office as one of the most powerful African American mayors in the country was controversial but largely successful. However, in 1990, at the end of his third term, his widely reported drug arrest (with accompanying video) shocked the nation. He chose not to run for re-election and served one year in a federal penitentiary.

But if his behavior appalled the rest of America, Marion Barry the politician was still beloved by minority voters in Washington, DC. And, within two years, he again was elected mayor. This fourth and final term was more contentious than controversial because the mayor and city council fought over a shrinking budget and chafed under federal oversight. Barry officially retired in 1999, explaining (probably correctly) that DC never would earn statehood as long as he was mayor. In 2005, despite another drug incident, Barry ran for DC City Council and won.

White House Press Secretary **James Brady**, who barely survived being shot in the head during the 1981 assassination attempt on President Ronald Reagan, became, along with his wife, the most passionate and successful gun control advocate in the country. **William DeVries**, the famous cardiothoracic surgeon, implanted the first artificial heart in a human being (Barney Clark) in 1982. Nixon's Assistant to the President for Domestic Affairs **John Ehrlichman** and White House Chief of Staff **H.R. Haldeman** were central figures, who had their careers destroyed in the Watergate scandal. **Andy Looney** became a cult figure among video game designers. **Henry Nicols**, a hemophiliac who contracted AIDS from one of thousands of blood transfusions became an internationally known AIDS activist in 1991 when he announced that he would use educating others about his illness as his Eagle service project. In 2000, he died at age 26 after a car crash on the way to a Scouting event.

David Lynch directed some of the most surreal and disturbing films ever to emerge from Hollywood. As an Eagle candidate, Lynch joined an honor guard outside the White House during the Kennedy inauguration. **Michael Moore** earned his Eagle in Flint, Michigan, at age 16, two years before he was elected to the local school board and embarked on his Academy Award-winning career of social activism and radical politics in film making. **George Moore** became writer and producer of *The Simpsons*, while **Bill Amend** created the comic strip *Fox Trot*. Television personality **Mike Rowe** became host of the popular cable series *Dirty Jobs*. Journalist **Ray Suarez** became a long-time news correspondent on the *PBS Newshour*.

Paul Theroux, who earned his Eagle with a Medford, Massachusetts, troop in 1955 became a novelist and one of America's most celebrated travel writers. **Leonard Tower** was a computer hacker before helping found the Free Software Foundation. **David Foreman** was co-founder of the environmental activist group Earth First!

When he was a schoolboy in the inner city of Los Angeles, **Chuck Smith** dreamed of ham radio and building rockets. But he was black, dyslexic and very shy. When he finally built up the courage to tell his teacher of his dreams, "She looked at me and said, 'Get away from me. You'll be lucky if you ever get out of school.' I went home, and I just cried."

But Smith's parents introduced him to a fellow ham radio enthusiast, who was also a Scoutmaster. He told the boy, "You not only can learn about radio, but there's a way you can learn about life—how to survive, how to be a leader. I've got just the organization for you." Smith not only earned his Eagle but went to college and soon thereafter, joined Pacific Bell (later Pacific Telephone). "Many of the things you do as a first-level manager, I did as a senior patrol leader. They weren't difficult, so I immediately started to rise in the telephone business."

Forty years later, Chuck Smith, now a Distinguished Eagle, was president and CEO of the 42,000 employee AT&T West, serving customers in California and Nevada. "I attribute that all to my Scouting education and background."

In 1982, symbolically closing the door on Scouting's recently troubled past and opening a new one on a more stable and optimistic future, a young, 13-year-old Life Scout named **Alexander Holsinger**, from the unlikely named city of Normal, Illinois, become the 1 millionth Boy Scout to earn his Eagle award.[25]

Alex Holsinger as he takes the call from President Ronald Reagan congratulating him on being America's 1 millionth Eagle Scout in 1982.

The year before, 30,000 Scouts had poured into the 11th National Jamboree at its new location at Fort A.P. Hill, Virginia—the first increase in attendance in nearly a decade. By the time Scouting celebrated its 75th anniversary in 1985 with the theme: "The Spirit Lives On," the missteps of the previous decade had been all but forgotten. The next two jamborees would continue to see increases in attendance. In 1988, showing its renewed prowess, Scouting successfully attempted a new national initiative, "Scouting for Food." The program, designed to gather food and clothing for the homeless and poor, drew headlines when it collected more than 60 million food items.[26]

Boy Scouting was back.

EAGLE SCOUT, SUPERSTAR

On May 24, 1989, crowds formed long lines in front of theaters across America in anticipation of the opening of the third installment of one of the most popular movie series in history.

Early reviews were strong. Not only did the film have a fast-moving and entertaining plot, it also had an impeccable pedigree: the producer and director were the most successful ever in their respective professions and to the cast had been added an older, legendary movie idol and the hottest new teen star.

The rapt audiences, in hundreds of movie palaces and strip mall multiplexes cheered as the opening scene—a vista of Arches National Park in Moab, Utah—unfolded across the screen and the title appeared:

INDIANA JONES and THE LAST CRUSADE

As the names of the lead actors—Harrison Ford, River Phoenix, Sean Connery—appeared one after another in the foreground, the background filled with a line of figures on horseback in wide-brimmed campaign hats, yellow neckerchiefs, dark khaki uniforms, and puttees. They are wearing backpacks, and the second horseman—the guidon bearer—holds a staff with a pennant.

These aren't the modern Boy Scouts of iPhones and rules about rope bridges being no taller than five feet because of legal fears, this is the Scout troop of myth—riding horses into the wilderness and led by a mustachioed Scoutmaster.

Beneath a tall rock arch, that Scoutmaster, Mr. Havelock, who wears a high-collared uniform, binoculars slung over his shoulder, and a whistle dangling from his left pocket, orders a halt. As he commands, "Dismount" everyone climbs out of the saddle crisply and in unison—except for the inevitable chunky Scout, who catches a foot in his stirrup and tumbles into the dust.

The next shot shows the Scouts climbing a jumble of rocks to enter the vast mouth of a cave. Inside the cave, one of the Scouts, apparently the senior patrol leader, hears a noise emanating from a side chamber. He pauses as the other Scouts pass on and, his face still in shadows, listens. Joined by the chunky, disheveled Scout, Herman, he heads into the side chamber.

He sees an opening to a chamber below, then a rope, and then the silhouette of a figure wearing a leather jacket, khakis, and a wide-brimmed fedora. The figure—whom the audience instantly assumes is Indiana Jones—is leading a work party and as the Scouts look on, one of the workers brings over an old wooden box. As the rest of the crew watches, the Jones figure sits at a table and carefully opens the lid. He pulls out an old golden crucifix: the Cross of Coronado. As the leader lifts his head to look at the dazzling artifact, the audience is stunned to discover that he isn't Jones, but some other person in identical dress.

The camera cuts to the two Scouts, who sit back in amazement at what they've just seen. The senior Scout takes off his campaign hat and leans forward—his face caught in the lantern light for the first time: he resembles nothing less than a cross between a Leyendecker Apollo and Norman Rockwell's third edition *Boy Scout Handbook* cover painting.

"Indiana," pleads Herman, "Indiana." The audience suddenly realizes that the senior patrol leader is, in fact, the young Indiana Jones. And in light of all that it has learned about Jones from the first two movies, it instantly is appropriate that his younger self should be a Boy Scout.

The caption reads "Utah 1912." The chubby Scout wants to run but young Indiana will have none of it. "That cross is an important artifact," he tells Herman. "It belongs in a museum." And that means, left unsaid, is that he will have to steal it.

The idea to open *Indiana Jones and the Last Crusade* with the creation of the Jones persona came from the film's producer, George Lucas. But the execution was in the hands of two Eagle Scouts: film editor **Michael Kahn** and, most of all, director **Steven Spielberg**.

Spielberg was born in 1946 Cincinnati to an orthodox Jewish family. During his childhood, his family moved first to Haddon Heights, New Jersey, then to Scottsdale, Arizona. Young Steven entertained his friends by making Super 8 movies and charging them 25¢ to watch while his sister made popcorn.

Steven joined Scouting at age 12 and progressed through the ranks. And, like an estimated 40 percent of all Eagle Scouts, he found his adult career while working on a merit badge. In this case it was, not surprisingly, photography. As he later recalled, "My dad's still-camera was broken, so I asked the Scoutmaster if I could tell a story with my father's movie camera. He said yes and I got an idea to do a Western. I made it and got my merit badge. That was how it all started."[27]

Spielberg earned his Eagle in 1961 at age 15. By then he was busy making movies, even showing one at a local theater for a profit of $1.

When his parents divorced, Steven moved with his father to Saratoga, California, while his mother and sisters remained in Arizona. It was a difficult time—Steven later said he experienced anti-Semitic attacks during his single, senior year at Saratoga High. Nevertheless, this connection to the emerging Silicon Valley would prove to be fruitful to his future.

After graduation, Spielberg applied three times to the famous film school at USC but was turned down each time (it later gave him an honorary degree). Instead, he attended Cal State Long Beach—and more importantly, interned at Universal Studios. Soon, the internship eclipsed school and it would be a quarter century before Spielberg finally finished his degree at Long Beach State.

After making a short film whose name (*Amblin'*) would become that of his production company, Spielberg became the youngest director ever signed to a long-term deal by a major movie production company. He was 22.

The rest, of course, is movie history. Spielberg's adventure films (the

Indiana Jones tetralogy, the *Jurassic Park* trilogy, and *Jaws*) and science fiction films (*Close Encounters of the Third Kind, E.T., A.I.,* and so on) are among the most successful movies ever made—most becoming, each in turn, the highest-grossing films of all time. His "serious" films, from the TV movie *Duel* to *Schindler's List* and *Saving Private Ryan*, are among the most honored.

Both Spielberg and his films are regularly listed among the top 10 directors and movies in the film industry. In 1996, *Life* magazine named him the most important figure of his generation.

In 1989, when he was making *The Last Crusade*, Steven Spielberg was 43 years old, with a son of his own. Scouting also was at the forefront of his mind because he would be attending the national jamboree and introducing the new Cinematography merit badge he had helped to develop. And so, when the time came to shoot the "early Indiana Jones" opening of the film, Spielberg publicly announced that he had decided to make Young Indy a Boy Scout in honor of his Scouting experience.

In part because of the BSA's long-standing wariness of representations of Scouting on the silver screen (and in part because of the social upheavals of the previous two decades) Boy Scouts had not appeared prominently in a movie since at least the 1966 Fred MacMurray/Kurt Russell comedy *Follow Me, Boys!* and not in a serious role since long before that. And now, thanks to a middle-aged Eagle, the most famous action hero in movie history was appearing in a blockbuster film dressed in a Scout uniform—not for laughs, but as part of the explanation for how he had *become* such a hero.

And as the millions of audience members watched, River Phoenix as the Young Indian Jones crept down into the chamber and stole the cross, bent on returning it to the right authorities.

But he soon is spotted and takes off running into what would be the most expensive allegory of the Trail to Eagle ever made.

Emerging from the cave at full speed, Indiana looks around desperately for his fellow Scouts, he shouts for his Scoutmaster. There's nobody. With the perspective of the true hero, Indy mutters, "Is everyone lost but me?"

He looks back to see that he is still being chased by the men, so he runs to a rock ledge, whistles, and leaps to the back of his horse—and misses. Finally, he manages to mount and takes off at a gallop across the desert, the tomb raiders in hot pursuit in a car and truck. Ahead is a passing steam locomotive—pulling a circus train. Indy rides up and leaps aboard, the pursuers just behind him.

What follows is five minutes of classic Spielberg set-piece action, as young Indiana races from car to car, the others in hot pursuit, facing one outrageous situation after another: an anaconda emerging from a basin of water, a rhinoceros trying to impale him, a lion, a tank full of snakes. Spielberg makes this action even more engaging and entertaining by having each of these encounters serve as the obvious source of one piece or another of the fully formed Indiana Jones persona. Thus, the snakes are the source of his pathological fear of the creatures. The whip he grabs to hold off the lion—with which he manages to cut his chin—becomes not only the inept beginnings of Indiana's later mastery of the bullwhip, but also the fictional source of actor Harrison Ford's real-life chin scar.

The opening ends with young Indiana, having escaped his pursuers, arriving in town, and rushing into his father's study—only to discover that the man in the fedora and leather coat is right behind him, with the sheriff. The man takes the crucifix. As he does, we see the heart shape of the Life rank on the chest of Indy's Scout uniform. The man gives Indiana a look of admiration and says, "You lost today, kid, but that doesn't mean you have to like it." Then he takes off his fedora and places it on Indiana's head, hiding the boy's face.

When Indiana Jones lifts his face again, he is the middle-aged hero known to all.

Having passed a series of challenges, each of which in some way changes him forever; having, in the course of this, encountered the profession that will one day be his own; and having been almost invisibly guided towards this future by men who have served as his mentors, Life Scout Indiana Jones surely will earn his Eagle.

It is a path that Steven Spielberg knew well—one that he had once taken himself. And if his Trail to Eagle hadn't been quite as cinematic that of young Indiana Jones, it had affected Spielberg's adulthood just as deeply. Now, with his unequaled talent, he transformed that memory into an unforgettable fictional experience to be shared by the world—putting the cap on Scouting's return.

CHAPTER SEVEN

EAGLES ALL

T o the outside world, being an Eagle Scout typically is seen as learning to become accomplished at a particular portfolio of practical skills—camping, first aid, leadership, and other talents. But those who have experienced Scouting—especially Eagles themselves—know that the Eagle Scout award ultimately is about *character*.

The central role of character building in Scouting is visible most obviously whenever Scouts gather and recite the Scout Oath and Law—the former a direct descendant of the oaths of loyalty and honor sworn by elected officials, leaders, soldiers, and members of professional societies for millennia; the latter echoing those self-improvement lists of proper behavior, first created in the Enlightenment and studied assiduously by generations of young men—most famously, the young George Washington.

But the cultivation and celebration of character is, in fact, implicit in every part of Boy Scouting. That hoary old cliché of the Scout helping the old lady across the street endures because at its heart it captures something true about Scouting. Scouts are not only expected to help others but to go out of their way to do so. That imperative, embedded in the Scout slogan "Do a Good Turn Daily," is observed to a degree that often surprises people not involved in Scouting. Indeed, at his Eagle board of review, the honoree can expect to be asked what good turn he *did that day*. So deep is this notion of service as character that many adult Eagles still feel impelled to perform daily good deeds decades long after they've left Scouting. It is not surprising to learn that the favorite phrase of Scouting founder Lord Baden-Powell came from the diary of Captain John Smith, founder of Jamestown, in 1609: *We were born into this world, not for ourselves but to help others.*[1]

At every rank, Scouts are required to perform service within their community, to teach at least one skill to younger Scouts, and (at the higher ranks) to hold a leadership position in the troop. Each of these roles is more than it appears. For example, *service* to the community for a young Scout may mean a few hours with his patrol raking leaves at a local school, washing dishes at the sponsoring church, serving at a soup kitchen or devoting time to the Eagle service project of an older Scout in the troop.

Brief as this service may be, it also sets a pattern of behavior that will be cultivated with ever-greater commitments (for example, Life Scout candidates are required to perform six hours of service after earning their Star rank) through the boy's Scouting career and, with luck, through their entire lives. The culmination of this commitment is the Eagle Scout service project that must be devised, initiated and managed by the Scout, must make a real contribution to the community, and can consume scores, even hundreds, of hours. So consuming (and absorbing) is the Eagle service project that it typically sets a pattern of service that defines the rest of the Eagle's life.

Similarly, the *teaching* requirement that appears at every rank serves both an explicit and hidden role. Requiring a Scout at one rank to teach a Scout at a lower rank both adds to the instructional capital of the troop (that is, it doesn't put the entire task upon the adults) and reconfirms that the teaching Scout has indeed learned the skill. Scouting supports this process by providing a proven methodology—EDGE: Explain, Demonstrate, Guide, Enable—that can be used through his adult career.

But, once again, hidden behind this explicit requirement lies a second motive, *inclusiveness*—a philosophy Scouting developed decades before it became a cultural movement.

Boys tend to be naturally exclusive, typically clustering by class, age, talents, and attitudes. The 17-year-old athlete who spends his life thinking of cars, girls and college applications typically has nothing to do with an 11-year-old computer nerd who likes to draw superheroes and fly model airplanes.

But Scouting, from the beginning, shattered those boundaries. Requiring an older Scout to teach a younger Scout is part of this connection that almost never happens in daily life. During this encounter, the older Scout is dependent upon the younger one to succeed—a reversal of the natural order that teaches humility to one even as it motivates the other.

This inclusiveness is made even more enduring (and formal) in the third set of requirements found at every rank from Second Class to Eagle: *leadership*. Scouts, as they progress through the ranks, are required to assumed ever-greater responsibility for the successful Scouting experience of others, typically younger than themselves. At Second Class, this typically is the job of the assistant patrol leader, the back-up to the leadership of a patrol of six to ten other young Scouts.

The leadership roles then progress upwards through patrol leader, to assistant senior patrol leader, and ultimately to senior patrol leader—the last a job, usually held by a Life or Eagle Scout, that puts the Scout in the position of chief executive of a multi-level Scout troop with as many as one-hundred boys and an annual budget in the thousands of dollars. This level of training (the equivalent to an MBA with the experience of running a small enterprise) almost has no equivalent in American boyhood. And thus, it is no surprise that the roll of Eagle Scouts over the last century contains so many corporate CEOs, university presidents, and government officials.

But once again, there is another motive to this leadership training. That 17-year-old senior patrol leader likely will spend more of his six-month or year-long tenure interacting daily with the layer of management (13- and 14-year-old patrol leaders) than he will with his peers (who themselves will be managing other inclusive jobs, such as instructor). In the modern

Scout troop, this senior patrol leader and Eagle (or soon to be) probably will manage scores of Scouts just out of elementary school, a middle management composed of eighth graders and high school freshman, a multi-racial/multi-ethnic troop with a diverse range of needs ranging from vegetarianism to different religious rules, and all the while reporting to a Scoutmaster and troop committee of adults of similar diversity. It is hard to imagine a better training program for leaders in the 21st century global economy.

What ties all of these threads together (and finds its fullest embodiment in the Eagle Scout) is at the heart of Scouting as far back as the first experimental Scout camp on Brownsea Island off the southern coast of England in Poole Harbor in 1907: *character*. And, as reinforced by Scouting's rules and requirements, this notion of personal character takes several forms:

Character as honor – The Scout Oath famously begins with "On my honor..." It is a phrase that is more than mere promise but rather a statement of personal integrity. That is, in taking the Oath, the Scout or Scouter, also is placing his or her personal reputation for integrity on the line. This notion is echoed in the Scout Law's first tenet—Trustworthiness. This is an almost medieval notion of "honor," one that reaches beyond the shallowness of mere reputation to a core body of inviolate values. It is perhaps not surprising that knighthood, chivalry, and the "sacred honor" of the nation's Founders regularly reappears in Scouting iconography, from the Knights of Dunamis to the Scouts standing alongside George Washington in the Norman Rockwell posters.

Character as duty – The Oath continues with " ... to do my duty to God and my Country," which is again echoed in the second tenet of the Law, "Loyalty." In practice, it means that a Scout not only has a set of useful skills – notably first aid, outdoorsmanship, and leadership–but understands that he is obliged to use them when needed. The 45-year-old Eagle, who may have long forgotten how to tie a sheepshank, nevertheless understands when he encounters an injured individual or is asked to join a search party on a camping trip or to volunteer at an understaffed local charity, knows where his duty lies and steps up to the task, bringing his special skills with him.

Few young Eagles appreciate the power of this duty until they get to college. Then, when someone is hurt or a fire needs to be built or luggage strapped to the roof of a car, every head turns to him.

<u>Character as service</u> – One of the most compelling findings that came out of the Baylor University survey referenced elsewhere in this book is that adult Eagle Scouts on average *perform* much more service in their community than men who never were in Scouting—and even more than former Scouts who didn't earn their Eagle. It seems that from all of those service hours performed by these men on their Trail to Eagle in their youth, they somehow inculcated "serving others" into a pattern of behavior—a moral imperative. And America has benefitted greatly from it.

<u>Character as judgment</u> – A useful portfolio of skills, combined with a strong sense of duty, honor and service is not enough. The choice of when and how to apply those attributes is at least as important. The wrong treatment in first aid can have a devastating effect. That is why Scouts are regularly re-tested on their skills at meetings, camp-o-rees, and Scout-a-ramas. It also is one reason why adult Eagles regularly update their skills or re-connect with Scouting in some capacity.

But good judgment must also rule in the totality of a life lived with good character, in long-term choices, as well as decisions of the moment. At the macro level, the history of World Scouting is filled with examples of how a sense of duty can be misplaced, most notably in those ersatz "Scouting" organizations created by tyrannies and totalitarian states (most infamously, in Nazi Germany).

That's one reason why the Scout Law speaks of "God and Country" but yet the BSA itself has consistently stayed away from endorsed political parties or candidates. Each year, Scouting makes its *Annual Report* to the president of the United States, whoever sits in the Oval Office. Again, Scouting is inclusive and it consistently works to embed that inclusiveness into the judgment of Scouts, especially Eagles. That this judgment still will vary from Eagle to Eagle is proven by the wide range of individuals listed in this book who have earned their Eagle.

But in the end, the Boy Scouts of America believes–though it has sometimes taken time for it to reach this wisdom that good judgment always is made in the direction of human liberty (the ability to live according to one's conscience) and *freedom* (the ability to enjoy the same rights as the rest of society).

It goes without saying that sometimes these two forces collide. That is, after all, the history of the United States of America. But, like the country it serves, the BSA is willing to accept this contradiction and do so in a spirit of compromise (though it can sometimes lead to friction and pain). And, as a matter of "Honor," it expects its Eagles, even long after they've left Scouting, to do the same. That too is part of "Always an Eagle."

Indeed, as we'll see in the rest of this chapter, it is Scouting's Eagles who have presented the biggest challenges to Scouting's vision of itself, to its definition of true character, and to its claims of inclusiveness.

INDIVISIBLE

To its credit, from the very beginning the Boy Scouts of America established the standard that all boys in America would be eligible to join the organization. If today that seems a negligible achievement, it certainly wasn't the case in an early 20th century America that still featured legal black/white segregation, Jewish university admission quotas, and anti-Catholic/anti-immigrant societies.

It remains one of Scouting's greatest achievements that it accepted African American boys–some of them the actual sons of former slaves—from its beginning. In fact, one of America's first unofficial "Negro Boy Scout troops" was established in Elizabeth City, North Carolina, on July 31, 1911—just a year after the BSA's founding. The unit met with prejudice from the start but persevered and grew.

Also in mid-1911, African American Scoutmaster A.H. Edmonds of Evanston, Illinois, petitioned national BSA officials to grant a charter request for his unit. It was approved on May 6, 1912, probably making his Troop 1 the first officially sanctioned all-black troop in the country.

Four years later in 1916, the BSA officially recognized Troop 75 in Louisville, Kentucky. And within a year, four more official black troops had been founded in the region.

A.H Edmonds of Evanston, Illinois—recognized as the Scoutmaster of the first officially chartered African American troop in the nation in 1912.

By 1926, the year of **Edgar Cunningham Sr.** and the first African American Eagles, there were 248 black Boy Scout troops with nearly 5,000 Scouts. The next year, the BSA established an "Inter-Racial" committee led by Stanley Harris to establish program outreach to minorities. Progressive as it was, this committee still exhibited some of the unenlightened nature of the era: it combined black Scouts with rural, poor, and disabled boys, as well as new immigrants—all perceived as outsiders to national life. Obviously, Scouting's sense of inclusiveness still had a ways to go, but it still was astonishing for the time, and for a national organization.

Though some segregated councils still could be found well into the 1920s (especially in the South), they operated in violation of the BSA's by-laws and eventually were weeded out—making Scouting one of the first national institutions to be fully integrated by the 1970s. By then, there were tens of thousands of black Boy Scouts in the United States and hundreds of Eagles. And it was from the ranks of the latter that would come the Tuskegee Airmen and the African-American officers who helped to integrate the U.S. armed forces.

Still, it should be noted that desegregation was one thing, full integration at the troop level was another. Until World War II, separate black and white troops were the rule with the former often suffering from shortages of equipment and uniforms. By the beginning of the 1940s, that began to change in many parts of the country. But even as late as 1954, there still was only *one* integrated troop in the Old South. And the KKK still was occasionally breaking up camp-o-rees and other Scout gatherings, not just in the name of segregation, but also anti-Catholicism. However, black Scouting continued to grow, now producing thousands of Eagles each year.[2]

African Americans weren't the only minority to find a path into the American mainstream through Scouting early on. Given that much of the iconography of the organizations (notably Seton's Woodcraft Indians) as well Scouting itself (most famously, the Order of the Arrow) derived from Indian lore and legend, it's not surprising that one of the first ethnic groups to establish itself in Boy Scouts were Native Americans. Indeed, like African American Scouting, American Indian Scouting also is nearly as old as the organization itself.

The most venerable and storied Native American Scout institution is Troop 1 of Tulsa, Oklahoma. Founded February 8, 1910, it is the oldest troop in Oklahoma, the oldest BSA troop in the Indian Nations Council, and very nearly the oldest Boy Scout troop in the United States.[3]

Initially sponsored by a Sunday school class at the local First Christian Church, Troop 1 soon found itself rootless when the church school's superintendent saw the boys' uniforms and feared they were running a paramilitary organization. Troop 1 eventually decamped to the basement of the nearby First Presbyterian Church—which has remained its sponsoring organization for more than a century. For more than eighty of those years, the troop met in a "Sooner" log cabin built into the basement of the church. It was so iconic to Oklahoma Scouting that when the troop had to move in 2009, the cabin was dismantled painstakingly and moved to the new meeting site across the street.

Carved and burned into the logs of this cabin not only is the history of Troop 1, but also, like many old troops, the list of its Eagles. Thus, we know that the troop's first Eagle was **G.T. Bynum** in 1914. It would be nine years before the troop saw its second Eagle, **E.E. Shelby**. Over the subsequent century, Troop 1 has produced nearly 300 Eagles—and those Eagles have led the troop through a number of historic events, from serving as the honor guard to General Pershing on his return from World War I to attending BSA's 1st National Jamboree to the measurable impact of all of those scores of Eagle service projects on the city of Tulsa.

But Troop 1's greatest moment may have come in 1921. After race riots swept the city, many of its African American victims found shelter in Troop 1's basement, sleeping on the Scouts' summer camp cots. Meanwhile, the

Scouts themselves spent the days after the riot helping register a number of the victims for food and clothing relief.

Native American Scouting largely owed its strong and early start to government-run Indian schools that found in Scouting not only a familiar group activity for energetic boys, but also support in teaching about patriotism and Western culture.

The most famous Native American Scouting program is the Koshare Indian Dancers of Troop 232 in La Junta, Colorado.

Founded in 1933, it is dedicated to maintaining Native American culture through traditional Sioux, Kiowa, and Pueblo ceremonial dances. The Dancers utilize two parallel yet connected advancement tracks: one moves upwards through positions in each Scout's tribe, the other through the traditional Scout ranks (the former also requiring advancement in the latter). Thus, for the rank of Brave, a Koshare Dancer must not only make his own dance costume, learn several dances and study Indian lore, but also reach the rank of First Class and earn several related merit badges.

At the highest level, to become a clan chief of one of the three tribes, a Dancer must earn his Eagle Scout award. And each year, the troop elects one Eagle as Head Chief.

The Koshare Indian Dancers began in a chicken coop and a backyard. Today it practices at its kiva at the Koshare Indian Museum and present as many as sixty summer and winter ceremonial shows each year. Over the years, the Dancers of the troop have performed in 47 states.

The story of Asian American Scouting has taken a very different trajectory. Chinese immigrants in the U.S., especially in California, had been entering mainstream society for a half-century by the time of Scouting's founding and had created extensive and wealthy communities in San Francisco, Los Angeles, and New York City. These communities began forming Scout troops from the first days of the organization.

At the beginning of the 20th century, Japanese immigrants began arriving to work in agriculture. Ironically, Japanese American Scouting, after a comparatively slow start, received an impetus from World War II. Interned in camps across the West, Japanese American parents found few outlets for their children—except Scouting.

Soon, troops were springing up in all of the camps. They proved to be a useful tool for socialization and skill training in the bleakest of settings. It also was a powerful way for boys to reach out beyond the barbed wire. Some were allowed to camp with non-Japanese Scout troops—and to forge friendships that sometimes lasted a lifetime. The most famous of these took place at the internment camp at Heart Mountain, Wyoming, between future Congressman and Secretary of Transportation **Norm Mineta** and future Senator **Alan Simpson**.

Initially, the internment camp troops were led by young adult men (often former Scouts and Eagles), who themselves were looking for an outlet from the boredom of camp life. Then, when the U.S. government allowed these men to serve in the U.S. Army in Europe (notably in the 442 Regiment, the most decorated military unit of its size in American military history), they were replaced as Scoutmasters of their units by older Scouts, usually Eagles.

These Scoutmaster-soldiers, Eagles, and Scouts returned to their communities after the War often to discover they had lost everything. And it was these same individuals who helped to lead the Japanese American communities to one of the strongest economic revivals in the nation's history.

In 1975, **De Tan Nguyen**, 14 years old and already a veteran hospital worker in Vietnam, escaped from Saigon by boat just two days before the city's fall to the North Vietnamese Army. "I was one of the lucky ones," he recalls. "Two days after I left, the city was so chaotic I couldn't have gotten on a boat."

His subsequent journey took him first to the Philippines, then to a refugee camp on Guam. Finally, he reached Fort Indiantown Gap, a new refugee camp in Lebanon County, Pennsylvania, where he joined tens of thousands of Vietnamese and Cambodian refugees already in residence.

The official portrait of the BSA's National Director of Training De Tan Nguyen.

"I was a sixth-grade dropout with no English," says De Tan. "But many people pitched in to help me" he says, "particularly the Boy Scouts of America, the YMCA, and the Methodist Church."

He soon joined the local Troop 146 and in just three years, earned his Eagle. His service project? Restoring and refinishing totem poles—items he never had heard of just months before. Nguyen's decision to devote his life to helping others is, in part, his way of paying back those people who helped him in those difficult days.

"I decided to work for the Boy Scouts because I felt I grew up in the Scouts. I knew the good they do. I could help them help others."

Today, he is the National Director of Training/Learning Delivery in charge of personnel training at the Center for Professional Development (CPD) in Westlake, Texas, for the national office of the Boy Scouts of America. His staff trains both newly hired and experienced BSA employees from across the nation.

"De is an inspiration for all us," says John Erickson, former CPD director.

"Only in America could this happen," Nguyen says, "Where else in the world would such an opportunity be offered to an uneducated boy who, separated from his family, had been fending for himself on Saigon's war-torn streets since age 11"?

Hispanic immigrants have long proven a particular challenge to the Boy Scouts of America. Many of the parents of these young citizens have been refugees from nations where uniforms represent brutal and oppressive regimes. Not surprisingly, many are suspicious of official organizations of any kind–even one dedicated to camping and character-building. The Roman Catholic Church, one of the few trusted institutions in these often insular communities, has proven a great help, but the challenge remains a large one.

Hector A. "Tico" Perez is the child of Cuban immigrants living in Sanford, Florida. He earned his Eagle at age 15 and served as the local Order of the Arrow Lodge Chief and Section Chief. As an undergraduate at the University of Central Florida, he was both student body president and—a sign of things to come—and a volunteer fireman.

After graduating from Georgetown University law school, Perez joined a legal firm in Orlando. Though he remains an active attorney to this day, the law wasn't enough to occupy Perez's restless spirit and desire to serve his community. Returning to Florida, he ran for Congress in 2000, served as the political analyst for a local radio station, became a nationally syndicated commentator, started his own talk radio show ("Talkin' with Tico"), hosted his own Spanish-language weekly radio and television programs, and sat on numerous arts and government boards in Orlando and for the state of Florida that included the United Arts of Central Florida, the University of Central Florida, Alumni Association, the Orlando Utilities Commission, and the Greater Orlando Chamber of Commerce—being the first Hispanic ever to do so.

The official portrait of the BSA's National Scout Commissioner Tico Perez in 2010.

Through it all, the tireless Perez remained devoted to Scouting, first as a council president in Florida, next as area president, and then as president for BSA's entire Southern Region. He also earned Scouting's highest honors, including the Distinguished Eagle Scout Award, the Silver Buffalo for service to national Scouting, the Distinguished Service Award of the Order of the Arrow, and the Whitney M. Young Jr. Service Award for his support of minority Scouting.

In 2008, Perez was named BSA's National Scout Commissioner—being the highest volunteer position in Scouting after the National President—further underscoring Tico Perez as a likely candidate for the most successful Hispanic Eagle in Scouting history.

The United States always has been a nation of immigrants. There's no reason to believe that will not continue to be the case for generations to come. In recent years, the nation's high-tech communities, such as Silicon Valley, have seen an influx of immigrant professionals from China and India. And it is a rare troop in those communities that doesn't feature a number of new Scouts from those immigrant groups. Many already have graduated their first Eagles.

For more than a century now, the Boy Scouts of America has dedicated itself to accepting every boy who wants to join. No doubt that will be true of Scouting for the next century, as well.

Character, after all, has no color.

ON THEIR OWN

One challenge Scouting faced in being open to all boys (even greater than in its early years) was that of the isolated boy. In today's increasingly urbanized and suburbanized America, it is a rare young man who is so far from any Scout organization that it is, practically speaking, impossible for him to participate.

But that wasn't always the case. In the second decade of the 20th century there still were hundreds of thousands of young men scattered across the landscape in homesteads and very small towns for which there wasn't the critical mass of young people to create a Scouting patrol, much less a troop. Moreover, unlike today's wired world, many of these boys had no access even to school libraries; rural mail delivery was irregular, and some even lacked electricity. If Scouting was going to live up to its promise of inclusiveness, it knew it would have to come up with a radical solution.

That solution came in 1915 with the creation of the Lone Scouts of America (LSA), founded by Boy Scout co-incorporator William D. Boyce specifically to serve Scouts who were unable to participate in traditional Scouting. That list—with its echoes of child labor, harvesters moving across the prairie, reform schools, and quarantine signs nailed to front doors—includes the following reasons:

- Children of American citizens who live abroad,
- Exchange students who live outside the United States,
- Boys with disabilities,
- Boys in rural communities,
- Sons of migrant farm workers,

- Boys who have jobs that conflict with troop meetings,

- Boys who have alternate living arrangements with parents who live in different

- Boys who are unable to attend unit meetings because of life-threatening communicable diseases.

The implicit goal of Lone Scouting was to enable isolated boys across the country (and around the world in the case of children of diplomats and businesspeople living in foreign lands) to enjoy as much of the Scouting experience as possible alone and without the usual benefits of patrols, troop members, and campouts.

Establishing himself as "Chief Totem," Boyce developed a series of alternative requirements, the training for which came from a library of official manuals, and a substantial correspondence program between the Lone Scout and LSA headquarters. Lone Scouting ultimately offered seven ranks, or degrees, the lowest being First or Lone Scout. Scouts earned these ranks through three paths: degree work, literary achievement, and promoting the organization.

Just how many Lone Scouts actually earned the Seventh Degree is unknown. It is known that by 1922, there were 490,000 Lone Scouts—an extraordinary number and a measure of the demand across America for this program. That said, it also was hugely expensive and difficult to manage. So, in 1924, Boyce decided to merge the LSA into Boy Scouting. Henceforth, Lone Scouts, with the assistance of some alternative requirements, would peruse the same trail to Eagle as all other Boy Scouts.

An estimated 45,000 Lone Scouts crossed over to the BSA. The rest, it is assumed, continued with the residual LSA program, then aged out. Henceforth, the Lone Scout would be a Boy Scout.

Lone Scouting continues to be a part of Scouting to this day, though the social and economic changes that have swept across America over the last century have kept its membership quite small—especially after overseas Lone Scouts were merged into special international Scout troops. In fact, by the end of the 20th century there were just 364 active Lone Scouts with many of them living on islands or in the backcountry of Alaska.

No more books and letters for this latest generation of Lone Scouts—they use the Internet for skills training, advancement, and are advised and signed off for advancement via email or Skype to counselors assigned to them by the nearest BSA council.

As one might imagine, being a Lone Scout was, and is, not an easy task. And advancement, without the hands-on support of adult Scouters and the teamwork of fellow patrol members, is harder still. And yet Eagles are a breed apart, even when they have to advance on their own, and an impressive number of Lone Scouts have managed to earn Scouting's highest rank. These "Lone Eagles" may be the rarest of all Scouts to earn this award.

One survey, among East Texas councils, found a total of 10 Lone Eagles from 1925 to 2000. The first, in 1929, was **Harvey Blailock** of Sweetwater, Texas. Given that this was just four years after the merger with the BSA, it is possible that Blailock was the very first Lone Eagle in the country.

In January 1985, two brothers named **Aaron** and **Mark Miles** of Barksdale, Texas, advanced through the ranks both through their Lone Scout work at home and through attending summer camp with the nearest troop, 227, located in Rocksprings. They also participated with the troop in camp-o-rees and joined the nearest council for a Canadian canoe trip. Though, as Lone Scouts, they were not eligible to join the Order of the Arrow; both brothers did so through an arrangement with Troop 227–Aaron even became a Vigil Honor member. Through it all, the Miles brothers managed to earn their Eagle.

One of the most recent Lone Eagles was even more isolated from traditional Scouting. Fifteen-year-old **Andrew Riddle** of the village of Put-in-Bay on Bass Island in northwest Ohio longed to be an Eagle Scout, but his tiny troop had neither the leaders nor the resources to help. So he signed up to be a Lone Scout—the only one of the 3,500 Scouts in his Council—and set out to do it on his own.

Less than two years later, he earned his Eagle—making him, it is believed, the only Lone Eagle in that area's history. "It just goes to show, if you want it bad enough, you can get it," he told the local newspaper.[4]

Riddle's advisor on his Trail to Eagle was the local school superintendent, Jim Stauffer. And he had to find his own merit badge counselors—sometimes having to leave the island to do so. For example, to earn the Personal Management merit badge, he had to take the ferry to Port Clinton. For Camping, he attended a district camp-o-ree with a Port Clinton troop. Moreover, he had to time these efforts to those seasons of the year when that part of Lake Erie wasn't frozen and the ferry not running.

Said Stauffer, "To go through the Eagle Scout program alone, that's a tough way to go because there's no one to help you. He's a hard worker. He's committed. He knows where he's headed, and he'll get there."

For his Eagle service project (five-day-long sports camps to help elementary school kids deal with the isolation of winter) Riddle used his high school classmates as volunteers.

Riddle later recalled, "[If] there wasn't one way we could do it, we found another. Improvised, I guess you could say." Asked if he had any regrets about missing the camaraderie and activities of being in a troop, Riddle replied in a common theme of most Lone Eagles: "I cherish the life that I live here on the island. I would not move for anything."[5]

THE CHARACTER OF SCOUTING

In its own way, the greatest achievement of the Boy Scouts of America–and its own greatest character test—has been its willingness to honor individuals with its highest award whom society traditionally has shunned, marginalized or made ineligible for honors. This has been the greatest test of its avowed commitment to inclusiveness; its claim to the primacy of character.

And nowhere has this been tested more often than with the rank of Eagle Scout. Eagles, after all, are supposed to be Scouting's shining exemplars, its paragons of the Scout Oath and Law, the tall, confident older boys in the Norman Rockwell paintings leading America into a shining future. But what of the boy in the wheelchair who can't hike the 50-miler or the young man with diminished capacity who can't possibly finish 21 merit badges by his 18th birthday or the Scout who has completed all of his Eagle requirements but who's lifestyle doesn't match the traditional meaning of the line in the Scout Oath about being "morally straight"? If the Eagle Scout award is ultimately about character, can any of these Scouts be judged wanting?

Scouting always has wrestled with these challenges to its vision of itself. To its credit, it never has been fully satisfied with its answers and regularly challenged itself to think again. And if sometimes it only found those answers after the rest of American society, to its greater credit, it often reached those answers—as with race—long before the rest of the country. And in one particular case, that of modifying the Eagle age requirements for Scouts of diminished mental capacity, the BSA exhibited a particular nobility of purpose and reminded the world that the Eagle award is about character above all.

Eagle Scout William J. McCanless, deaf, with the captain and staff captain of the S.S. Aquitania *upon his return from attending the 3ʳᵈ World Jamboree in Hungary as part of the BSA's contingent in September 1933.*

Scouting has continuously modified its special rules for Scouts with special needs for decades, trying to find the right balance between the abilities of young men to earn ranks and awards, while still providing sufficient challenges to help those same Scouts grow in character, skills, and confidence. These special rules take three forms:

Modifications – Upon application, Scouts may be allowed to modify existing requirements to match their disabilities, such as being able to push a wheelchair, rather than walk, to pass a hiking requirement. In some cases, Scouts may be allowed to earn alternative merit badges to those required for Eagle.

Alternatives – The BSA also has created a series of alternative rank requirements for special needs Scouts, who, with approval, may pass them instead while still earning the standard ranks, including Eagle.

Extension – Scouts who suffer a grievous illness or injury that keeps them temporarily from participating in the Scouting program may apply for a time extension on the 18th birthday deadline for membership in Boy Scouts and earning their Eagle. Scouts with mental diminishment or serious impairment, upon approval from the BSA, have no time requirement. They may take as much time as necessary, even well into adulthood, to earn their Eagle.

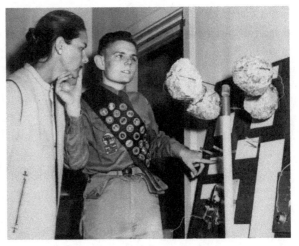

Richard Dwight of Berekely California, who's both blind and deaf, qualifying for his final merit badge for the Eagle Scout award with his teacher, Miss Jean Pollard, in March 1960.

Thanks to Scouting's willingness to modify the requirements for Eagle in special cases, every year we hear of numerous stories of the estimated 100,000 mentally or physically disabled Scouts overcoming unusual obstacles on their Trail to Eagle. As one might imagine, the stories of these young men are among the most moving in the history of the Eagle Award

In 2008, **Mathew McClain**, a 41-year-old Scout with special-needs Troop 216 in Anne Arundel County, Maryland, earned his Eagle after 23 years of regular attendance with his troop. McClain had not been expected to survive long after birth. And now, at an age when many of his contemporaries were returning to Scouting as middle-aged parents, McClain, with the new Eagle medal pinned to his chest, stood before a large crowd (including a state senator) and proudly thanked them for their help.[13]

In the coastal city of Bandon, Oregon, **Kyle Lawrence** completed his Eagle while attending a local junior college and preparing to transfer to Oregon State. A high school track, cross-country, and soccer athlete, Lawrence had been hit by a car in 2010 while walking home on Highway 101. He sustained life-threatening injuries and spent months in the hospital, well after his 18th birthday. He still was recovering from his injuries when he received his Eagle.

Said his Scoutmaster Jim Proehl to an audience that included many of Kyle's old high school classmates, "There are some things that, because of the accident, Kyle never will have a do-over." For example, his first day of senior year, playing soccer or running cross-country. "But this was one of the things that he did get a second chance—and we were glad the Boy Scouts of America [was] able to give him that."

Eagles run in the family of Philadelphia Scout **Brian Miller**, whose grandfather, father, and brother had earned the award. But there was some question how Brian, a student at the Overbrook School for the Blind, could complete the requirements even with Scouting's alternate requirements for the rank.

But Miller persevered, and against all odds, managed to earn his Eagle before his 18th birthday and to use the standard requirements. With one exception: in earning the Bird Study merit badge (that once-required badge that had ended the dreams of generations of potential Eagles), Miller was allowed to identify species of birds by their calls rather than by sight.

At one point along the trail, Miller came close to giving up. But, while working one summer at his council's Camp Ockanickon, Miller had an epiphany: "I could finally see the mountaintop," he recalled. "It would take serious devotion, but I could do it, and I did." He earned his Eagle in January 2010.

In 2009, **Justin Simmons**, 17, was completing his Eagle when he was killed in an automobile accident. At his funeral three high school friends and fellow Eagles, **Leighton Cline**, **Zach Colby**, and **Zack Owings**, approached Justin's mother and promised that they would complete his Eagle service project—building storage cubicles for the pre-school rooms of a local church in Jamestown, North Carolina where Justin had spent many hours as a volunteer.

Said Justin's father, "They wanted some kind of memorial to Justin that would remind people for years to come that he made a difference."

Upon completing the project, the three friends added one more item that wasn't in Justin's original plan: a plaque that reads "Eagle Scout Project of Justin Simmons—Completed by His Family, Friends and Troop 17 – 2010."[5]

For a small troop of just 22 Scouts, Troop 409 of Pensacola, Florida, is weighty with honors, including eight Eagle Scouts, a Scout whose story was covered on National Public Radio, and one Scout who earned the Honor Medal saving his father with the Heimlich Maneuver. Also, uniquely, as of 2010, Troop 409 still had ten of its original Scouts from the troop's original chartering 27 years before.

That last is possible because Troop 409, sponsored by the local Optimist Club, is a special needs troop whose members are not limited by the usual rank deadlines. They suffer a range of disabilities including Down syndrome, spina bifida, and autism

The troop members, most of whom either still live at home or group facilities and work day jobs in the community, are dedicated attendees at the Thursday night meetings. One Scout even puts on his uniform the day before to ensure everything is correct (giving his mother time to make any adjustments or sew on badges).

In action, Troop 409 is like every other Scout troop, learning skills at meetings, going on campouts, and attending summer camp. The difference, says Scoutmaster **Richard Coleman** is that they just take a bit longer to do things with some individual tasks being solved with group effort. As an example of the latter, Coleman points to a problem for one of the Scouts (who is in a wheelchair) getting around the sandy soil of camp. His fellow troop members came up with a solution: tying ropes to the wheelchair and, working together, pulling him to wherever he needed to go. "It was like a giant dogsled," recalled Coleman. "They saw the problem; they overcame it; it was a group effort."

Coleman himself is a remarkable figure. Earning his Eagle at 13, he stayed involved with Scouting wherever he traveled over the course of a 20-year Air Force career. Retiring to Pensacola, he once again set out to volunteer with local Scouting, which led him to becoming Scoutmaster of Troop 409—a job he took in 1988 "just on a temporary basis until we find someone." He and his wife had planned to spend their retirement sailing. Instead, Coleman stayed on as Scoutmaster for twenty-four years until his death in 2012.

One of the early members of Troop 409 was **Derek Connell**, now 59, who is still a Scout. Connell, who suffers from severe Asperger's Syndrome, earned his Eagle in 1995. His service project was refurbishing Pensacola's historic St. John's Cemetery, where his ancestors are buried. Connell's sense of duty didn't end with that project. For many years he has volunteered in a nearby park picking up pine cones before they jam up the city crew's mower. "And they never stop falling," he says.

Over the course of his Scouting career, Connell has earned more than 40 merit badges. His favorite is Disability Awareness—not least because he often is invited to teach about the badge and the life of the disabled to non-disabled Scouts from other troops.

In 2010, as troop historian, Derek was invited to record his troop's story, which later was aired on National Public Radio and currently is preserved in the Library of Congress.[7]

In 2006, Scout **A.J. Trueblood** completed the almost superhuman challenge of earning his Eagle while still in his 18th year. Trueblood, who suffers from Down Syndrome, refused to follow any special disabilities path but instead insisted on pursuing the official one to Eagle Scout. He didn't even list his disability when sending in his paperwork for the completed rank.

In making this decision, Trueblood presented himself with some singular challenges—not least, the requirements for public speaking—that were particularly difficult due to his speech impediment. There also were the various reports required for many of the merit badges and even the paperwork for the rank itself—all of which A.J. insisted on doing himself.

For his Eagle project, Trueblood landscaped Noah's Nest, a home for people with developmental disabilities. He drew the plans for the landscaping and grew the plants himself. He convinced a local company to donate a cement slab to serve as a patio and build a trellis.

One hundred people attended A.J. Trueblood's Eagle Court of Honor. True to form, he played the "Star-Spangled Banner" himself on the piano.[8]

Kurt Kozeny, a young man with Down Syndrome, poses for his official Eagle Scout portrait holding with his well-thumbed Handbook in September 1986.

As his 18th birthday approached, **Derek Slinger** raced to come up with a worthy Eagle service project. It wasn't easy, as Slinger, who already had 51 merit badges and was heavily involved in student government and theater at his high school, also was battling with the return of his cancer, a lethal form of osteosarcoma. Hospital stays already had cost him much of his junior year—though he still managed to attend Scout summer camp and continue his work with special-needs kids.

In light of his situation, the BSA gave Slinger an extension on his Eagle. It was time he used wisely. Having spent so much time in hospitals, Slinger knew as much as anyone of its boredom and isolation, especially for young people. His solution was to create a comic book, drawn by his friends, fellow Scouts, and his mother's co-workers to be handed out to young patients.

Unfortunately, the first attempt was a failure; the drawings just didn't work. But Derek Slinger didn't give up—and set out to create a different book, designed to help his 12-year-old sister, Leslee, and others deal with sibling illness.

Enter the Elves of Christmas Present, a voluntary group dedicated to helping fulfill the wishes of people facing difficult times at Christmas. The Elves had heard of Slinger's predicament and secretly set out to create this new book—not with amateur drawings but with the help of the Universal Press Syndicate, the world's largest newspaper syndicate. Universal Press in turn approached its legendary stable of cartoonists.

Fourteen cartoonists agreed (including Eagle Scout Bill Amend, creator of "Foxtrot," Jim Davis of "Garfield," and Tom Wilson of "Ziggy") with each contributing one or more cartoons for the Leslee book.

On Christmas Eve, as is the Elves' practice, there was a knock at the door of the Slinger home. The family answered and found themselves facing a group of young boys in elf costumes, each emblazoned with the title "Rookie Elf" led by a grown man dressed as "Chief Elf".

Derek and Leslee each were handed a gift. Leslee opened hers to find the first copy of the coloring book, "My Best Friend," filled with the cartoonists' drawings.

Derek opened his gift box to find an Eagle badge. Almost before he could react, the house had a second visitation, this time from three adult Scouters from the local district. They had come to conduct Derek's Eagle board of review—an experience he long had dreaded—in the family kitchen. As expected, he passed with flying colors.

Within months, 20,000 copies of the book, the printing costs donated by a publisher, were distributed to young patients in hospitals around the country. Calling Derek "a brave warrior," Carlos Castellanos, creator the comic "Baldo," would say, "I'm hopeful his project will offer, if even in a small way, enough of an escape from the daily rigors these children surely will have to endure, allowing them the focus, strength, and hope to overcome."

In 2005, Derek earned a standing ovation from nearly two thousand members of the audience at the Boy Scout's National Annual Meeting. In August 2006, after a three-year fight, Derek Slinger lost his battle with cancer.

Not all young men marginalized by society find themselves in that position because of geography, race or physical or mental abilities. One of the greatest challenges Scouting ever faced to its philosophy of inclusion and its commitment to character above all, came in the 21st century, when the organization's traditional rules—ones that reflected the larger society—were caught unprepared by a sudden shift in that society.

The larger issue of gays in Scouting is discussed elsewhere in this book (as are the critical role of gay Eagles, such as **Tim Curran** and **James Dale**). They drove the Movement towards the acceptance of homosexual youth in the organization—an inclusion that was voted upon and accepted at the 2013 BSA National Annual Meeting held in Grapevine, Texas.

What matters in this section about that debate and vote was that ultimately it came down, as it should have, to the questions of character (i.e., was it possible to be homosexual and of good character?) and inclusion (should the BSA deny the Scouting experience to a young man because of his sexual orientation?). Thus, even at a critical, even existential, moment in Scouting's history, the program still adhered to its core principles. And, probably because it did so, Scouting was able to navigate through these rough waters with a minimum of rancor or loss of membership.

OTHER TRAILS

Not every Scout pursuing a pinnacle achievement in Scouting chose the trail to Eagle Scout. And Scouting—not always without resistance to the latest competitor to the Eagle award—accommodated.

For example, from the early days of the BSA, Scouts have been able to earn religious medals of often considerable complexity for learning and service in their faiths. By the 21st century, Scouting offered more than three score medals and emblems representing more than 30 different religious groups, from Roman Catholicism (Ad Altare Dei, the first such medal, created in 1926 for the Archdiocese of Los Angeles) to Buddhism to Zoroastrianism, each with a difficult set of requirements that often took years to earn.

There also was the Hornaday Medal, one of the nation's most respected conservation awards—bestowed at the highest levels to only a few Scouts and Scouters each year for extraordinary contribution to the field. Exploring also had its own top medal, the GOLD (Growth Opportunity in Leadership Development) Award.

Sea Scouting presented the most venerable counterpart to the Eagle. This nautical wing of Scouting, which largely operated in its own world of sailing ships, power boats and regattas, was older than the BSA, having been founded in the UK in 1909 by Henry Warrington Baden-Powell, the oldest brother of Scouting's founder. In the United States, a distinct organization, the Rhode Island Sea Scouts briefly represented a real competition to the Boy Scouts of America in its earliest days—leading the BSA in 1912 to create its own organization, Sea Scouting, in response. Thus, Sea Scouts are as old as Eagle Scouts.

Though they never numbered (except during wartime) more than a few thousand members, they nevertheless remained an enduring and cherished part of Scouting. Where other Scouting organizations, such as the Knights of Dunamis, Air Scouts, and Rovers, faded away, Sea Scouting endures—and its highest honor, Quartermaster is fully the equal of the Eagle (it even has its own service requirement) and far, far rarer. In 2011, just forty Sea Scouts earned the Quartermaster medal—the Boy Scout emblem atop an anchor atop a ship's wheel on a dark blue ribbon—compared to more than 50,000 Eagle medals awarded that year.

Not surprisingly, given its rarity, the arcane skills required to earn it and its specialized subject, the Quartermaster Medal is one of the most admired and desired in all of Scouting. And given the number of Sea Scouts who go on to careers in the U.S. Navy and commercial shipping, the Quartermaster medal also is seen as a ticket to the fast track to ship command.

In its original incarnation, Exploring also had a supreme award, the Ranger Award. This program underwent a number of changes over the years after World War II—initially becoming part of Senior Scouting that encompassed Sea, Air, Rover, and Explorer Scouts (the last seen as the camping/outdoors continuation of traditional Boy Scouting). By the 1960s, only the first and last remained, with Exploring taking on the dual duties of traditional Scouting and career training, the latter in the form of specialized Explorer posts.

While most of these career-oriented posts provided apprenticeship training for such careers as law enforcement, emergency preparedness, and medicine, others took a more unusual path. Easily the most remarkable of these was created at Moffett Naval Air Station/NASA Ames Research Center in Mt. View, California, in the early 1970s. This post, filled with many future players in the then-emerging Silicon Valley, focused on programming, computer networks, and other digital technologies. Many of its Explorers would go on in the next few years to help found the Homebrew Computer Club, which in turn, through such new members such as Steve Wozniak, would go on create the personal computer revolution and transform the modern world.

This new, fast-moving society, created in part by those "computer Explorers," made the schizoid nature of traditional Exploring untenable. So, in 1998, the BSA split the program in two, creating Learning for Life that retained the Exploring label, and Venturing that operated as an extension of traditional Scouting to age 21.

For its first 15 years, Venturing offered its Scouts a combination of skill awards (including the enduring Ranger medal) and advancement awards. For the latter, Venturing restored the Silver Award, which had been Exploring's supreme award from 1948 to 1956, and which had been earned by about 18,000 Scouts. Then, at the end of 2014, Venturing, in a major reorganization, retired much of its existing awards system and replaced it with a new set of awards (though the legendary Ranger award managed to survive) that included as its supreme award the Summit Medal. This new medal paid homage to the original Explorer Silver Medal, but its requirements placed much greater emphasis on leadership and personal growth over skill acquisition.

Whatever its title, the Silver Medal likely will continue to play its unspoken role as Scouting's great "second chance." For many young men who came to Scouting late or who didn't appreciate the Eagle award until they ran out of the time, or who just missed earning the award by their 18th birthday, the Silver medal (and the Quartermaster medal) gives them an additional three years to reach Scouting's pinnacle.

Though this alternative scenario rarely is discussed, Scouting understands that many Scouts take this path and has accounted for it. Thus, any Scout or Scouter who has earned his Eagle, Quartermaster or Summit/Silver medal (as well as the Denali Medal of Scouting's less-formal Varsity program) is entitled to wear on his uniform the tri-color square knot normally associated with the Eagle award. It also works the other way: members of these "other" Scouting organizations may choose instead to pursue the traditional Scouting requirements and ranks—and, if they are not yet 18, can still earn their Eagle.

In 2012, the BSA announced a new initiative that stretched from Cub Scouting to Venturing. STEMNova was Scouting's response to the growing concern that America's youth were falling behind in the development of science, technology, engineering, and mathematical skills. It had two tiers: the basic STEMNova program in which younger Scouts in each program could earn badges for learning and practice in different disciplines, and SuperNova, for older Scouts, in which they could earn a bronze, silver or gold medal (each named for a famous scientist) for a more challenging combination of merit badges, research and study, teaching and field experiments. In Boy Scouts, the highest award that could be earned was the Thomas Edison SuperNova Silver Award. In Venturing, a Scout could go one step higher and earn the supreme Dr. Albert Einstein Supernova Gold Award.

In January 2015, Eagle Scout **Justin Kerr** became the first Scout ever to earn the SuperNova Einstein gold medal. In three years, he had earned 15 merit badges specifically for the award, read and watched numerous scientific articles and documentaries, taught science to a Cub Scout pack, participated in a national mathematics competition, devised the requirements for a new STEMNova badge, and, ultimately, conducted a professional-level scientific experiment. And he was presented his awards in turn by astronaut Dr. Bernard Harris, personal computer pioneer Steve Wozniak, and microprocessor inventor Federico Faggin.

But what made Kerr's achievement even more remarkable—and likely unique in Scouting history—was that he had been the first person in the nation to earn these awards at *every level*.

Kerr's Troop 466 in Sunnyvale, California, was one of the small cohort of packs, troops, and crews around the country as the beta site for the program—and one of the few to stay with it. As a result, Justin was in the first group of Scouts to earn a badge, and then a second and third. After that, with a small group of the troop's Eagles, he was the first in the nation to earn the Bronze (Dr. Sally Ride) and Silver (Wright Brothers) medals—the latter being the supreme STEMNova award in Scouting.

But that wasn't the end of it. After aging out of Scouting, Justin joined the troop's associated Venturing Crew 466 and left to study bio-engineering at the University of California, Irvine. And there, now working on his own, Justin set his mind to earning the SuperNova Gold. He completed it in late 2014. And like Arthur Eldred Jr. and BSA National more than a century before, the Silicon Valley Monterey Bay Council had to scramble to form a board of review to meet with him. And also like Eldred, the quiet and studious Kerr seemed, on reflection, the perfect first recipient of Scouting's newest top award.

Meanwhile, the title of Kerr's experiment and paper for his Einstein medal, "Expression, Purification and Biophysical Characterization of Reflectin Isoforms from *Doryteuthis Pealeii* and *Doryteuthis Forbesi*" should dissuade anyone who doubts the seriousness or the challenge of Scouting's STEMNova program. And, as with the Eagle service project, it points towards the level of competition to come.

CHAPTER EIGHT

GOLDEN EAGLES

Sergey's life Had the most difficult start imaginable. Born in 1994 at L.S. Berzon City Clinical Hospital no. 20 in the Siberian city of Krasnoyarsk, Russia, little Sergey was both premature—he weighed less than 2 pounds—and suffered from cerebral palsy.[1]

Sergey's parents, faced with huge costs and an uncertain future, abandoned him to what they assumed would be a life of perpetual care and institutionalization. But the hospital didn't give up on the baby boy and thanks to the heroic efforts of doctors and nurses (and a well-used incubator) little Sergey survived. And, although still very ill as he neared his first birthday, it was apparent that he would survive and that even his cerebral palsy was minor in severity.

That's when little Sergey got his second chance. L.S. Berzon City Clinical Hospital No. 20, like many Russian hospitals after the fall of the Soviet Union, was overwhelmed with orphans, and was regularly visited by childless Western married couples hoping to adopt and give those orphans an unimaginably better life.

Dwight and Jenny Griffith of the Baltimore suburb of Forest Hill, Maryland was just such a couple. And when they toured the hospital in Krasnoyarsk, they spotted tiny Sergey and fell in love with him.

They knew what they were getting into. Little Sergey, whom they soon would rename "Alexander," now was 11-months-old, but still in very bad shape. Recalled Dwight Griffith, "The first time we saw Alex, he had rickets and he was malnourished. At first Alex did not smile and hardly moved."[2]

But the Griffiths (Dwight is a successful home builder) were prepared to do whatever it took to give Alex a happy and healthy life and soon the little boy found himself with a new name—**Alex Griffith**—living with a new family, in new home, and on the other side of the world. And thanks to that loving family and world-class medical care, Alex grew into a healthy and typical suburban American boy, his days filled with school, life with his four adopted siblings, riding his dirt bike, and playing video games. Russia, of which Alex had no memory, existed only as anecdotes told by his parents and a few snapshots taken by them during their visit.

Still, Alex hadn't fully escaped his nightmarish beginnings. The symptoms of the cerebral palsy eventually disappeared but there proved to be other aftereffects—including attention deficit/hyperactivity disorder and impulsivity—that likely were the result of the limited medical care the hospital could give baby Sergey. So too, Alex's small size and fragile frame were a reminder of the rickets and other signs of malnutrition the Griffiths saw that first day.

By nature a plucky kid, Alex didn't let those limitations slow him down. And when he turned 11 in 2005, Alex joined Boy Scout Troop 809 in Forest Hill. A clever and committed kid, he quickly rose through the ranks, and at the comparatively young age of 13, Alex reached the point that comes in the career of every successful Scout—when he began to ponder the ultimate challenge that lay ahead: the Eagle Scout service project.

Most Scouts, when faced with their Eagle project, look to local institutions—church, school, the local parks, and recreation department—for potential project ideas. A small fraction (probably no more than a few percent) have greater ambitions: they want to leave their mark on the world.

Alex Griffith was one of this group. And unlike most other Eagle candidates, especially the ambitious ones, Alex didn't have to look far. He knew exactly whom he wanted to help with his project: the boys and girl sat the L.S.

Berzon City Clinical Hospital No. 20 in Krasnoyarsk, Russia, where Alex once had been.

"Russia is part of me and this hospital is part of me," said Alex. "They gave me life, so I [wanted] to give back to them, to give them a fun place to play."[3]

But how? All Alex had to work from was his parent's limited memories of their brief visit to the hospital more than a dozen years before (and they had been looking for a child, not running an inspection) as well as a handful of quick, barely composed, snapshots of the place.

It was one of those photographs, easily overlooked by an uninvolved viewer that haunted young Alex. It showed a sad and dreary "playground" at the hospital that consisted of little more than a rusted swing set with a single rotting wooden seat and a sandbox that Alex characterized as "a mud pit because of all of the rain." The image captured a world so very different from the one that fortune had allowed Alex to grow up in.

Studying the photograph once more, now with a different eye, Alex Griffith knew what he had to do: he would build a new, state-of-the-art playground at the hospital where he was born.

The "Krasnoyarsk Playground Project," as it came to be called, consumed the next two-and-a-half years of Alex's life. During that time, he took advantage of his father's membership in the Rotary Club to convince that organization to mobilize in support of the project—an operation that eventually engaged 500 volunteers in five countries, including more than 100 in Russia. At the same time, Alex organized Scouts in the Baltimore area to conduct fund-raising through barbecues, car washes, and candy sales.

In the end, these many efforts raised $60,000—enough to enable Alex, who had also been doing extensive research on playground equipment, to purchase exactly the setup he wanted for the hospital. It also was enough money to ship the heavy parcels to Russia. Alex, his parents, and a small group of volunteers followed, arriving in early August 2009.

On August 12th (Alex's 16th birthday) at a dedication ceremony, the playground was unveiled. Hospital 20's young patients and their families were awestruck by the sight: swings, a rock wall, a climbing bridge, zip lines and, of course, a new sandbox. To capture the international spirit of the project, the entire playground was painted with a red, white, and blue motif. And, flanking the entrance stood two carved wooden statues, one of the Russian bear, and the other the American eagle.

As Alex told CNN, which named him one of its annual "Heroes," "It makes me feel awesome opening the playground on my 16th birthday. It's just made me really happy just being here."[4]

For Alex, as it is for many Scouts working toward the ultimate rank, the Krasnoyarsk Playground Eagle service project was a life-changing experience. During his visit, he and his father toured the hospital including the pediatric intensive care ward. There they saw, still in use, the ancient incubator that was Alex's home for the first months of his life. "It kept you alive," his tearful father told him.

It goes without saying that the children of Hospital 20 were thrilled by their new playground—a feeling made even richer by the knowledge that Alex Griffith was one of their own. Said 11-year-old Sonja Sultanova, a patient at the hospital, "I like this playground because when you slide on it all the sadness goes away. I think that Alex is a noble person."[5]

NESA REDUX

In January 2010, almost 60 years after it began, the largest youth community service project in history finally found its voice.

Like many important events in the story of Scouting, this announcement was made almost as a whisper, with considerable confusion, and it was destined to be heard—at least at first—by only a few.

The news announcement first appeared on the website of the National Eagle Scout Association (NESA), the BSA operation that manages all communications with Eagle Scouts new and old.

After its big launch at the two national jamboree sites (as well as the National Order of the Arrow Conference) in 1973, NESA had experienced a slow start—if not in membership, but in content. This was in large part because Scouting really did not know what to with it, other than use NESA as a giant mailing list/database it could tap someday as needed for local, regional, and national fund-raising, talent, and political support.

But for the hundreds of thousands of Eagles across America who allowed their connection to Scouting to lapse, NESA at first seemed little more than yet another alumni fund. And for older Eagles, especially those who had seen the lively, albeit small-scale, efforts of the Knights of Dunamis, its replacement seemed pretty short on either action or ambition.

Indeed, for the first two decades of NESA, the only contact most Eagles had with the organization occurred every few months with their receipt of the *Eagletter*, a three-times-per-year newsletter of the organization. A low-budget production, the *Eagletter* nevertheless became the de facto bulletin board for Eagles of every age.

Before the *Eagletter*, the BSA always had tried to sublimate Eagle Scouting into the larger Scouting universe. The Boy Scouts always had attempted to maintain a balance between celebrating the Eagle as the zenith of the Scouting experience; while at the same time, for fear of losing those same Eagles too early, never labeling Eagles as different from the rest of Scouting.

The half-century experiment of the Knights of Dunamis may have proven the desire of Eagles to stay engaged with Scouting, but also it warned the BSA that any such organization, if not tightly constrained, eventually would go renegade and set its own terms for that engagement.

The *Eagletter*, designed essentially as a newsletter for dues-paying NESA members, inadvertently proved a valuable touchstone for the Eagle Brotherhood, reminding its members that they still were part of a great, if almost invisible, Movement.

Subscribers (i.e., current and lifetime NESA members) quickly would skip to the middle pages to read about Eagles around the United States who had earned recent honors and promotions. Some were young men who had just earned their medal a year or two before and now were joining the military, heading off to a service academy or graduating with honors from college. Others were elderly men reaching the highest levels of government, the corporate world or their professions. Not until Wikipedia and other websites began publishing lists of famous Eagles a quarter-century later, would there be another location where older Eagles could revel in the success of their peers.

Less obvious but perhaps even more engaging was the page or two in each issue filled with photographs of "Eagle Families": two, three, even fourgenerations of men in a single family, all of whom had earned their Eagles, sometimes a half-century apart. If the member achievement pages were a reminder of the extraordinary career successes of Eagle Scouts, the "Families" page was the first real celebration of Eagle Scouting as a living tradition, and an enduring presence in American life.

Finally, more solemnly, there was a page or two dedicated to Eagle Scouts who recently had died. It was a standard obituary page with an important exception: along with the men of great age and accomplishment, there were also a surprising number of young men. Achievers also are often risk takers or young men and women in a hurry before their clock runs out. And to read these memorials to young men killed in battle or in a high adventure or from a fatal illness was to take consolation in the knowledge that, because of their Eagle, even their short lives had contained at least one enduring achievement.

Each spring issue of the *Eagletter* also would carry news of that year's newest crop of Eagle scholarship winners. A careful reader would notice that the number and size of these scholarships seemed to grow by the year. In time, NESA would manage a score of such scholarships offered to as many as 100 finalists and ranging in awards from $500 from the Epsilon Tau Pi Alpha Chapter of the University of Dayton to the $48,000 ($12,000 per year) Mabel and Lawrence S. Cooke Scholarship. In between were numerous scholarships from NESA and the BSA at the regional and national level, from religious institutions (with the most coming from the National Jewish Committee on Scouting), to academic institutions (from small regional Bible colleges to giants such as Stanford University and Texas A&M), to nonprofit associations such as the American Legion, VFW, and the National Society of the Sons of the American Revolution.

By the mid-1990s, these scholarships had become so numerous and large that they became their own source of identity (even the defining purpose) for NESA itself. Before the advent of the Web, many young Eagles joined NESA just for the *Eagletter* and its access to scholarship information (as well as for the distinctive neckerchief).

But beyond the scholarships, the newsletter (that slowly metamorphosed into a true magazine), the neckerchiefs, and other swag, NESA had little impact in the lives of America's Eagles. At the quadrennial national jamboree, the National Eagle Scout Association inevitably set up a tent to serve as a meeting place for visiting Eagles. The Association also held its own convention every four years, largely as an exercise in solidarity. In all, for its many achievements, in the 1990s NESA largely remained a giant organization without a greater purpose than to stand and wait, as the BSA's de facto reserves, for a call to action.

RETHINKING THE MODEL

As Eagle Scouting inched its way forward towards an independent purpose and identity, Scouting continued on its own hike home. The retrenchment began with Green Bar Bill's landmark 1979 *Handbook* had by the early 1990s pervaded all of Scouting with a new generation of Scouts and leaders never having known the Improved Scouting era. The baby boomers, who had swelled the ranks of Scouting in the 1950s and 1960s, and who had been largely absent now for two decades, began to return with their own sons— causing a secondary membership boomlet across the BSA, as well as a jump in adult Scouter volunteers.

Through these years, Scouting seemed content to keep its core operations while fine-tuning its specialty programs on the margins. The BSA opened the 1990s with the establishment of a new classroom program called "Learning for Life". Learning for Life, open to students from kindergarten through high school, evolved out of the inner-city programs first created in the 1970s by Improved Scouting. At that time, a number of schools in low- income neighborhoods had asked if Scouting could be integrated into the curriculum rather than be an after-school program.

At the end of the 1970s, as Scouting returned to its traditional philosophy, the In-School Scouting programs (often organized with the Girl Scouts and Campfire Girls) slowly evolved into Learning for Life, which was instituted formally in 1991. Learning for Life was distinctly different from Scouting not just because it eschewed such BSA stalwarts as the Oath and Law, but in a concession to the changing larger culture, one that would soon prove very important. Learning for Life didn't restrict membership by gender or residence.Still, one legacy matter did prove to be vexing: Exploring. This third major program of the Scouting triumvirate, designed for older teen boys to focus on both high adventure and career training, had become increasingly schizophrenic. There always had been "Scouting" Explorer posts that camped and hiked and focused on helping young men reach Eagle (if they were under 18) or the Silver Award (if they were beyond that birthday). At the same time, by the mid-1960s, a second and even more celebrated type of Explorer post—this one affiliated with law enforcement, law, medicine or other professional careers and serving as a kind of apprenticeship program—began to appear.

With the arrival of Learning for Life, these "worksite-related" Explorer posts migrated to that program—and kept the Exploring name. Meanwhile, the traditional posts, now orphaned, founded a new organization in 1998 with "Venturing." Exploring now largely focused on a new set of awards, notably the Young American medal, while Venturing retained the Eagle and Silver awards.

One obvious effect of this reorganization was that Scouting's rolls instantly lost a couple hundred thousand members. Given the BSA's still depressed numbers in the post-baby boom era, this kind of drop was dispiriting—even if it was easily explainable. After all, strictly speaking, this wasn't just a bookkeeping entry transfer: those Learning for Life Explorers no longer were on the Trail to Eagle or even the Silver Medal; they were gone from Scouting forever. Not surprisingly, jamboree attendance in the 1990s still hovered down around 30,000. Meanwhile, Learning for Life, that saw 700,000 members in its first year alone, was by any measure a huge success.[6]

But once again, Eagle Scouting—with its uniquely ambitious and disciplined aspirants—ran counter to expectations. At the dawn of the 1990s, the number of Scouts each year earning their Eagle once again crossed the 30,000 threshold—a number not seen since the early 1970s at the peak of the baby boom (where it peaked in 1973, at 46,966). One might have predicted a long-term slump in these numbers as Learning for Life drew away a sizable pool of potential Eagles. But, in fact, other than a brief dip in 1995, the number of new Eagles continued to advance year-by-year right through into the new century. In 1997, the number broke the 40,000 threshold for new Eagles, crossing that barrier for the first time in a quarter century.[7]

And it just kept going—despite the fact that the total membership of Scouting had continued to hover around 3 million, as it had for 20 years. In 2004, another barrier was broken: 50,377 Scouts earned their Eagle.[8] The legendary "2-percent" ratio of the number of Eagle Scouts to the overall total of all Scouts still held—but only because (thanks to recessions, depressions, war, and the Bird Study merit badge) the ratios were even lower in Scouting's first half century. Now, in a given year, that ratio was more like 4 - 6 percent—and in some competitive areas, where an Eagle was seen as an especially valuable line item on a university application, it was even higher than that.

It wasn't surprising, then, that in 2009, Scouting saw its 2 millionth Eagle Scout: **Anthony Thomas**, a 16-year-old Scout from Troop 471 of Burnsville, Minnesota. Thomas had been born just about the time Alexander Holsinger had earned the 1 millionth Eagle medal. In 2010, the centennial year of American Scouting, 56,176 Scouts earned their Eagle medal—the greatest single year number ever.[9]

Anthony Thomas of Burnsville, Minnesota—America's 2 millionth Eagle Scout in 2009.

Why this sudden increase in the percentage of new Eagles? One answer, as already noted, was the restored worth of the award (after the devaluation of the 1960s and 1970s) on college applications and in job interviews. For large sections of the population (both educated professionals and upwardly mobile blue-collar families) earning the Eagle was seen as just as much a teenage ticket to adult success as a high SAT score or a transcript full of AP courses.

A second reason was the growing systematization of the Trail to Eagle. A Boy Scout working toward his Eagle in 1925, 1945 or 1965 faced a truly difficult uphill path. For one thing, for those past Eagle candidates, each merit badge was major challenge: the Scout not only had to fulfill the requirements of the badge (many of which had heavier writing requirements than for modern Scouts), but also had to locate, contact, visit, and work with an adult who usually was a stranger. And then, having earned the requisite 11 required and 10 optional merit badges, the Eagle candidate then typicallyhad to submit to the grilling of a council board of review, again by adult strangers, in some distant courtroom or office building.

But, by 1985, and especially by 2005, the process had changed radically. Because of the new BSA Youth Protection Rules, Scouts now typically earned their merit badges with at least one other Scout or adult nearby, and from a merit badge counselor who was most likely a familiar parent from his troop. And there was an even easier way than that: week-long summer camps geared to enable dedicated Scouts to earn a half-dozen merit badges or more in just a matter of days or even more extreme: day-long local merit badge "midways" that typically made the merit-badge-earning process so systematic and easy that many troops banned their Scouts from attending them.

It wasn't surprising then to see Scouts going into their Eagle board of reviews—now typically manned by a couple troop parents and a district representative—with a once unheard-of 30 or more merit badges.

A third reason was the changing nature of the Scouts themselves. It is not a coincidence that Alex Griffith, whose story began this chapter, was a Russian baby adopted by American parents—or that Anthony Thomas, the 2 millionth Eagle, was adopted from South Korea. Early Scouting almost was exclusively white European, black African, and a small percentage of Native American boys. But, beginning with the end of the World War II and accelerating in the decades that followed, the United States absorbed one wave after another of new immigrants—Mexican, Southeast Asian, Russian, Saharan African, Indian and Pakistani, Latin American, Chinese and Korean, and South Sea Islander.

Like immigrants everywhere, most of these new Americans were anxious to dive into the daily life of their new country, to assimilate and succeed. And, as in the past, many of these immigrants focused on making sure their children participated fully in the life of the new culture—including Scouting. The BSA, which a generation before had been reviled for its perceived connection to the nation's establishment, its patriotism, and its traditional values, now saw that liability turn into an asset with millions of new immigrant families.

As a result, Scouting, which always had prided itself on ecumenicalism and tolerance, now found itself living out those ideals to a degree it never before had imagined. It wasn't surprising to find a 21st century Scout troop with parents speaking both English and a dozen different languages and dialects, and with the Scouts themselves professing to a score of different religious faiths and denominations. Those changes were dealt with through training, changes in official imagery, and new programs (such as "Interpreter" badges, changes in the required Citizenship in the World merit badge, and special adult awards for work with minority communities), and ultimately, with an ease that belied the conventional view of a "traditionalist" BSA.

Immigrant families answered Scouting's hospitality and easy assimilation by making it a popular doorway into American life. Many troops, especially on the two coasts, found themselves with new Scouts whose parents spoke little or no English, but who saw in troop meetings and campouts a way for their sons to enter daily life in the United States that wasn't possible in the increasingly immigrant-dominated public schools. Just as important, they saw the Eagle Scout award as the most American of childhood achievements— the ticket to adult success in the New World.

Though there is no official BSA record of the ethnic background of new Eagle Scouts in the 1990s and 2000s, even a brief glance at the names on the annual lists—or, better yet, attendance at a council annual awards dinner in, say, California, Florida or Texas—suggests a sizable and growing presence of first-generation American Eagles. It is from these ranks that much of the annual growth of new Eagles likely came during those two decades. And that in turn argues that not just Scouting, but the lure of the Eagle rank, has played a significant role in the assimilation of new Americans at the turn of the 21st century.

THE FINALISTS

In January 2010, the National Eagle Scout Association announced the creation of the *Glenn A. and Melinda W. Adams National Eagle Scout Service Project of the Year Award.*

As was often the case with 21st century Scouting, the announcement was low-key—little more than an announcement on the NESA website and in some other Scouting publications. It had been many years since the traditional media had covered anything Scouting other than various lawsuits and the quadrennial jamboree.

Even those Scouts and Scouters who read the announcement probably only saw it as yet one more Eagle scholarship program. But the nation's new Eagle Scouts, almost alone, had a glimmering that something fundamental had changed in the nature of being an Eagle—one that could prove to be turning point in the BSA—and that ultimately might even have a material impact on the world.When the figures came in about the total number of Eagle service hours per year, Glenn Adams was as thunderstruck as everybody else: "I remember looking at those figures in disbelief. Like every middle- aged Eagle, I assumed that today's Eagle projects were pretty much the same as my own and others I remembered from the 1970s. Even as a Scoutmaster, it hadn't registered with me that many of the new generation of Life Scouts were taking on Eagle projects far beyond anything we ever had imagined."

"When I saw those figures, especially the 200-hours-per-project average, and then as I read the workbooks and saw some of the amazing projects being done by these boys, I was staggered. It suddenly struck me that what I was seeing was not only the biggest untold story in Scouting, but also of American boyhood. Here was a leadership, management, and entrepreneurship program for teenage boys that was the equal of any MBA or executive development program offered anywhere. And because no one had ever seen the Big Picture before, no one had noticed."

For Adams, it was an epiphany. "It struck me that we were seeing, for the first time, the ultimate purpose of Scouting in the modern world— and that anything we could do to support the advancement of this purpose would benefit everyone on the planet. It also struck me that the best way to accomplish this would be to create a competition—Scouts love competition—for the best Eagle project of the year."

Adams was so convinced of the value of such a competition that, after conferring with his wife, he decided that the two of them would endow the annual competition with their own money.

The nature of this competition had yet to be finalized. Being Eagles themselves, the troika of Adams, NESA Director Bill Steele, and Chief Scout Executive Bob Mazzuca had a unique understanding of what motivated Eagles. And all agreed that while college scholarships would be a good start, the kind of Eagles likely to win such a competition probably would be top students already loaded up with scholarships from top schools. No, they agreed, what was needed for this competition was a new kind of award, one that would figuratively and literally attach to a Scout's Eagle medal for the rest of his life. The new Adams Award, they decided, would combine a scholarship and a special device that would be pinned to the Eagle medal ribbon.

That couldn't fail to capture the attention of every new Eagle in the country. After all, the last time the BSA had allowed anything to be pinned to the Eagle medal ribbon was the Eagle palm—and that was in 1927. So, this addition of the Adams Award device (it too would be in bronze, gold, and silver for the council, regional, and national levels) would, by Scouting standards, be a momentous event. With just a few dozen council, four regional, and one national award each year, the "Adams" quickly would become among the rarest and most desirable of all Scouting awards.

In an unconscious, and ironic, tribute to the creation of the original Eagle medal, NESA didn't actually have a design for the device when it announced the Adams Award. But it didn't need to: as with Arthur Eldred a century before, Eagle Scouts only needed to know that such an award *would* exist for thousands to begin pursuing it.

The January 2010 announcement made all 52,470 Eagles eligible for the competition, who had earned the rank in 2009. This group of applicants were made doubly unique: not only would the winners be the first to ever receive the Adams Award, but they would be the very last to conduct their Eagle service projects outside the influence of that award. There was no doubt in anyone's mind, especially after they saw the applications flowing in, that the lure of the Adams Award would take the Eagle project to a whole new level of achievement. And thus, the 2009 finalists would represent the last "pure" Eagle projects done entirely for the sake of earning the Eagle, and not with one eye on an even higher glittering prize.

NORTHEAST REGION		
Keith Edmund Brown	*Patriots' Path Council*, Florham Park, NJ	Built a 40-foot bridge across a stream on the Middle Brook Trail in Bridgewater Township, New Jersey. He did much of the work in mid-winter to be able to work on frozen ground, rather than mud.
Brian Hong-sui Ching	*Monmouth Council* Morganville, NJ	Built swimming pool cubbies for YMCA Camp Topanemus in Millstone, New Jersey.
James E. Collins Jr.	*Narragansett Council* Providence, RI	Made knotted rosary beads for men and women in the armed forces. His original goal was 200 beads, but thanks to community help, made a total of 700.
John A. Heck	*Greater Niagara Frontier Council* Buffalo, NY	Restored the german Evangelical Church Cemetery in West Seneca, New York.
Aaron E. Kreimer	*Greater Pittsburgh Council* Pittsburgh, PA	Built a memorial walkway for the Charles Morris Nursing Facility in Pittsburgh.

J. Colin McCormick	*Chester County Council* West Chester, PA	Provided school equipment for 405 students at Sixth Ward Elementary School in Pearl River, Louisiana.
Thomas R. Ritterhoff	*Southern New Jersey Council* Millville, NJ	Designed, built, and installed artificial fish reefs in Union Lake, Millville, New Jersey to create habitat for local fish.
Benjamin Shavitz	*Greater New York Council* New York, NY	Conducted a book drive benefiting the Metropolitan Hospital Center in East Harlem, New York.
Tyler L. Sibley	*Connecticut Rivers Council* East Hartford, CT	Built a one-acre public dog park for the town of Middlefield, Connecticut. The park featured fenced areas for large and small dogs.
Brian Elliott Slatky	*Suffolk County Council* Medford, NY	Built a Holocaust memorial garden, using "green" materials, at Congregation Sholom in Babylon, New york.
Zechariah D. Sparrow	*Transatlantic Council* Livomo, Italy	Refurbished the memorial to a crashed and killed Berlin Airlift pilot in Heroldishausen, germany. Sparrow and his crew traveled 400 km to complete the project.

CENTRAL REGION

Joshua Broze	*Blackhawk Area Council* Rockford, IL	Built a memorial garden for VFW Post 1461 in Belvidere, Illinois.

Derrick L. Gregg	*Lewis & Clark Council* Belleville, IL	Built an emergency helipad for the city of Highland, Illinois.
Timothy Crosby Judge Jr.	*Miami Valley Council* Dayton, OH	Organized a Memorial Day recognition event at the Dayton National Cemetery in Dayton, Ohio. Judge led 65 volunteers for three months sorting through 40,000 American flags to repair or retire damaged ones.
Christopher LaMarche	*Hiawathaland Council* Marquette, MI	A diver, LaMarche worked with the Coast guard to replace the navigational buoys on a historical shipwreck, the *E.R. Williams*, in Lake Michigan.
Charles J. Livesay III	*Greater St. Louis Area Council* St. Louis, MO	Organized an awareness event for the National Alopecia Areata Foundation in San Rafael, California.
Jacob Paul Edward Music	*Sagamore Council* Kokomo, IN	Renovated the playground at the St. James Lutheran Church and School in Lafayette, Indiana.
Thomas Geoffrey Reuter	*Samoset Council* Weston, WI	Created diagrams with safe- landing zones for medical helicopters serving Taylor County, Wisconsin.
Bryan Rothmeier	*Northern Star Council* St. Paul, MN	Organized a send off for the local National guard unit deploying to Iraq.

Jacob Peter Schowalter	*Bay-Lakes Council* Appleton, WI	Built a bell tower for the St. Peter of Alcantara Church in Port Washington, Wisconsin.
John Sewell	*Northeast Iowa Council* Dubuque, IA	Removed one mile of barbed- wire fencing from the Lost Canyon Wildlife Area near Cascade, Iowa. The project restored ancient animal movement patterns in the region.

SOUTHERN REGION

Preston F. Boyles	*Cherokee Area Council* Bartlesville, OK	Beautified two public parks in Nowata, Oklahoma.
Richard Denson	*Alabama-Florida Council* Dothan, AL	Upgraded access for those with disabilities to a playground at St. Columbia Catholic Church in Dothan, Alabama.
Alexander Scott Hutchins	*Piedmont Council* Gastonia, NC	Built an honorarium to Floyd's Creek veterans in Forest City, North Carolina.
John Anderson Morse	*Daniel Boone Council* Asheville, NC	Created four murals for ABCCM Veterans Restoration Quarters in Asheville, North Carolina.
Christopher A. Pyle	*Stonewall Jackson Area Council* Waynesboro, VA	Installed a memorial garden at the Emmanuel Episcopal Church in Harrisonburg, Virginia.

Zachary Wright	*Lincoln Heritage Council* Louisville, KY	Constructed a team-building course at the Pleasant Valley youth Camp in New Albany, Indiana.
Justin Aaron Yourman	*Tukabatchee Area Council* Montgomery, AL	Built accessible shooting platforms for those with disabilities for the Alabama Department of Conservation.
WESTERN REGION		
Johnathan Douglas Baird	*Los Padres Council* Santa Barbara, CA	Organized a multiphase organ and tissue donor awareness campaign.
Eisen Clark Gross	*Denver Area Council* Denver, CO	Replaced a 255-foot boardwalk over a wetland area along Bear Creek greenbelt in Lakewood, Colorado. The 1,300-hour project required replacing hundreds of boards with new pressure-treated ones, as well as building handicap-safe areas.
Michael Stephen Polowski	*Grand Canyon Council* Phoenix, AZ	Designed and built a rosary garden for the good Shepherd Center in Mesa, Arizona.

As such, these finalists, as they might be called, represented a new baseline of achievement for those Eagle candidates aspiring to do something great with their service projects. The finalists now were the new version of The List for the Adams Award generation. And, like The List before them, the impact of the finalist might well last for generations. For that reason, they deserve closer scrutiny. The table that follows lists the council and regional winners by region.

Each of these Eagles was the first to earn the bronze Adams Award device for their medals. Here are the first four regional winners of the gold Adams Award device. They also were council winners. In these four can be found a glimpse of what the best service projects will look like for at least the next generation of Eagles.

NORTHEASTERN REGION
Alex Griffith
Baltimore Area Council—Baltimore, MD
Alex Griffith's story, of building a playground for a children's hospital in which he was born in Krasnoyarsk, Russia began this chapter. Alex's project, which consumed nearly 2,000 hours, was carried by CNN, and was the cover of Eagle Scout magazine (the much-upgraded successor to the NESA *Eagletter*).

CENTRAL REGION
Justin Lee Mengon
Buckeye Council—Canton, OH
Justin Mengon renovated the Canal Fulton Heritage Society Museum building in Canal Fulton, Ohio. The tiny museum, housed in a two-century-old historic home that once was called the "smallest museum in America". Combined with an additional structure, it now holds one of the country's largest collections of canal-era artifacts. Justin and his team cleaned up the interior of the museum, restored parts of the damaged structure, and then gave the facility a new paint job—creating a regional showpiece.

SOUTHERN REGION
Torey McCleskey
Central Florida Council—Apopka, FL
Torey McCleskey, an avid diver, working with as many as 20 fellow Scouts at a time, as well as with members of the local Lockheed Martin dive club, fabricated a dozen "reef balls"—sophisticated four-foot diameter, multi-chambered, and perforated concrete domes that were designed to serve as the foundation of an artificial reef. Torey first had to construct the complex

molds out of fiberglass (with removable metal inserts for the perforations) then carefully fill those models with the rough liquid concrete. Meanwhile, he raised enough money to pay for the transport by truck of these heavy structures to the Reef Ball Foundation in Sarasota, where they became part of a local artificial reef construction. An interesting side note is that McCleskey, like Arthur Eldred before him, earned the Boy Scout Honor Medal for saving a life—while he was working on his Eagle.

WESTERN REGION
Patrick Talmadge Malone
Santa Clara County Council—San Jose, CA

"Tad" Malone convinced a famous Silicon Valley venture capitalist to purchase a 40-foot shipping container for him, which Tad then filled to the brim with thousands of textbooks, hundreds of used school uniforms, desks, computers, pianos, and school supplies donated from a half-dozen local public and private schools. Dubbed a "classroom in a box," Tad then convinced other Silicon Valley executives to fund the shipping of the container to Children's Town AIDS orphanage and school in Zambia, Africa—a process that took more than a year. The Zambian Minister of Education officially opened the container at a regional gathering and it was emptied and converted into the

school's new library. Tad's project, which took three years and consumed more than 3,000 hours, earned local and national network news coverage in the United States and a documentary on Zambian television.

On May 28, 2010, during the Boy Scouts of America's centennial year, at the

Tad Malone with Zambian children upon delivery of the "classroom in a box" container for his award winning Eagle Scout project.

Americanism Breakfast during the BSA's National Meeting in Dallas, Texas, NESA committee member and Distinguished Eagle **Thomas Owsley** was joined on stage by Glenn and Melinda Adams to announce the first-ever national winner of the Adams Award: Alex Griffith of Baltimore's Troop 809. And to great applause, Alex—now much taller and lankier than the boy who had returned to L.S. Berzon City Clinical Hospital No. 20 in Krasnoyarsk, Russia—took the stage to receive his award. It was apparent that not only had he changed since completing his Eagle project, but so had Eagle Scouting itself. As he reached out to take the award box from Glenn Adams, Alex was symbolically leading his fellow Scouts out of the second great epoch of Eagle Scouting—the Service Project Era—into something new and as yet unknown.

Already evident was that this new era, as defined by the Adams Award and its finalists, would have an even greater impact on Scouting and American life than the two eras that preceded it. And that the Eagle Scout project, the greatest youth volunteer community service initiative in history, was only just beginning.

Alex Griffith, the first recipient of the Adams Award, being congratulated by Glenn and Melinda Adams at the Americanism Breakfast at the BSA's National Annual Meeting in Dallas, Texas, in 2010. Photo courtesy of NESA.

In the years since those inaugural awards, Adams Award winners have only further burnished the reputation of the Eagle medal—and continued to set ever-higher standards for what constitutes a great Eagle service project. These have included: the restoration of several pioneer and veterans cemeteries that had fallen into decay, rejuvenating a memorial to a Vietnam War soldier, creating a ten-mile historic bike trail complete with historic markers, building numerous hiking trails, designing and building gardens and meditation areas at hospitals, nursing homes and women's shelters, establishing a free oil change program for single mothers, planting thousands of trees, sending 20,000 meals to flood victims in Colombia, organizing a rock concert to support a local food bank, organizing a Veterans Day parade and ceremony, building a venomous snake enclosure in a Florida zoo and a camel shelter in a California zoo, and restoring numerous creeks and streams.

The 2013 Adams Award national winner was Eagle **Elijah King**. He had been volunteering at the Cincinnati Veterans Administration Medical Center when he learned that the VA was helping put homeless veterans in apartments—but it can't provide furniture, kitchen items, or anything else. King set out to change that. Traveling 2,800 miles, raising $2,600, and logging more than 420 volunteer hours, King successfully furnished ten veteran's apartments.

Each year, the Adams competition seems to grow fiercer—just as Glenn and Melinda Adams planned—taking the nation's best Eagle service projects to levels, and scales of service no one would have imagined a half-century before when the requirement first was published. Who can doubt the next half-century will see prodigies of service unimaginable today? After all, that's what Eagle Scouts do—and always have done.

A BREED APART

As the 2012 Eagle Scout centenary approached, Baylor University set out to determine if America's Eagle Scouts were as special as they were claimed to be. Backed by a grant from the John Templeton Foundation, sociology professor Sung Joon Jang and Byron R. Johnson, distinguished professor of social sciences (they later were joined by post-doctoral fellow Young-Il Kim) set out to compare Eagle Scouts to their fellow Americans.

They began with this goal:

Previous studies have shown that participation in Scouting produces better citizens. And, there is no shortage of examples or anecdotal accounts that would affirm these findings. Surprisingly, however, there is very little scientific evidence to confirm the pro-social benefits associated with

Scouting or earning the rank of Eagle Scout. Thus, the central question of this study is to determine if participation in Scouting and ultimately becoming an Eagle Scout is associated with pro-social behavior and positive youth development that carries over into young adulthood and beyond.

And asked these questions:

Do youth participating in Scouting receive character-building advantages over youth that have not participated in Scouting? More specifically, do Eagle Scouts, because of the additional commitment and effort required to reach this rank, experience additional positive attributes that provide advantage and benefits to them over non-Scouts as well as other Scouts who never attain the rank of Eagle?

Their survey, which was conducted by the Gallup Organization, took place in October and November 2010. Gallup initially contacted 81,000 potential respondents then narrowed the number to 2,512 randomly selected adult male participants. Of this group, 134 were Eagle Scouts, 853 were former Scouts, and 1,502 never had been Scouts. The survey questions focused upon three main subjects: well-being, civic engagement, and character development.

The results astonished even adult Eagles who always had known they were special. Though former Scouts and non-Scouts sometimes approached them in specific areas, *Eagle Scouts showed greater, sometimes vastly greater, health in every category.* The following compares America's Eagles to non-Scouts. In summary, Eagles:

Established greater lifelong connections to family, friends, and neighbors. They were 46 percent more likely to say they talk with their neighbors at least once a month; 38 percent more likely to be close with their brothers and sisters; and 37 percent more likely to have extremely close friends.

Exhibited a higher sense of responsibility to give back through volunteering and donating. They were 73 percent more likely to have voted in the last election; 66 percent more likely to volunteer their time to a religious organization; 53 percent more likely to donate to a religious institution; and 34 percent more likely to donate money to nonreligious institutions or charities.

Enjoyed a greater connection and concern for their community. Compared to non-Scouts, America's Eagles were 87 percent more likely to belong to four or more civic or social groups or clubs; 76 percent more likely to have held a leadership position in their local community; and 56 percent more likely to indicate they have worked with neighbors to solve a community problem.

Exercised more self-discipline to plan ahead, set, and achieve goals. Compared to non-Scouts, Eagles were 84 percent more likely to keep a disaster supply kit in their home; 81 percent more likely to say they achieved a spiritual goal in the last year; 64 percent more likely to say they achieved a personal goal in the last year; and 49 percent more likely to say they achieved a financial goal in the last year.

Held higher self-expectations. Eagles were 52 percent more likely to agree they always try to exceed people's expectations; 47 percent more likely to agree they always try to do what is right; and 40 percent more likely to agree they work hard to get ahead.

Demonstrated greater appreciation and concern for the environment. Contrary to the myth held by many that Scouting was not a progressive movement, America's Eagles, compared to non-Scouts, were 92 percent more likely to be active in a group that worked to protect the environment; 50 percent more likely to agree they find a spiritual presence in nature; 42 percent more likely to visit a local, state, or national park; and 31 percent more likely to avoid using products that harm the environment.

Displayed increased respect for religion and religious diversity. Contrary to any myths about the intolerance of Scouting; Eagle Scouts were found to be 45 percent more likely to say they always treat people of other religions with respect; and 29 percent more likely to agree that most religions make a positive contribution to society.

Enjoyed an increased variety of hobbies and interests. As might be expected, Eagles were 95 percent more likely to go camping than their non-Scouting counterparts; but they also were 72 percent more likely to attend plays; concerts or live theater; 59 percent more likely to participate in boating activities; 39 percent more likely to read books; and 38 percent more likely to play a musical instrument.

Developed a greater commitment to lifelong learning. Compared to non-Scouts, America's Eagles were 80 percent more likely to have taken a course or class in the past year; and they were 40 percent more likely to say it is extremely important to learn something new every day.

Taken in isolation, any of these results would be impressive and a credit to Scouting. But taken as a whole, they are mind-boggling. It is as if you were to design the profile of the perfect American citizen—only to discover that it already had been done decades before and that millions of American men, young and old, could be found throughout the country who already fit that profile.

It should be noted, again to Scouting's credit, that the survey also found that adult men who had experienced *any* amount of Scouting showed better scores in most of these measures than those with no experience. That said, it was the Eagles who truly were off the charts—almost as if they were the product of a different, more enlightened society altogether. They were healthier, more patriotic, better neighbors, more conscientious, better stewards of nature, more committed to volunteer work and dedicated to self-improvement for the entire lives. Eagle Scouting, it seemed, not only was the "PhD of Boyhood," but also an unmatched preparation for a happy and enlightened adulthood.

Through its Eagles most of all, the Boy Scouts of America had fulfilled its own Oath to the United States made a century before: to create better citizens. It was a stunning, largely unheralded, achievement; one of the biggest in the nation's history.

So, why wasn't this better known? Why did it take a century and the research of a university sociology department, a religious foundation, and polling company finally to disclose this truth?

One obvious answer is that Scouting never really has known what to do with its Eagles—they always were too old, too independent, too dissimilar from the rest of Scouting, and too often, too much trouble. It wasn't, in fact, until the 21st century that Scouting finally found an organization with the right charter and the right leadership—the National Eagle Scout Association—to at last get its arms around that army of overachievers and success stories.

A second answer is that, though there was no empirical measure until the Baylor study, both Scouting and the general public always had known that Eagle Scouts were different and special. This book has charted just how Americans have long awarded Eagles with a distinct role in our society as the embodiment of integrity, competence, and character. And certainly the value of Eagles to our national life has long been implicit in our attitudes towards them.

But in the end, it just may be that the enduring low-key attention towards the towering success of America's Eagle Scouts is due to the Eagles themselves. For these millions of men, becoming an Eagle was one of—perhaps the—signal experience of their youth; the event that sent their lives on a very different trajectory. They cherish that experience and they privately honor their achievement. But, for most, it is almost sacred—not something to boast about or tower over others, because that would dishonor the rank and their own accomplishment.

However, these men know, more than anyone because they regularly test themselves, that ultimately the Eagle Scout award is about character.

And character speaks softly; it never shouts.

A GATHERING
OF EAGLES

*Washington, DC, July 2010—When it is 95 degrees,
the two guys you don't envy are Santa Claus and
the man in the bomb disposal helmet and gear.*[1]

There were a couple hundred of them, mostly old guys, hiding from the heat by standing under the trees on the Capitol Mall. What distinguished them from the 10,000 or so other marchers resting under the trees beside us was that the others all were under 18-years-old and wearing Boy Scout uniforms. The men hiding under the trees ranged in age up to 71 and mostly were wearing white shirts and khaki trousers.

They were the Eagles, designated as the closing contingent/grand finale of the 100th anniversary parade of the Boy Scouts of America—and their task was to march with the parade down Madison, turn right on 7th, then left for about a mile down Constitution Avenue—all the while trying to look like exemplars of that most famous of boyhood achievements: Eagle Scout.

Toward that end, other than the white shirt/khakis ensemble, the men were asked to wear symbols of their professions. Hence the heavily sweating, white-bearded guy in the Santa outfit. "It's all velvet," he said with dismay, holding an ice pack to his neck. And miserable as he was, it must have been nothing compared to the military officer in full camouflage fatigues who, just before the Eagles formed up, put on his thick, heavy "Hurt Locker" ensemble, complete with massive helmet.

There were others. An Army colonel in full dress uniform and ribbons. A doctor in his white smock. A couple younger guys in their old Scout uniforms, both with more than 100 merit badges each on their sashes. An old Scout in a uniform that must have been from the 1940s. Even the Bermudan diplomat with his blazer, tie, red shorts, and knee socks looked visibly uncomfortable. I stood by as a veteran journalist with a satchel over my shoulder and a MEDIA identification card around my neck. Several of the older men were among the last surviving Knights of Dunamis. And a few of the old-timers had been New Deal babies the last time Scouts had marched from the Capitol Mall.

The Gathering of Eagles processing down Constitution Avenue in Washington, DC, during the BSA's centennial year celebrations. Photo courtesy of NESA.

Many of these men had come thousands of miles to be here and planned to head down into Virginia, to Fort A.P. Hill, after this event to attend the Centennial Scout Jamboree. But, before everything else, they had to survive this parade.

After a couple hours of waiting, a young man with a bullhorn got the old Eagles to their feet and into formation on the street. The heat and humidity were overwhelming. And in the few minutes the men waited there, the hot asphalt already had begun to burn through the soles of their shoes.

Finally, with a cheer, they began to move, taking their place in the parade between an Eagle float and a big, helium-filled Eagle balloon. Somehow, the bomb disposal guy (everyone was worrying how he was managing inside his personal sauna) remained upright and moved forward. He probably was thinking that this was a cakewalk after Fallujah.

In the front row, Santa looked like he was melting. The merit badge boys seemed fresh, but some of the elderly guys in the back of the cohort already appeared soaked.

But the men held their heads high, sipped on water bottles, and tried to keep their ranks straight as they marched. That task became easier when, after the asphalt blast furnace of the intersection of 7th and Constitution, the roar of the crowd met the men.

The reviewing stand announced their arrival: "Ladies and Gentlemen, *America's Eagle Scouts!*"

A roar went up from the thousands lining the route. People cheered, waved, pointed out the men to their children, even saluted as the men— many now with eyes filled with tears—marched past. After all of the controversies and changes, America never had forgotten its Eagles.

Here in the 21st century, after more than a decade of controversy, Scouting was something many of these gentlemen rarely spoke of with their more sophisticated, right-minded friends and neighbors. And so, to now find themselves marching with legions of Scouts, representing its pinnacle of achievement, before thousands of people cheering their childhood accomplishment, was far more dumbfounding than even the heat.

Eagle Scouts marching during the BSA's centennial year parade.
Photo courtesy of NESA.

At the beginning of the parade, each of the Eagles had been given a small American flag. Now, with the crowds cheering, the men held those flags just a little higher. For each of them, becoming an Eagle was one of the defining events of their lives—their first truly important achievement— and now they had been allowed to honor that award by representing it before the world.

Or at least a small part of the world. What was equally striking about the parade (besides how many people were there), was just who wasn't there. Unlike 1937, when a Progressive president had embraced Scouting as an ally against Depression and war, the new Progressive president (and much of Congress), during a time of Recession and war, had decided to stay away. It was a stunning, even appalling, disconnect at a time of unprecedented numbers of fatherless boys and unemployed teenagers, when the United States had an unequaled need for trained young leaders. The unspoken message at the front of Sunday's parade was: *Here is the bright young future of America.* And at the back of the parade, the message of the Eagle ranks was: *Here's what Scouting can do.* But many people no longer were listening. Perhaps one day their children would.

The Eagles understood that. And still, as they started to drip with sweat and the older guys started to limp on their bad hips and arthritic knees, the men who once had conquered 50-mile hikes and Philmont's Tooth of Time, kept their pace with their chins up and acknowledged every cheer.

Even Santa and Bomb Disposal Guy maintained their stride. Once an Eagle, always an Eagle.

A Scoutmaster takes a photo of participants in the BSA's 2010 Anniversary parade in Washington, DC. Photo courtesy of NESA.

As the Eagles—to their great relief—neared the end of the parade at the Washington Monument, one of the men spotted a little Cub Scout, no more than seven and one of the tiniest on the parade route, waving his own flag. The gray-haired Eagle finally broke ranks and hobbled over to the boy. The Cub and his parents were astonished to see the man.

"Here," said the Eagle, handing the boy his flag, "I'll trade you." With the briefest hesitation, the Cub Scout made the swap.

"This was in the Parade of Eagles," the man told the boy before he turned to rejoin the march. "Keep it with you. And ten years from now bring it to your own Eagle Court of Honor. Then pass it on."

NOTES

CHAPTER ONE: THE PHD OF BOYHOOD

1. Calculations in support of this figure can be found in Chapter 7.
2. Boy Scouts of America, *Annual Report 2010*, p. 4.
3. Virtual Boy Scout Museum, Boy Scout Stuff 1910–1919. "The World and Scouting," http://www.virtualscoutmuseum.com/timeline.html; BSA National Archives.

CHAPTER TWO: PATHFINDER

1. David C. Scott, "The Origins of BSA's 1910 Handbook." *International Scouting Collectors Association (ISCA) Journal 6* (4; 2006): 6–13; BSA National Archives; David C. Scott, *The Scouting Party* (Irving, TX: Red Honor Press, 2010), p. 128.
2. Gary Twite, "BSA's First Eagle Scout," Eagle Scout.org (2005), http://www.eaglescout.org/history/ first_eagle.html.
3. Throughout its early history, the BSA claimed that 2 percent, then 3 percent of all registered Scouts would earn their Eagle. Today the BSA claims that number is about 4 percent historically, although the current rate approaches 8 percent annually.
4. Approximately 2 million merit badges are currently awarded each year (http://meritbadge.org/wiki/index. php/Merit_Badges_Earned). This means a modern Scout would have to earn an impossible 300,000 merit badges to match Eldred's ratio; Terry grove, *A Comprehensive Guide to the Eagle Scout Award* (Winter Park, FL: T. grove, 1991), p. 18.

CHAPTER THREE: SIR KNIGHT

1. National Eagle Scout Association (NESA) Archives, www.nesa.org.
2. Much of the Knights of Dunamis material for this chapter comes from three surviving notebook volumes (1925–1942, 1943–1972, and Manuals & Pamphlets of archival history from Knights of Dunamis, 1925 to 1974, including Raymond O. Hanson's correspondence, KD newsletters and flyers, and minutes from annual meetings and conferences. These volumes were provided by Kelly Williams of Pueblo, Colorado, and were used with the author's deep appreciation.
3. US Scouting Service Project, "Merit Badge History," http://usscouts.org/mb/history.asp.
4. Ward's Book of Days, "February 22," http://www.wardsbookofdays.com/22february.htm.
5. Chuck Wills, *Boy Scouts of America: A Centennial History* (BSA and New York: DK Publishing, 2009), p. 66.
6. J.C. Leyendecker, "Weapons for Liberty," 1917. (Poster and magazine cover), http://en.wikipedia.org/ wiki/File:Weapons_for_Liberty.jpg.
7. Boy Scouts of America, "History of the BSA—Highlights" (August 2009), http://www.scouting.org/ about/factsheets/bsa_history.aspx; "Effect of World War I on Children in the United States: Boy Scouts," Wikipedia, http://en.wikipedia.org/wiki/Effect_of_World_War_I_on_children_in_the_ United_States#Boy_Scouts.
8. History of the BSA, http://www.scouting.org/about/factsheets/bsa_history.aspx; William D. Murray, *History of the Boy Scouts of America* (New York: Boy Scouts of America, 1937), p. 112.
9. For a complete history of the BSA WWI war bond effort, see T.P. McDermott, "USA's Boy Scouts and World War I Liberty Loan Bonds," *SOSSI Journal*, May–June 2002, http://www.sossi.org/journal/ scouts-ww1-liberty-bonds.pdf.
10. Boy Scouts of America, "1910," *Decades Fact Sheet*, BSA, 2010, http://scouting.org/100years/100years/ SiteFiles/1000/Celebrating100years/100yearcds/docs/FactSheets/1910.pdf.
11. Murray, *History of the Boy Scouts of America*, pp. 126–127.
12. Boy Scouts of America, "Senior Scouts brochure," 1938.
13. "History and growth of Dunamis," *Dunamis Doings*, April 1934, p. 1.
14. Ibid., p. 2
15. Raymond O. Hanson, "Knights of Dunamis Manual of Ritual," 1936, p. 20.
16. Robert Peterson, "gathering of Eagles," *Scouting*, May–June 2000, p. 13.
17. *Knights of Dunamis* (1925–1942), from contemporary letters and correspondence.

18. "Program guide of Activities for Local Chapters issued by the grand Chapter of the Knights of Dunamis," January 1936.

19. "Dunamis Doings," June 1935, p. 7.

20. Boy Scouts of America, *The Guide Book of Senior Scouting* (New York, BSA, 1938), http://www.seniorscoutinghistory.org/archive/NationalDocs/3442.pdf.

21. Peterson, "gathering of Eagles," p. 13.

22. Indy Nelson, comp. *The History of Camp Royaneh, Operated by the San Francisco Bay Area Council* (2009), p. 10, http://sfbac-history.org/History%20Of%20Royaneh.pdf.

23. Boy Scouts of America, San Francisco Bay Area Council. "Knights of Dunamis, National Eagle Scout Honor Society History," San Francisco Bay Area Council History, http://sfbac-history.org/SFC-KOD. html.

CHAPTER FOUR: FIRE AND ICE

1. The primary source for the Siple section is Patricia Potter Wilson and Roger Leslie, *Eagle on Ice* (New York: Vantage Press, 2008).

2. Those who have read the history of polar exploration will know that there is some question whether Byrd and Bennett really did fly over the North Pole.

3. *Eagle on Ice*, p. 14.

4. *Eagle on Ice*, p. 28.

5. John T. McQuiston, "Milt Caniff, 81, creator of 'Steve Canyon' dies", *New York Times*, April 4, 1988, http://www.nytimes.com/1988/04/04/obituaries/milton-caniff-81-creator-of-steve-canyon-dies.html.

6. West Texas Scouting History, "Eagle Scouts," http://www.westtexasscoutinghistory.net/award_eaglepage.html.

7. National Eagle Scout Association, *Eagle Scout Roll of Honor: National Eagle Scout Registry*, "The History of the Eagle Scout Award," p. xiv, http://www.nesa.org/PDF/58-435.pdf.

8. Wills, *Boy Scouts of America: A Centennial History*, p.106.

9. Christopher Wagner, "Boys' Historic Uniforms: the 1930s," Historic Boy's Uniform Chronology Pages, http://histclo.com/youth/youth/chron/c1930.htm.

10. "The History of the Eagle Scout Award," p. xiv.

11. Wills, *Boy Scouts of America: A Centennial History*, pp. 114–116.

12. "National Geographic Society Presents Hubbard Medal to Dr. Paul A. Siple," *National Geographic*, June 1958, p. 793.

13. Ibid.

CHAPTER FIVE: SHOOTING THE MOON

1. The details of the Apollo 11 moon landing are from the official NASA archives, posted at The History Place, "Apollo 11," http://www.historyplace.com/unitedstates/apollo11/land.htm; orbital data from NASA, "Apollo 11," http://www.nasa.gov/mission_pages/apollo/missions/apollo11.html.

2. Ibid.

3. Wills, *Boy Scouts of America: A Centennial History*, pp. 111–112.

4. "The History of the Eagle Scout Award," p. xvi, http://www.nesa.org/PDF/58-435.pdf.

5. Ibid., p. xviii.

6. Ibid., p. xvii.

7. Wills, *Boy Scouts of America: A Centennial History*, p. 127.

8. Ibid.

9. Ibid., chart, p. 122.

10. "Scouting Quotes," Boy Scouts of America, Orange County Council, http://www.ocbsa.org/category/ about-ocbsa/scouting-quotes.

11. "Walmart," Wikipedia, http://en.wikipedia.org/wiki/Walmart.

12. Grand Teton Council, "Boys' Life Magazine," http://www.grandtetoncouncil.org/index.cfm?pageid=506.

13. Wills, *Boy Scouts of America: A Centennial History*, p. 122.

14. Ibid.

15. "National Scout Jamboree (Boy Scouts of America)," Wikipedia, http://en.wikipedia.org/wiki/National_ Scout_jamboree_(Boy_Scouts_of_America).

16. "The History of the Eagle Scout Award," p. xvi, http://www.nesa.org/PDF/58-435.pdf.

17. Boy Scouts of America, "History of the BSA—Highlights" (August 2009), http://www.scouting.org/ about/factsheets/bsa_history.aspx.

18. "The History of the Eagle Scout Award," p. xvi, http://www.nesa.org/PDF/58-435.pdf.

19. "Eagle Scout Requirements," http://www.troop97.net/bseagle.htm.

20. Gerald R. Ford Presidential Library and Museum, "gerald R. Ford Biography," http://www.ford.utexas.edu/grf/fordbiop.asp.

21. "Leslie Lynch King, Jr.," Wikipedia, http://en.wikipedia.org/wiki/Leslie_Lynch_King,_Sr.

22. Mark Ray, "Eagle Scouts Welcome President Gerald R. Ford Home," Scouting, March–April 2007.

23. goDeke.org, "Brother Gerald R. Ford, Jr., Omicron '35 Remembered," http://www.godeke.org/History/ gerald_Ford_Remembered.htm.

24. "Gerald Ford—Football Player," *Packerville U.S.A.*, October 31, 2007, http://packerville.blogspot. com/2007_10_01_archive.html.

25. Gleaves Whitney, "Model Ford," *National Review Online*, November 14, 2006, http://www. nationalreview.com/articles/219249/model-ford/gleaves-whitney.

26. James Cannon, "Gerald R. Ford," PBS.org, Character Above All, http://www.pbs.org/newshour/ character/essays/ford.html.

27. "President Gerald R. Ford Remarks on Taking Office," The History Place, great Speeches Collection, August 9, 1974, http://www.historyplace.com/speeches/ford-sworn.htm.

28. "Remarks by President Gerald Ford on Taking the Oath of Office as President," watergate.info, August 9, 1974, http://watergate.info/ford/ford-swearing-in.shtml.

29. "Jimmy Carter Remembers Gerald Ford," CNN (Transcript), January 3, 2007, http://www. jimmycarterlibrary.gov/documents/carter_ford.pdf.

30. John R. Fulton, Jr., "Eagle Scouts Welcome Gerald Ford Home," *Scouting*, Mar–Apr 2007, http://www. scoutingmagazine.org/issues/0703/a-ford.html.

31. Bryan Wendell, "Adventure Base 100, Vol. 18 grand Rapids, Michigan," Bryan on Scouting (blog), May 24, 2010, http://blog.scoutingmagazine.org/category/adventure-base-100/page/2.

32. Phil Gioia, interview by the author, January, 2011.

33. Ibid.

34. Ibid.

35. "National Scout jamboree (Boy Scouts of America)," Wikipedia, http://en.wikipedia.org/wiki/National_ Scout_jamboree_(Boy_Scouts_of_America).

36. Wills, *Boy Scouts of America: A Centennial History*, pp. 161, 164.

37. Eric M. Jones, "One Small Step," Apollo 11 Lunar Surface Journal, http://www.hq.nasa.gov/alsj/a11/ a11.step.html.

38. Ibid.

CHAPTER SIX: LOST AND FOUND

1. Wills, Boy Scouts of America: A Centennial History, p. 187.

2. Ibid., p. 159.

3. Robert Peterson, "The Perfect Book for a Desert Island," *Scouting*, September 1999, http://www.scoutingmagazine.org/issues/9909/a-book.html.

4. Wills, *Boy Scouts of America: A Centennial History*, p. 171.

5. Ibid., p. 173.

6. Ibid., p. 171.

7. "The Nation: Windmill Power," *Time*, Dec. 2, 1974, http://www.time.com/time/magazine/ article/0,9171,945280,00.html.

8. Steve Henning, comp., "Merit Badges, Past and Present, and Their Evolution," Henning's Scouters' Pages, http://www.scouters.us/homemb.html; Terry grove, A Comprehensive guide to the Eagle Scout Award, (Winter Park, FL: T. grove, 2004) p. 19.

9. Ibid.

10. "Twelve for '12", Eagle Call magazine, Fall 2013, pg. 21.

11. "Distinguished Eagle Scout Award," Wikipedia, http://en.wikipedia.org/wiki/Distinguished_Eagle_ Scout_Award.

12. Wills, Boy Scouts of America: A Centennial History, p. 181. 12. Ibid., p.188.

13. "National Scout Jamboree (Boy Scouts of America)," Wikipedia, http://en.wikipedia.org/wiki/National_ Scout_jamboree_(Boy_Scouts_of_America).

14. Robert Peterson, "Bill Hillcourt—Still going Strong on the Scouting Trail," Scouting, September 1985, p. 26.

15. Wills, Boy Scouts of America: A Centennial History, p. 147.

16. Ibid., p. 147.

17. "National Scout jamboree (Boy Scouts of America)," Wikipedia, http://en.wikipedia.org/wiki/National_ Scout_ jamboree_(Boy_Scouts_of_America).

18. Wills, Boy Scouts of America: A Centennial History, p. 196.

19. Ibid.

20. "William Hillcourt," Wikipedia, http://en.wikipedia.org/wiki/William_Hillcourt.

21. Scout Handbook, eighth edition, 1973, pp. 79–81.

22. Wills, Boy Scouts of America: A Centennial History, pp. 199–200.

23. Richard H. Truly (Vice Admiral, USN, Ret.), NASA Astronaut (former). Biographical data, National Aeronautics and Space Administration, http://www.jsc.nasa.gov/Bios/htmlbios/truly-rh.html.

24. Peggy Mihelich, "Adventure Defines Steve Fossett" CNN, September 4, 2007, http://articles.cnn. com/2007-09-04/ tech/fossett.profile_1_single-engine-turbofan-aircraft-solo-balloon-flight-steve- fossett?_s=PM:TECH.

25. "The History of the Eagle Scout Award," p. xvi, http://www.nesa.org/PDF/58-435.pdf.

26. Boy Scouts of America, "History of the BSA—Highlights" (August 2009), http://www.scouting.org/ about/factsheets/bsa_history.aspx.

27. "Nickelodeon Magazine Interviews Steven Spielberg." Nickelodeon Magazine. http://www.nick.com/ shows/nick_mag/lookInside/index.jhtml?pagenum=8.

CHAPTER SEVEN: EAGLES ALL

1. Baden-Powell letter, December 1919.

2. http://www.aaregistry.org/historic_events/view/african-american-boy-scout-movement-story.

3. http://www.troop1tulsa.com/aboutus.

4. http://www.toledoblade.com/frontpage/2004/04/25/A-Lone-Scout-flies-high-as-an-Eagle.html.

5. Ibid.

6. Eagle Scout Magazine, winter 2010, back cover.

7. "The 409 Formula" by Mark Ray, Eagle Scout Magazine, Summer 2010, pg. 22-23.

8. http://www.theledger.com/article/20060814/NEWS/608140355?p=2&tc=pg.

CHAPTER EIGHT: GOLDEN EAGLES

1. "Boy Scout Turns 'Mud Pit' into a $60K Playground," September 10, 2009, CNN, http://www.cnn. com/2009/ LIVINg/wayoflife/09/10/cnnheroes.alex.griffith/index.html?iref=newssearch#cnnSTCVideo.

2. Ibid.

3. Ibid.

4. Ibid.

5. Ibid.

6. Boy Scouts of America, "History of the BSA—Highlights" (August 2009), http://www.scouting.org/ about/factsheets/bsa_history.aspx.

7. "Number of Eagles per year," Boy Scouts of America, NESA; Jon C. Halter, "A Plan and a Vision," Scouting, September 1998, http://www.scoutingmagazine.org/issues/9809/a-plan.html.

8. "Number of Eagle Scouts year by year (2000–2005)," College Confidential, Dec. 1, 2006, http://talk. collegeconfidential.com/parents-forum/269133-number-eagle-scouts-year-year.html; "Number of Eagle Scouts by year (1991–1998)," US Scouting Service Project, http://usscouts.org/usscouts/eagle/numbers.asp.

9. Ibid.

POSTSCRIPT: A GATHERING OF EAGLES

1. Adapted from Michael S. Malone "A gathering of Eagles," PJMedia.com, July 2010.

PHOTO CREDITS

Ebenexer A.M.E. Church, Souvenir program and Directory of the 31st Annual Session of the Chicago Conference (Illinois) - 204

Gerald R. Ford Presidential Library (Michigan) - 142, 146

Dr. Terry Grove Collection (Florida) - 23

Harbin Scout Museum, Camp Wisdom, Circle Ten Council (Texas) - 126

William "Green Bar Bill" Hillcourt Trust (Texas) - 123

Library of Congress (DC) - 6, 13, 46, 47, 73R

Michael S. Malone Collection (California) - 246

National Archives, Boy Scouts of America (Texas) - 12, 28, 33, 36, 45, 51, 91(upper), 101, 106,
116(lower), 129(lower), 131, 134, 141(right), 168, 187, 210, 235, 247, 254, 255

De Tan Nguyen Collection (Texas) - 208

David C. Scott Collection (Texas) - 5, 20, 22, 41, 48, 50, 73, 89, 90, 91(lower), 92, 104, 105, 110,
116(upper), 120, 126, 127, 129(upper), 133, 136, 141(left), 144, 149, 163, 172, 189, 192, 215, 218

Harry S. Truman Library and Museum (Missouri) - 14

Gary Twite Collection (Washington) - 34

Kelly Williams Collection (Colorado) - 59

Patricia Potter Wilson Collection (Texas) - 73L

INDEX

Michael S. Malone is one of the world's best-known technology writers. He has covered Silicon Valley and high-tech for more than 25 years, beginning with the *San Jose Mercury News* as the nation's first daily high-tech reporter, where he was nominated twice for the Pulitzer Prize for investigative reporting. His articles and editorials have appeared in such publications as the *Wall Street Journal, The Economist,* and *Fortune.* And for two years he was a columnist for the *New York Times.* He was editor of *Forbes ASAP,* the world's largest-circulation business-tech magazine, at the height of the dot-com boom.

Malone is the author or co-author of nearly twenty award-winning books, notably the bestselling *The Virtual Corporation, Bill and Dave, The Future Arrived Yesterday, The Intel Trinity,* and *Four Percent.*

Malone also has hosted three nationally syndicated public television interview series and co-produced the Emmy-nominated primetime PBS miniseries on social entrepreneurs, "The New Heroes." As an entrepreneur, Malone was a founding shareholder of eBay, Siebel Systems (sold to Oracle) and Qik (sold to Skype), and is currently co-founder and director of PatientKey Inc. An Eagle Scout and recipient of both the NESA Outstanding Eagle Scout Award and the Distinguished Eagle Scout Award, Malone was a chapter commander of the Knights of Dunamis and on the staff of the 1973 National Jamboree. He currently is an Assistant Scoutmaster of Troop 466 in Sunnyvale, California, president of the Silicon Valley chapter of NESA, and a member of the Santa Clara County Council board of directors.

Malone holds an MBA from Santa Clara University, where he currently is an adjunct professor. He also is an associate fellow of the Said Business School at Oxford University and a Distinguished Friend of Oxford.

Scan for more resources.

ABOUT WINDRUSH PUBLISHERS

Dallas, Texas

Founded in Dallas, Texas, WindRush Publishers excels at bringing books of exceptional quality and content to the minds of discriminating readers everywhere. With an eye for excellence we are always on the search for new inspirational and motivational topics by expert authors in a variety of subjects. With more great books to follow, WindRush remains devoted to producing exciting works designed for audiences of all ages and interests.

Stay Informed and Inspired at www.WindRushPub.com

**Scan for more
resources.**